PLEASE RETURN TO
LEARNING SUPPORT OFFICE
B336

The Editors

Charles Hulme is Professor of Psychology at the University of York. His main research interests are in the development of memory and reading skills in children.

Margaret Snowling is Professor of Psychology at the University of Newcastle upon Tyne. Her main research interest is in the cognitive bases of children's reading difficulties.

Reading Development and Dyslexia

Edited by
CHARLES HULME and MARGARET SNOWLING

Selected papers from the Third International Conference of the
British Dyslexia Association 'Dyslexia: Towards a Wider
Understanding', Manchester, 1994

Whurr Publishers Ltd
London

© 1994 British Dyslexia Association
First published 1994 by
Whurr Publishers Ltd
19b Compton Terrace, London N1 2UN, England

Reprinted 1995, 1997 and 1999

Published and distributed in the USA and Canada by
SINGULAR PUBLISHING GROUP, INC.
4284 41st Street
San Diego, California 92105

British Library Cataloguing in Publication Data
A catalogue record for this book is available from the
British Library.

ISBN 1-897635-85-0

Library of Congress Cataloging-in-Publication Data
A catalog record for this book is available.
Singular number 1-56593-368-0

Photoset by Stephen Cary
Printed and bound in the UK by Athenaeum Press Ltd,
Gateshead, Tyne & Wear

Preface

The chapters in this book represent a small selection of the papers presented to the Third International Conference of the British Dyslexia Association, held in Manchester in April 1994.

In the last few years, an appreciation of the importance of adopting a developmental framework (Snowling, 1987) when considering disorders of learning to read has gained widespread acceptance. In this view disorders of learning to read must be interpreted in the context of understanding normal development. It is only from an understanding of how normal children learn to read that we can hope to understand the difficulties that some children encounter in such learning. A corollary of this view is that the development of adequate theories of the nature and causes of reading difficulties are, in turn, crucial to the development of soundly based teaching strategies to overcome such difficulties.

The selection and organisation of the chapters here reflect this developmental perspective. The chapters in Part I deal with the normal development of reading skills, those in Part II go on to consider the nature and causes of reading difficulties, whereas those in Part III deal with strategies for helping to overcome reading difficulties. This organisation reflects our conviction that a developmental framework should guide our efforts both to understand and to overcome children's reading difficulties.

Consideration of the normal development of reading skills starts with Marilyn Jager-Adams' chapter. This chapter reviews some theories of reading and learning to read and relates them to recent advances in the development of connectionist computer models. Jager-Adams shows considerable enthusiasm for these models (an enthusiasm we share!) while also emphasising the difficulties that still remain to be addressed by this approach. Usha Goswami's chapter focuses upon the importance of one particular strategy in early reading: reading by analogy. Goswami proposes that children who are sensitive to the rhyming relationships between spoken words use this knowledge to direct their attention to shared letter strings between words. This affords them the possibility of reading new words by analogy with others that they already know. This strategy has obvious advantages and, in the course of the chapter, Goswami draws out the practical implications of studies in this area for the teaching of reading.

The chapter by Siné McDougall and Charles Hulme, and the one by Valerie Muter, deal with factors that are predictive of success in learning to read. McDougall and Hulme present data from a study of the correlates of reading skill in a large group of 8- to 10-year-old children. Consistent with previous research, they show that individual differences in reading ability are not predicted by differences in visual memory but, rather, by differences in phonological skills. Among these, both verbal short-term memory and phonological awareness are good predictors of reading, once IQ has been controlled. A new, and surprising, finding that has arisen from their study is that speech rate (literally, the speed with which familiar words can be articulated) makes an independent contribution to reading ability. Moreover, the contribution made by short-term memory is no longer significant once speech rate has been accounted for. These results underline the special significance of speech processing in learning to read. The data presented by Muter from a longitudinal study of children between the ages of 4 and 6 years is consistent with this view. She identifies two independent factors which account for the performance of 4 year olds on tests of phonological awareness: rhyme and segmentation. She goes on to show that segmentation ability influences the development of reading and of spelling, but not of arithmetic ability, in the subsequent 2 years. The finding of quite independent segmentation and rhyming factors in this study is a novel one, and the suggestion that segmentation rather than rhyming skill is the crucial determinant of progress in learning to read is likely to generate some controversy!

Taking the developmental studies as a back-drop, Part II of this book is concerned with the nature and causes of reading difficulties. Philip Seymour considers how best to understand the variability found among developmental dyslexic children. He argues that the processes used to read and spell familiar and unfamiliar words are at least partially separable and that they may show differential impairments in different dyslexic children. A challenge that remains for this approach is to relate this variability in reading and spelling processes to differences in underlying cognitive skills, most obviously the phonological and visual skills that children bring to the task of learning to read.

A similar theme is taken up by Maggie Snowling, Nata Goulandris and Joy Stackhouse, who present evidence from three single cases of children with reading difficulties. Two of these children were dyslexic, the third had a phonological speech disorder. They use data from these cases, in particular from their relative difficulties in speech processing, to hypothesise that the nature and prognosis of a child's reading difficulty is determined by the extent and severity of their phonological deficit. This hypothesis is tentative. However, it would find favour with Mary Kibel and Tim Miles whose chapter is concerned with the spelling errors that are made both by normal and by dyslexic children. Kibel and Miles present qualitative analyses of a large corpus of children's spelling errors, arguing that primarily they are phonological in nature. Strikingly, dyslexic children who have been systematically taught sound–spelling relationships persist in making phonological spelling errors to a greater extent than normal children who are matched for spelling age. Although the dyslexic children had mastered specific orthographic conventions adequately, they had persisting difficulty with the analysis of speech sounds and their relationship to spelling.

The final chapter in Part II pursues a different theme, but one that is critical for our understanding of the consequences of reading difficulties both in the short and the longer term. Barbara Maughan reviews a large number of studies which have examined the relationships between reading difficulties and various aspects of social and emotional adjustment, such as anxiety, depression, hyperactivity and aggressive or antisocial behaviour. There is a vast literature which indicates that there is an association between reading difficulties and such emotional and behavioural problems. In this area, it is very difficult to establish the direction of causation, but the evidence reviewed does suggest that reading difficulties may exacerbate the behavioural difficulties shown by some children, particularly in the early school years. If this is true, this may be an important 'hidden' cost of reading difficulties and one with important social implications. There is clearly a need for well-designed, prospective studies which will address these important questions of obvious social relevance.

Part III of the book turns to the remediation of reading difficulties. Bill Tunmer and Peter Hatcher have similar concerns with what types of intervention can promote the reading skills of young children who are failing, and how these interventions relate to theories of normal reading development. The research reported in both these chapters has been influenced by the pioneering work of Marie Clay in New Zealand. The research from these two independent groups argues strongly for procedures that emphasise teaching children about the interrelationships between the sound structure and spelling patterns of words to provide the most effective treatment for children's reading difficulties. Notwithstanding this excellent research, it can always be argued that prevention is better than cure. In this vein, Ingvar Lundberg provides a useful overview of his team's work aimed at reducing reading failure through the implementation of pre-school phonological training programmes in Scandinavia. These three chapters lead to some very optimistic conclusions about the feasibility of predicting and overcoming many cases of reading difficulty. These findings, we believe, have very important practical implications and the time is now ripe to put them into practice.

The final chapter by Susan Stothard considers the nature and treatment of specific reading comprehension difficulties in children. This is an area which, in comparison to children's decoding difficulties (which is the focus of the other chapters in this book), has been relatively neglected. Although reading comprehension difficulties are not usually seen in dyslexic children, any complete theory of reading difficulty must also address the causes of comprehension difficulties and their interrelationship with decoding skills. Stothard provides a useful guide to the nature of the cognitive difficulties that characterise children with specific comprehension difficulties, and goes on to consider evidence about the kinds of teaching procedures that are likely to be helpful to these children.

We have chosen to emphasise a developmental perspective here. We believe that any adequate theory of dyslexia and other reading difficulties in children must be developmental in nature. Such a theory can account for the considerable variability seen among dyslexic individuals while also adhering to the belief that it has a biological origin. Ultimately, as the research in this volume shows, this approach will not only lead to a better understanding of reading and its disorders; it will also lead to rationally based improvements in teaching programmes both to promote literacy and to prevent reading failure.

Reference

Snowling, M. (1987). *Dyslexia: A Cognitive Developmental Perspective*. Oxford: Basil Blackwell.

Charles Hulme and Maggie Snowling
January 1994

Contents

Contributors

Usha Goswami, Department of Experimental Psychology, University of Cambridge, UK

Nata Goulandris, National Hospital's College of Speech Sciences, London, UK

Peter Hatcher, Cumbria Education Authority, UK

Charles Hulme, Department of Psychology, University of York, UK

Marilyn Jager-Adams, Bolt Beranek & Newman Inc., Cambridge, Massachusetts, USA

Mary Kibel, Devon Dyslexia Association, UK

Ingvar Lundberg, Department of Psychology, University of Umeå, Sweden, and Center for Reading Research, Stavanger, Norway

Siné McDougall, Department of Psychology, University College Swansea, UK

Barbara Maughan, MRC Child Psychiatry Unit, London, UK

Tim Miles, Department of Psychology, University College of North Wales, Bangor, UK

Valerie Muter, Department of Neurology and Developmental Paediatrics, Institute of Child Health, The Wolfson Centre, London, UK

Philip Seymour, Department of Psychology, University of Dundee, UK

Margaret Snowling, Department of Psychology, University of Newcastle upon Tyne, UK

Joy Stackhouse, National Hospital's College of Speech Sciences, London, UK

Susan Stothard, Department of Psychology, University of Newcastle upon Tyne, UK

William Tunmer, Department of Education, Massey University, New Zealand

Acknowledgements

The chapters in this book are based on papers presented at the Third International Conference of the British Dyslexia Association 'Dyslexia: Towards a Wider Understanding'. We would like to thank our colleagues on the Conference Organising Committee, and particularly the Chairman, Steve Chinn, for their help and support. We also thank all the contributors for the efficiency and good humour with which they responded to the tight deadlines necessitated by our need to publish in time for the conference. Finally we are most grateful to Kate Nation and Jane Sugarman for editing the editors.

Charles Hulme and Maggie Snowling
January 1994

Dedication

To the memory of Jean Augur

Part I
The Normal Development of Reading Skills

Chapter 1
Learning to Read: Modelling the Reader versus Modelling the Learner

MARILYN JAGER-ADAMS

> Problem enough, this, for a life's work, to learn how we read! A wonderful process, by which our thoughts and thought-wanderings to the finest shades of detail, the play of our inmost feelings and desires and will, the subtle image of the very innermost that we are, are reflected from us to another soul who reads us through our book....
>
> And so to completely analyze what we do when we read would almost be the acme of a psychologist's achievements, for it would be to describe very many of the most intricate workings of the human mind, as well as to unravel the tangled story of the most remarkable specific performance that civilization has learned in all history.

Thus wrote Edmund Burke Huey (1908/1968, pp. 5–6), nearly a century ago. Both before Huey's writings and since, we have been offered a variety of more or less complex models of how the workings of the human mind might combine to create meaning from print. More or less in common, such models have envisaged the relevant information and processes to be anchored at one end in the text and, at the other, in the reader's understanding and perspective on its meaning and message. The struggles, both within and among ourselves, have been over the flow of knowledge and activity in-between: is it bottom-up from print to meaning, or top-down from meaning to print? Are there alternative routes, short-cuts or cognitive strategies for saving time and effort? More generally, what's involved and how is it learned?

Only very recently, and only through a convergence of lots of research along with significant advances in psychological, mathematical and computational sciences, have we begun to see models that appear capable of mimicking the processes of reading and learning to read. Whether they portray beginners or experts, the key to these models is that they are neither top-down nor bottom-up in nature.

3

Instead, all of the processes within are simultaneously active and interactive, with every awakened cluster of knowledge and understanding at once both issuing and accommodating information, both passing and receiving guidance, to and from every other. The key to these models is not the dominance of one form of knowledge over the others, but the coordination and cooperation of all with each other (see Adams, 1990).

In fact, this class of models fits well with the recent paradigm shifts in the classroom, in that it emphatically reasserts that literacy development depends critically and at every level on the child's interest and understanding of what is to be learned. Further, to learn to be efficient and productive, literacy cannot be fostered one piece at a time. The relationships between the parts serve just as importantly in guiding the acquisition and refinement of the system as they do in its fluent operation. From the start, therefore, it is vital that literacy development involves reading, writing, spelling, language play, conceptual exploration, and all manner of engagement with text, in relentlessly enlightened balance.

Over the last few decades, we have learned much about how children learn to read words and about some of the reasons why such learning can be difficult. We have learned why poor word recognition is a stumbling block for so many young readers and why, too, it is so frequently associated with poor comprehension. In skilful reading, the mind works interactively and in parallel with as many cues as it can recognise as relevant – and that integrally includes words and their spellings. These models have served well to organise and make sense of the wealth of information we have gained about the nature of print processing, and how it feeds and fits into the rest of the reading system. At the same time, however, they underscore how much we have yet to learn.

Reading, Automaticity and Learning

There are two striking characteristics of skilful readers. One is the amount and texture of information and response which they generate in reading a text. The other is the ease and speed with which they are able to read it. Skilful adults can course through text at rates upward of 300 words per minute – upward of five words per second! Indeed, skilful readers can perceive whole words as quickly and accurately as single letters; they can perceive whole phrases as quickly and easily as strings of three or four unrelated letters.

Against such a backdrop, the idea that skilful readers might recognise words on the basis of their component letters seems almost ludicrous. Yet research indicates beyond a shadow of a doubt that that, in fact, is exactly what they do.

Over the last 20 years, research has demonstrated that for normal adult readers, meaningful text – regardless of its ease or difficulty – is read through what is essentially a left to right, line by line, word by word process. On top of that, skilful readers visually process virtually every letter of every word they read even while they tend rather irrepressibly to translate the print to speech as they go. They do so whether they are reading isolated words or meaningful connected text. They do so regardless of the semantic, syntactic or orthographic predictability of what they are reading. And they do so in spite of the fact that they generally do not feel like that is what they are doing. (For reviews, see Just and Carpenter, 1987; Patterson and Coltheart, 1987.)

As these findings began to accumulate, the first reaction was to search for ways to dismiss them. Perhaps they were the result of measurement error; perhaps they were misrepresentative, somehow brought on by one or another peculiarity of the laboratory tasks through which they were evidenced. Yet, as many times and through as many different paradigms as psychologists could invent, the results came out the same, over and over again: the skilful reader recognises the words of a text on the basis of the sequences of individual letters which comprise them. In the end, there may be no more broadly or diversely replicated finding in the field of modern psychology.

Perhaps it was also because we were so unwilling to accept this finding that it took us so long to understand it. True, skilful readers neither look nor feel like they attend to the visual details of print as they read. But this, as it turns out, is the crowning explanation rather than the refutation of such findings. In the end we realise that readers must read the words just as listeners must hear them. The words are the building blocks of language. It is precisely through their words and wordings that speakers and authors strive to evoke and refine the meaning and message of their intentions. Yet it is only because listeners and readers process the words so automatically and effortlessly that they have the mental resources left to construct and reflect on that meaning and message. For skilful readers, as G. Stanley Hall (1911) described it, 'the art has become so secondarily automatic that it can be forgotten and attention be given solely to the subject matter. Its assimilation is true reading and all else is only the whir of the machinery and not the work it does' (p. 445).

In the end, too, we realise that such automaticity is not odd at all, but quintessentially human. It is, in kind, a property that is common to virtually all of our complex and multilayered activities. When you walk, you do not think about each separate step you take. Once you have decided where you are going, something inside you generally takes care of the steps leaving your conscious attention free for conversations, daydreams or the view. When you type, you do not think about each separate letter and key as you stroke it. Indeed, when typing from copy, your eyes and mind tend to be well ahead of your fingers. Yet hit the separate keys you do, and something inside you must be controlling and monitoring your progress, for however far ahead your eyes may be, you very often know when you've made a typo. In the same way, the skilful pianist must meticulously read every note while guiding every touch and position of her hands and fingers. Still, it is not the separate notes or fingering to which she consciously attends as she plays, but the larger force and flow of the piece – that is what makes it music, after all.

For reading and listening, for walking, typing and playing the piano, and similarly for dancing, juggling, driving the car, peeling the carrots, buttoning your shirt, tying your shoes, playing sports, eating your dinner, shuffling and dealing cards, ...with time and practice, people become able to run off many such activities – not just with seamless fluency and remarkable precision, but even while their conscious attention is more or less preoccupied with other layers or even other topics of thought.

All such activities involve a host of small, relatively precise, often complex and deftly coordinated parts. Yet, their very speed and fluency makes clear that the doer *could* not execute them by thinking about each little part in turn. At the same time, the fact that such activities can be run off even while – or, equally, in *support* of – thinking about something else, makes clear that the doer *does* not execute them by working out each little part in turn.

What is the nature of such automaticity and how does it develop? The landmark study in this area was published nearly 100 years ago and was focused on mastery of the Morse code by students training to become professional telegraphers. By carefully observing and analysing performance, Bryan and Harter (1897) found that increases in speed and accuracy were coupled with qualitative changes in the way the students approached the task. At the first stage, the students concentrated on the individual letters of the incoming messages, learning, for example, to think 'A' on hearing '• –', 'S' on hearing '• • •', 'K' on hearing '– • –', and so on. Gradually, gradually, the students became able to listen for larger groups of letters and eventually to hear them as words. Finally, and only after many weeks of practice, a new level set in, and only after this point did coding speed and accuracy reach or surpass the minimal acceptable level for the job: the students developed a knack for letting their transcriptions lag behind the incoming signal by a whole phrase or even a short sentence 'just as the practiced oral reader lets his voice lag a half a line or so behind his eye' (Bryan and Harter, 1897, p. 507).

Bryan and Harter's explanation for the patterns that they witnessed was that learning was hierarchical: only when perception of the letters had become relatively automatic could the students elevate their active attention to words; only when the words had become relatively automatic could they elevate their active attention to sentences and larger units of meaning. Even today, this explanation seems essentially correct. On the other hand, it led to a number of strictly bottom-up and hierarchical models of teaching – which today seem both theoretically and pedagogically untenable.

In fact, substantial advances as to the nature and acquisition of automaticity have only appeared quite recently – and interestingly they have drawn on the same class of models that are proving so useful in the domains of language learning and comprehension. These newer models, alternatively known as connectionist, neural net or parallel distributed processing (PDP) models, are built on the assumption that learning progresses as people come to respond to the *relationships* between patterns or events. It is, for example, the overlearned relationships about its edges that enable people to recognise a shape as a triangle, just as it is the overlearned relationships among the letters of a printed string that enable people to recognise it as a word. Similarly it is the relationships among the pitch, timing and quality of its notes that evoke interest in a piece of music, just as it is the relationships among the meanings of its composite words that give texture and meaning to a sentence. As the models thus attribute higher-order knowledge and thinking to associations among the simpler parts of an experience, they have been peremptorily dismissed by some as 'behaviourist' in nature. But rest assured: these models are not repackaged Skinner.

First, although Skinner's claims to fame derive from his strong personal beliefs about the nature and control of human behaviour, those personal beliefs are quite independent of the larger history and spirit of associationist theories of knowledge. Indeed, to a striking extent, the history of Western philosophy and psychology, and the history of associationism, are one and the same. The associationist theories of knowledge were given to us first by Aristotle 2300 years ago. Recovered by John Locke and reinvented by Thomas Hobbes in the 1600s, they continued to be of focal interest throughout the Enlightenment. The theories were refined and deepened by Berkeley, Hume and Hartley; they were critiqued and extended by Kant and by the Mills. At one level or another, moreover, they have underlain a great many of the significant psychological theories of the twentieth century, from those of William James, G. Stanley Hall and John Dewey to contemporary schema theories.

In the latter half of this century, we were no longer content to discuss, describe or presume such models. We had computers. We wanted to build them. We wanted to see if they worked. And they did not. When we taught our computers what went with what, they obediently and stupidly overgeneralised what we wanted them to learn. When we added inhibition and taught them what did not go with what, they obediently and stupidly overgeneralised in the other direction. Stubbornly, we persevered. We tried again and again – tweaking this, fancifying that – but our computers' results were just as stubbornly disappointing.

Ultimately such disappointing results forced theorists to recognise that we cannot simply learn that X goes with Y or X does not go with Y. We also learn that X does or does not go with Y given certain contexts and conditions, and that X may go with other things besides Y. And however we learn, we learn in such a way that we not only recognise sameness and difference, but also vague similarities and subtle distinctions. We can recognise outliers and alternatives; our behaviour can become rule-like without rules and with sensitive respect for exceptions; we can extend our knowledge through induction, deduction and analogy; and we can understand that some parts of our knowledge and conclusions are solid whereas others are pretty iffy and diffuse. Further, although such reasoning sometimes depends on deliberate thought, it seems at other times to flow of its own accord. What the connectionists discovered was that, by linking the pieces of our knowledge not directly one to the other but indirectly via some hidden 'mediating' units, they could imbue the network of associations with the logical power and flexibility to support these characteristics of learning and thought. (For a description of the logic and dynamics of these models, see Rumelhart and McClelland, 1986; for a discussion of their importance and potential, see Bereiter, 1991.)

Using the connectionist architecture, computers have been shown to perform remarkably well on a host of once-elusive perceptual tasks, such as fingerprint recognition (Leung et al., 1991) and a variety of medical challenges such as tumour detection (Boone, Gross and Greco-Hunt, 1990; DaPonte and Sherman, 1991). At the same time, they have been shown to mimic both strengths *and* weaknesses of human beings in such tasks as speech recognition (McClelland and Elman, 1986), visual word recognition (Seidenberg and McClelland, 1989), learning the structure of complex event sequences

(Cleeremans and McClelland, 1991), and even in generating explanation and analogy in studies of literature and science (Holyoak and Thagard, 1989; Thagard, 1989). Whereas older computer models were generally helpless when presented with situations that mismatched their programmed knowledge, the connectionist models exhibit the abilities to make best guesses and to capitalise on partial information, passing gradually from vagueness to clarity and from uncertainty to decision. Interestingly, as the outward behaviour of these programmes becomes realistically sophisticated, their insides become so intricately interconnected that their own inventors find it impossible to figure out exactly how they behave as they do.

Modelling the reader

As applied to reading, the grand logic of these models is shown in Figure 1.1 (for fuller description and discussion, see Seidenberg and McClelland, 1989; Adams, 1990). Within each of the 'processors', knowledge is represented by lots of simpler units which have become linked, connected or associated to one another through experience. The oval labelled 'orthographic processor', for example, represents the reader's visual knowledge of printed words. Within it, individual letters are represented as interconnected bundles of more elementary visual features, whereas words are represented as interconnected sets of letters. Similarly, the meanings of any familiar word are represented in the meaning processor as bundles of simpler meaning elements, just as its pronunciation is represented in the phonological processor as a complex of elementary speech sounds.

I introduced the term 'processors' in quotes so as to emphasise that it is mostly in the interest of descriptive convenience that they have been separated from one another: the associations among the pieces of one's knowledge depend, not on the 'processor' in which each resides, but on the ways in which they have become interrelated or connected through experience. Indeed, the links among any set of representational units are nothing more than a cumulative record of the ways in which those units have been related to one another in a person's experience. The more frequently that any pattern of activity has been brought to mind, the stronger and more complete will be the bonds that hold it together.

Ultimately it is these bonds, these associations – as they pass excitation and inhibition among the elements that they link – which are responsible for the fluency of the reader and the seeming coherence of the text. For the skilful reader, even as the letters of a word in fixation are recognised, they activate the spelling patterns, pronuncia-

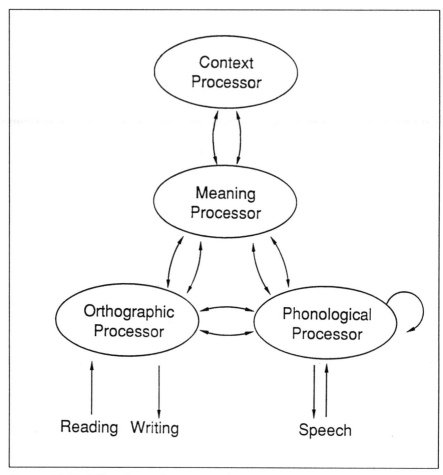

Figure 1.1 Modelling the reader

tions and meanings with which they are compatible. At the same time, using its larger knowledge of the text, the context processor swings its own bias among rival candidates so as to maintain the coherence of the message. Meanwhile, as each processor homes in on the word's identity, it relays its progress back to all of the others, such that wherever hypotheses agree among processors, their resolution is speeded and strengthened. In this way, as initiated by the print on the page and hastened through the connectivity both within and between the processors, skilful readers come to recognise the spelling, sound, meaning and contextual role of a familiar word almost automatically and simultaneously, leaving their active attention free for critical and reflective thought.

The connectionist models have captured the interest and imagination of psychologists precisely because they have given us a way to represent complex performance from the associative interactions of a data-flow which is initiated and ultimately constrained from the bottom up. At the same time, however, these models are qualitatively different from their behaviourist predecessors. The path from sensation to action does not consist of linear chains of stimulus–response linkages, but circuits instead. Through these circuits the system gains the capability to use its own prior knowledge and experience to select, structure and augment the sensory input into perceptual coherence. In other words, the models represent a way in which top-down and bottom-up processes can work together automatically, efficiently and with no need of the homunculus – provided, that is, that the system has been properly set up.

Modelling the Learner

In short, the excitement over the connectionist models is precisely an excitement at the prospect that, at some level, they may accurately model the skill-based performance of humans. Given also that their strongest empirical support comes from machine-training studies, an obvious question arises: should we not be able to learn much about the acquisition of such skills by human novices through study of their acquisition by the machines?

This strategy has recently been proposed and pursued by Seidenberg (1992, 1993). Major hypotheses about the underlying causes of dyslexia, argues Seidenberg, fall into three categories:

1. Abnormalities in visual perception (e.g. Livingstone et al., 1991).
2. Difficulties in phonological processing (e.g. Brady and Shankweiler, 1991).
3. General learning disability or, perhaps, resource limitations (e.g. Morrison, 1984).

Within the framework of his connectionist model of visual word recognition (Seidenberg and McClelland, 1989), Seidenberg then hypotheses that these shortcomings may respectively reflect computational limitations in the orthographic processor, the phonological processor and the hidden units connecting these two processors (see Figure 1.1).

Seidenberg has conducted two computational experiments to test this hypothesis. To simulate the effects of resource limitations, he reduced the number of hidden units that connect the orthographic and phonological processors. To simulate the effects of an early visual processing deficit, he degraded (diffused) the machine's representations of its orthographic input. (Note that the Seidenberg–McClelland simulation has not yet been developed to the point that would allow analogous treatment of phonological information-processing. Nor has the model been extended to include semantic or higher-order linguistic/conceptual representations.) Then, in each case, he re-trained the model through the same regimen (practice with feedback to approximately 3000 monosyllabic words) as has been shown, with the intact model, to result in an impressive simulation of 'normal' visual word recognition.

Interestingly, and despite the fact that Seidenberg's two types of computational dysfunctions were conceptually distinct from one another, the machine's performance was similar across the two conditions. In each case, performance of the disabled machines was poorer than that of the normal machine even on words with regular spelling–sound correspondences. However, both disabled systems demonstrated exceptional difficulties in generating appropriate pronunciations for both pseudo-words (e.g. *lome*) and irregularly pronounced words (e.g. *have*).

Significantly, observes Seidenberg, such differential impairment on pseudo-words and irregular words is also characteristic of real children with reading disabilities (Backman et al., 1984). He concludes that the strategy of selectively impairing the machine and evaluating its consequent performance holds considerable promise towards furthering our understanding of the underlying causes and expressions of dyslexia.

Maybe. But, by itself, this strategy can alternatively be seen as frustratingly risky and indirect. First, even where the output of a machine resembles the output of a human being, this is scarce indication that the inner workings of the machine resemble the inner workings of a human being. Second, even if Seidenberg and McClelland's connectionist model of normal visual word recognition were exactly correct, the strongest necessary interpretation of the dyslexic simulations is that, if the mapping process is anywhere impeded or weakened, so too is learning. Third, despite positive evidence of the heritability of dyslexia and its association with neurophysiological abnormalities, research increasingly points to the power of experiential factors in attenuating individual differences.

Again, what the connectionist research demonstrates is that, if the human mind were structured in a way that remotely resembles these models, then through nothing more than practice with a representative set of stimuli, it would automatically learn not only to recognise the trained stimuli, but also to abstract complex and interdependent packages of their perceptual commonalities in ways that enable remarkably well-tuned generalisation to novel members of their category. But even while we get excited about the consequentce of this demonstration, we must take care not to be glib about its antecedent: the connectionist model is a structural model. Moreover, its underlying structure has been built from empirical evidence about skilful readers. Perhaps, then, to move towards using the model to understand reading acquisition and its difficulties, it is necessary to examine the structural givens on which and from which it was built.

To begin with, the Seidenberg and McClelland machine takes it as given that print is print. Thus, whether it encodes the letters accurately or carelessly (as in the version with the 'orthographic deficit'), the machine automatically analyses its input into letters. In contrast, children's first words seem to be encoded more as pictures than as print, seemingly remembered less in terms of letters than more generic aspects of their pattern and appearance (see, for example, Masonheimer, Drum and Ehri, 1984; Byrne, 1992).

In addition, the connectionist machine necessarily encodes and works with the complete and ordered set of letters comprising the input string at once. It is on this basis that the machine acquires, adjusts or uses the associations among the letters for learning or recognising spelling patterns and words. In contrast, even after children have begun to attend to the letters within words, they seem not to attend to *all* of them for some time (see, for example, Juel, 1991; Ehri, 1992).

From the first word it sees, Seidenberg and McClelland's computer is programmed to associate letters with phonemes and, derivatively, spelling patterns with phonological patterns. Yet, this alphabetic insight – as well as the awareness of the phonemes that it presumes – is broadly documented to be among the most 'iffy' and troublesome requirements of the reading challenge for children (see, for example, Stanovich, 1986; Liberman and Liberman, 1990). Furthermore, the awareness issue itself is moot unless the child's phonological memory is differentiated into phonemes, and this may not be the case. On the contrary, Fowler (1991) has argued that beginning at age 2 years and typically continuing to at least age 7, phoneme-level representations emerge only gradually, at a pace depending not only on individual factors but also on language play, lexical expansion and, possibly, orthographic experience itself.

Every time the machine attempts to sound out a word, its response is automatically compared with the word's correct pronunciation and the weights on the relevant associations are adjusted accordingly. Again these are built-in features of the machine's learning regime. The correct pronunciation of each word is supplied to the machine, as are the algorithms by which the associative weightings within and between the orthographic and phonological nodes are adjusted towards the intended response. In fact, this sort of corrective feedback is key to the machine's human-like performance, because it constitutes the principal means through which it learns to recognise and respond to larger spelling patterns.

But what would a human reader need to do to accomplish the same effect? Minimally, she or he would have to *know* the intended word. Beyond *knowing* the word, however, the reader must *think* of it. This means first, and perhaps non-trivially, that the reader must have the inclination and confidence to think about what the word really could be. And more. Doing so successfully must depend on whether the text has been understood well enough and/or whether the tentative decoding of the print is close enough to boost (and not block) the availability of the intended word in memory. And still more. Successful word identification does not, in itself, result in learning. By analogy to the machine's error correction algorithms, the child must still take time to revisit the spelling of the word just identified and to reflect on its revised connections to sound and meaning. All together, this is a tall order for young readers, and certainly not to be taken for granted.

The developmental appropriateness of the connectionist machine's structural assumptions may also be questioned on theoretical grounds. As argued nearly 50 years ago by Donald Hebb, in order for connected structures of this sort to be establishable, much less to guide awareness and action, it is vital 'that reverberation continue in one of these structures long enough so that temporal overlap can occur' (Hebb, 1949, p. 100). Only where the relevant substructures are active at once can they support the associative interactions – the feedback and feedforward between themselves – which ultimately define their conjoint structure. Within limits, Hebb explains, the very circularity of these structures will extend the duration for which their parts remain active. Furthermore, the larger and more complex the structure, the longer the duration across which its activity will be maintained. Nevertheless, where the key components of the structure depend on external stimulation, there's no getting around the importance of perceptual speed. The very possibility of noticing *or* creating any relationship between the parts must depend on the speed of their arrival: the last to-be-connected piece must arrive before activation of the first has subsided. For the machine, this is not a problem. For beginning readers, in contrast, it clearly is and at every level.

Thus we are returned, full circle, to the issue of automaticity. The connectionist model demonstrates that, when the pieces of the puzzle have been put in place and provided that the system is disposed to look for the right kinds of relationships between them, then circuit upon circuit, sensation and knowledge can meld seamlessly, automatically into structured perception. As such, the model emphasises the importance of the young reader's knowledge at every level – one cannot, after all, interrelate what's not there. At the same time, it emphasises the importance of the young reader's understanding of the task (see also Downing, 1979) – how else could the relevant relationships gain focus and support against the background of simultaneous activity? Thus, even while the model provides strong hypotheses about what must be learned and also about where we might look for dysfunctions and weak, missing or misconstrued links, it leaves many mysteries for those of us concerned with the initial acquisition of reading. In particular, how does the system get set up and how can we tell if it's getting set up right?

In Charles Perfetti's words:

> 'The areas of knowledge and ignorance in the scientific study of reading are not, respectively, decoding and comprehension but rather skilled reading and the processes of becoming a skilled reader. What we know a lot about is *skilled* word recognition and *skilled* comprehension. What we still know much less about are the processes of word recognition (and comprehension) that serve a child as he or she learns how to read. Even less is known about the processes by which the learning reader acquires higher levels of word recognition skill, moving from "novice" to "expert."'

> (Perfetti, 1992, pp. 145–146).

Conclusion

Over the last few decades, we have learned much about how children learn to read words and about some of the reasons that such learning can be difficult. We have learned why poor word recognition is a stumbling block for so many young readers and why, too, it is so frequently associated with poor comprehension. In skilful reading, the mind works interactively and in parallel with as many cues as it can recognise as relevant – and that integrally includes words and their spellings. The connectionist models have served well to organise and make sense of the wealth of information we have gained about the nature of print processing, and how it feeds and fits into the rest of the reading system. At the same time, however, they underscore how much we have yet to learn.

References

Adams, M. J. (1990). *Beginning to Read: Thinking and Learning About Print*. Cambridge, MA: MIT Press.

Backman, J., Bruck, M., Hébert, M. and Seidenberg, M.S. (1984). Acquisition and use of spelling–sound correspondences. *Journal of Experimental Child Psychology* **38**, 114–133.

Bereiter, C. (1991). Implications of connectionism for thinking about rules. *Educational Researcher* **20** (3), 10–16.

Boone, J. M., Gross, G. W. and Greco-Hunt, V. (1990). Neural networks in radiological diagnosis: I. Introduction and illustration. *Investigative Radiology* **25**, 1012–1016.

Brady, S. A. and Shankweiler, D. P. (1991). *Phonological Processes in Literacy*. Hillsdale, NJ: Lawrence Erlbaum Associates.

Bryan, W. L. and Harter, N. (1897). Studies in the physiology and psychology of the telegraphic language. *Psychological Review* **4**, 27–53.

Byrne, B. (1992). Studies in the acquisition procedure for reading: Rationale, hypotheses, and data. In P. B. Gough, L. C. Ehri, and R. Treiman (eds), *Reading Acquisition*, pp. 1–34. Hillsdale, NJ: Lawrence Erbaum Associates.

Cleeremans, A. and McClelland, J. L. (1991). Learning the structure of event sequences. *Journal of Experimental Psychology: General* **120**, 235–253.

DaPonte, J. S. and Sherman, P. (1991). Classification of ultrasonic image texture by statistical discriminant analysis and neural networks. *Computerized Medical Imaging and Graphics*, **15**, 3–9.

Downing, J. (1979). *Reading and Reasoning*. New York: Springer-Verlag.

Ehri, L. C. (1992). Reconceptualizing the development of sight word reading and its relationship to recoding. In P. B. Gough, L. C. Ehri and R. Treiman (eds), *Reading Acquisition*, pp. 107–144. Hillsdale, NJ: Lawrence Erlbaum Associates.

Fowler, A. E. (1991). How early phonological development might set the stage for phoneme awareness. In S. A. Brady and D. P. Shankweiler (eds), *Phonological Processes in Literacy*, pp. 97–117. Hillsdale, NJ: Lawrence Erlbaum Associates.

Hall, G. S. (1911). *Educational Problems*. New York: Appleton.

Hebb, D. A. (1949). *The Organization of Behaviour*. New York: Wiley.

Holyoak, K. J. and Thagard, P. (1989). Analogical mapping by constraint satisfaction. *Cognitive Science*, **13**, 295–355.

Huey, E. B. (1908/1968). *The Psychology and Pedagogy of Reading*. Cambridge, MA: MIT Press.

Juel, C. (1991). Beginning reading. In R. Barr, M. L. Kamil, P. B. Mosenthal and P. D. Pearson (eds), *Handbook of Reading Research*, vol. 2, pp. 759–788. New York: Longman.

Just, M. A. and Carpenter, P. A. (1987). *The Psychology of Reading and Language Comprehension*. Boston, MA: Allyn and Bacon.

Liberman, I. Y. and Liberman, A. M. (1990). Whole language vs code emphasis: Underlying assumptions and their implications for reading instruction. *Annals of Dyslexia* **40**, 51–76.

Leung, W. F., Leung, S. H., Lau, W. H. and Luk, A. (1991). Fingerprint recognition using neural networks. In B. H. Juang, S. Y. Kung and C. A. Kamm (eds), *Neural Networks for Signal Processing*, pp. 226–235. Piscataway, NJ: IEEE.

Livingstone, M. S., Rosen, G. D., Dislane, F. W. and Galaburda, A. M. (1991). Physiological and anatomical evidence for a magnocellular defect in developmental dyslexia. *Proceedings of the National Academy of Sciences* **88**, 7943–7947.

Masonheimer, P. E., Drum, P. A. and Ehri, L. C. (1984). Does environmental print identification lead children into words reading? *Journal of Reading Behavior* **16**, 257–271.

McClelland, J. L. and Elman, J. L. (1986). The TRACE model of speech perception. *Cognitive Psychology* **18**, 1–86.

Morrison, F. (1984). Reading disability: A problem in rule learning and word decoding. *Developmental Review* 4, 36–47.

Patterson, K. E. and Coltheart, V. (1987). Phonological processes in reading: A tutorial review. In M. Coltheart (ed.), *Attention and Performance XII: The Psychology of Reading*, pp. 421–448. London: Lawrence Erlbaum Associates.

Perfetti, C. A. (1992). The representation problem in reading acquisition. In P. B. Gough, L. C. Ehri and R. Treiman (eds), *Reading Acquisition*, pp. 145–174. Hillsdale, NJ: Lawrence Erlbaum Associates.

Rumelhart, D. E. and McClelland, J. L. (eds) (1986). *Parallel Distributed Processing*, vol. 1: *Foundations*, pp. 216–271. Cambridge, MA: MIT Press.

Seidenberg, M. S. (1992). Dyslexia in a computational model of word recognition in reading. In P. B. Gough, L. C. Ehri and R. Treiman (eds), *Reading Acquisition*, pp. 243–274. Hillsdale, NJ: Lawrence Erbaum Associates.

Seidenberg, M. S. (1993). A connectionist modelling approach to word recognition and dyslexia. *Psychological Science* 4, 299–304.

Seidenberg, M. S. and McClelland, J. L. (1989). A distributed, developmental model of word recognition and naming. *Psychological Review* 96, 523–568

Stanovich, K. E. (1986). Matthew effects in reading: Some consequences of individual differences in the acquisition of literacy. *Reading Research Quarterly* 21, 360–406.

Thagard, P. (1989). Explanatory coherence. *Behavioral and Brain Sciences* 12, 435–502.

Chapter 2
Reading by Analogy: Theoretical and Practical Perspectives

USHA GOSWAMI

A Theoretical Perspective: Phonological Skills and Orthographic Analogies

It is now well established that phonological skills have an important connection with reading and spelling development. Phonological tasks such as recognising rhyme and alliteration in spoken words (CAT and BAT, SUN and SOCK), orally deleting phonemes (JAM–am), judging whether two words begin or end with the same sound (PLEA–PLANK, RAT–WIT), and tapping out the number of sounds in spoken words such as BUTTERFLY and SOAP, all show a significant relationship to reading (Bruce, 1964; Liberman et al., 1974; Bradley and Bryant, 1978, 1983; Treiman and Zukowski, 1991). Furthermore, research has shown that there are different *levels* of phonological awareness, and that these different levels are most strongly related to reading at different points in development. Phonological tasks which require children to make judgements about rhyme and alliteration in monosyllabic words require phonological skills at the *onset-rime* level. The onset in spoken syllables corresponds to the initial consonant(s) in the words ('pl-' in PLANK), and the rime corresponds to the vowel and to any final consonant(s) ('-at' in RAT). A *phoneme* is the smallest unit of sound that changes the meaning of a spoken word. RAT and RAP differ by a single phoneme, and so do SOAP and SIP. Onset-rime skills are present *before* children begin learning to read. Phonemic awareness seems to develop largely as a *consequence* of learning to read and to spell.

Analogies among spelling patterns in early reading

A theoretical explanation of the relationship between phonological skills at these different levels and the development of reading is

suggested by research on children's use of analogies as they are learning to read. An analogy in reading involves using the spelling–sound
relationship of one word, such as BEAK, to predict the pronunciation
of an unknown word which shares a similar spelling pattern, such as
PEAK. Children appear to be able to use this kind of analogy from the
start of learning to read (Goswami, 1986, 1988). However, analogies
need not involve shared spelling sequences which correspond to
rimes. It is logically possible to make analogies between words which
share only one or two letters, such as BEAK and HEAP (shared vowel
digraph), BEAK and BARK (shared initial and final phoneme), or
TRIM and TRAP (shared initial consonant cluster or onset). One plausible developmental hypothesis would be that, early in reading,
analogies might depend on a substantial proportion of the spelling
sequence being shared between two words, such as BEAK and PEAK,
or BEAK and BEAN. Later in reading development, analogies may be
based on shared spelling units that are as small as a single letter
(BUG–CUP).

Contrary to this proposal, however, detailed study of the kinds of
analogies that children use as they are learning to read suggests that
phonological knowledge is more important in early reading analogies
than the size of the shared spelling unit. Take the examples of BEAD
and PEAK, which both share three letters with BEAK. At the beginning
of learning to read, most analogies are based on spelling sequences
that reflect rimes (Goswami, 1986, 1988). Children who learn to read
a word such as BEAK can use that spelling pattern as a basis for
decoding a new word sharing the same rime, such as PEAK or WEAK.
The same children do not use the spelling pattern of BEAK as a basis
for reading other words that also share three letters with BEAK, such
as BEAN and BEAD. Slightly older readers *will* use BEAK as a basis for
an analogy to BEAN or BEAD, but these analogies (which correspond
to a phonological unit made up of the onset [b] and part of the rime
[ea]) are generally used less frequently than rime analogies. So
phonological knowledge at the *onset-rime* level seems to be more
important for early analogies than the size of the orthographic
sequence which is shared between words (Goswami, 1986, 1988).

Phonological knowledge in early analogies

If onset-rime knowledge is important for early analogies, then children should use analogies between spelling sequences which reflect
shared onsets, too. So far, onset analogies have only been studied in
words that share consonant blends (Goswami, 1990). A consonant
cluster at the beginning of a monosyllabic word, such as the cluster

'tr' at the beginning of TRIM, or the cluster 'gl' at the beginning of GLUM, correspond to the onsets of these words. A consonant cluster at the end of a single-syllable word, such as 'ft' at the end of LOFT, or 'sk' at the end of DESK, correspond to part of the rime. Research has shown that children who learn to read a word such as TRIM will use this word as a basis for making analogies to words like TRAP and TROT, which share the same consonant cluster. However, when the same children learn to read a word like DESK, they do not use it as a basis for analogies to words like RISK and MASK, which also share a consonant cluster. This seems to be a phonological effect. Although both TRIM–TRAP and DESK–RISK share consonant clusters, the use of analogy depends on the *phonological status* of these clusters. When they correspond to onsets, then children use analogies; when they correspond to parts of the rime, they do not. So spelling sequences which correspond to onsets or rimes are more likely to be used as a basis for analogy than spelling units of equal size which require segmentation of the rime.

Vowel analogies in early reading

So far we have seen evidence for an apparently close correspondence between phonological knowledge at the onset-rime level and children's use of orthographic analogies in early reading. If this close link between the level of a child's phonological skills and the kind of analogies that they use in reading continues, then we might predict that, as awareness of phonemes develops, children will begin using analogies among spelling units corresponding to single phonemes. In some recent experiments, I attempted to study this possibility by looking at children's analogies among vowels in single-syllable words. I chose to look at vowels because they are always part of the rime. Thus vowel analogies *demand* phonemic skills. Children who use the vowel in BUG as a basis for reading CUP, or the vowel digraph in BEAK as a basis for reading HEAP, must be segmenting the words *phonemically* in order to make these analogies.

In these experiments (Goswami, 1994), I found that the use of vowel analogies emerges gradually as reading develops. Beginning readers (5–6 year olds), whose phonological skills are strongest at the onset-rime level, restrict their use of analogies to shared rimes. A beginning reader who learns to read a word like BUG will use it as a basis for reading RUG (shares rime), but not for reading BUD (shares onset-vowel) or CUP (shares a phoneme). A child with better reading skills (the mean reading age of this group was 6;10 years) will use a word like BEAK as a basis for decoding words like MEAN and HEAP, as well as PEAK, WEAK, BEAD and BEAT. These vowel analogies involve phonemic knowledge, as MEAN and HEAP share a single phoneme with BEAK (represented by the vowel digraph 'ea'). BEAN and BEAD share spelling sequences which require some phonemic knowledge, as well, because children need to segment the rime to make an analogy from BEAK to BEAN (extracting the onset-vowel unit 'bea'). Thus as reading develops, analogies are no longer restricted to spelling sequences that reflect onsets and rimes. Analogies among spelling patterns that represent phonemes and groups of phonemes are also used.

An interactive analogy model of learning to read

The close relationship between phonological and orthographic knowledge in the early stages of reading development can be described by an interactive analogy model of learning to read (Goswami, 1994). This model has the theoretical advantage of proposing that the child is using the *same* strategy at every phase of reading development, namely a strategy of lexical analogy. The cognitive strategy of analogy is known to be present by at least 3 years of age (Goswami, 1992). The model is interactive because phonological knowledge and orthographic knowledge are seen as influencing one another throughout development. Phonological knowledge initially constrains the development of orthographic knowledge, with children focusing on spelling sequences corresponding to rimes. Developing orthographic knowledge then, in turn, refines phonological knowledge, with phonemic awareness emerging from a combination of factors, including learning about single-phoneme onsets and learning to spell (see Goswami, 1994, for a more detailed description of this model).

Although teaching experiences and differences in orthographic consistency will affect development, too (see Wimmer and Goswami, 1994), the general proposal is that English children begin to read by analysing the orthography at the level of the phonological skills available to them at school entry, which are usually onset-rime skills. Phonological and orthographic knowledge then continue to affect each other's development as reading progresses. A key assumption is that orthographic analysis is *founded* in phonological skills, at least for the phonologically able child (see also Stuart and Coltheart, 1988). I have also speculated that the orthographic knowledge to which children apply their phonological knowledge might develop in part from their 'emergent literacy' experiences, such as having stories read to them while they follow the text. Although this is a largely passive experience, children who have had many stories read to them could develop some implicit knowledge about recurring patterns in the orthography, and they could exploit this implicit orthographic knowledge once they start being taught to read.

If English children *do* focus on rimes in the initial stages of learning about the English orthography, then this would be extremely adaptive. Wylie and Durrell (1970) showed that knowledge of only 37 rimes enabled a beginning reader to decode 500 of the most frequently occurring words in primary grade texts. So a reading strategy of using analogies based on rime units in familiar words would allow a rapid growth in reading vocabulary. The rime unit is also comparatively *consistent* in terms of its pronunciation in different words, whereas single phonemes are not. For example, the word LIGHT is often considered to be an irregular word. Its spelling pattern is indeed irregular when grapheme–phoneme mappings are considered, as a child who tries to read LIGHT by sounding out each letter is doomed to fail. However, the rime 'ight' in LIGHT has a very consistent pronunciation. There are 90 other English words in which the rime 'ight' is pronounced as in LIGHT, and no exceptions (Stanback, 1992). Thus rime units are preferable to grapheme–phoneme correspondences as a way of introducing children to spelling–sound correspondence in written English.

A Practical Perspective: Teaching by Analogy in the Classroom

The practical implications of the theoretical analysis presented above appear quite compelling. Spelling patterns corresponding to rimes in single-syllable words are readily used by beginning readers as a basis for analogies. Rime-spelling patterns also offer the most consistent way of teaching children about spelling–sound correspondences in written English. A teaching programme based on reading by analogy appears guaranteed to succeed. Training children to use rime analogies in the classroom should result in significant progress in reading.

Although there is a growing body of data which supports the proposal that learning to use rime analogies benefits young children's reading, there are some important factors to bear in mind if an analogy training programme is to work. One is the phonological abilities of the children involved. In order to exploit rime analogies in reading, a certain level of phonological skill is required. Children need onset-rime awareness to use analogies in reading and, furthermore, children who have good rhyming skills make more analogies (Goswami,

1990; Goswami and Mead, 1992). Thus children with *poor* rhyming skills, such as backward readers, may not readily benefit from being taught to read by analogy, or may only benefit *after* intensive phonological training.

A second factor is the length and depth of the training provided. Short-term training studies which give brief training in analogy by highlighting shared rimes in words have short-term effects. Such studies tend to find no gain in generalisation to untrained words, and no long-term retention of the words taught during training (e.g. Bruck and Treiman, 1992). Studies that provide training over a longer period of time are more successful (Peterson and Haines, 1992). The depth of training is also important. Successful training programmes teach children about *both* phonology and orthography, and stress the links between rhyming sounds and spelling patterns for rimes.

Finally, it is important to ensure that the children taking part in the training have the blending and segmentation skills that they will need to apply analogies to unfamiliar words. To read PEAK by analogy to BEAK, you need to be able to detach the initial 'b' from BEAK, leaving the spelling sequence 'eak' (segmentation). You also need to blend the sound for 'p' onto this rime unit, which further entails knowing the pronunciation of the initial 'p' in PEAK (the onset). Thus some training in segmentation and blending, and some explicit teaching of the sounds of onsets in words, may also be required if analogy training is to succeed. Each of these three factors, and the experimental evidence for them, will now be considered in more detail.

The importance of training phonological skills

The interactive analogy model of reading development described above proposed that orthographic analysis may be founded in phonological skills, at least for phonologically able children. This assumption entails the prediction that children who are not phonologically able may have difficulties in analysing the orthography. Their phonological skills may be inadequate for the task.

Consistent with this prediction, it has been shown that dyslexic children, unlike normal readers, do not spontaneously use analogies between spelling patterns in words (Lovett et al., 1990). Lovett and her co-workers trained one group of dyslexic children to read a list of single-syllable words like PEAK and CART. A control group who did not receive any training were given the same list of words to read in pre-test and post-test sessions. In contrast to the control group, the experimental group improved significantly on the taught words from pre- to post-test, showing that they had learned the spelling patterns of the words on the training list. Lovett et al. (1990) then went on to examine reading by analogy in the two groups. Both groups were given a second list of words to read, made up of words that shared rimes with the first list, like BEAK and PART. This time the experimental group failed to out-perform the control group. In fact, they showed an equivalent level of performance in reading these new words to their controls. Although a reading level control group of normally developing readers was not included in this study, the results suggest that the dyslexic children were unable to make analogies from the spelling patterns that they had learned in the trained list. This could either have occurred because the list presentation format meant that they did not notice that the rimes of the new words were familiar, or because they were unable to exploit the correspondence between the two lists because of their weak phonological skills. The inclusion of a normally developing control group in the study would have helped to clarify this point.

In a larger-scale study based in Hawaii, White and Cunningham (1990) tried training children to use rime analogies in the classroom. Although the children that they studied were not dyslexic, they were disadvantaged because they were from low socioeconomic and minority groups, and attended schools ranked in the bottom 15% of the state. White and Cunningham noted that reading problems were traditionally over-represented in these schools. Two training studies were conducted over two consecutive years, one involving 290 seven year olds, and the other 305 six year olds.

The analogy training that White and Cunningham used was part of regular classroom reading teaching, and was conducted by the teachers themselves, who had been trained to use a specially developed analogy programme for this purpose. An important feature of this analogy programme was that it provided training in *both* phonological and orthographic skills. The initial part of the programme, which lasted for a year, concentrated on rhyme training. After this, the teachers began to introduce the notion of analogy via a word family format. For example, a teaching session might focus on the known words JOB, NINE and MAP. Children were told that they would be shown words that rhymed with these key words, such as SPINE. They had to decide which family the new word belonged to, and then to read it aloud. Instruction in writing the words (spelling analogies) was also provided. As key words were learned, they were displayed on a wall of the classroom, to help the children to remember their spelling patterns. By the end of the year, the children had learned about 200 key words, and had had extensive practice in decoding and spelling by analogy.

To assess the effects of analogy training on reading development, standardised tests of reading accuracy and comprehension were given to the children in the analogy classrooms. Children in comparable control classrooms who had not received analogy training were given the same tests. White and Cunningham (1990) found that the children in the analogy classrooms achieved significantly higher scores than the children in the control classrooms in measures of *both* decoding and comprehension – an exciting result. The gains in comprehension as well as in decoding suggest that learning to read by analogy leads to a general improvement in reading skills as well as a specific one. Reading by analogy leads to better decoding, which in turn enhances reading comprehension. Although this study is weakened by the use of an unseen control group, the gains in reading made by the analogy group provide support for the idea that children will benefit by being taught to read by analogy in the classroom.

The length and depth of analogy training

The children in White and Cunningham's (1990) training study were given instruction in reading by analogy that lasted for a whole year. This is unusual in an experimental study. Training periods are usually fairly short, with consequent problems in interpreting negative results. Such negative results leave open the possibility that longer or more intensive training *would* have improved performance on the outcome measure.

Below two shorter training studies are contrasted, one that provided analogy training for two brief sessions of 10–15 minutes on consecutive days, and one that provided similar training over a period of a month. Both studies concentrated on analogy training (highlighting shared rimes), and neither provided additional phonological training. However, whereas the shorter training study did not result in significant gains in reading for a rime-trained group, the longer study did. This suggests that the length and depth of the analogy training is itself an important variable.

Bruck and Treiman (1992) conducted the shorter training study. In their study, 6-year-old children were taught to read a list of ten simple CVC words, such as PIG and HOP. One group of children were then given rime analogy training. They were shown ten new words that shared rimes with the taught words, such as BIG and TOP, and were taught to decode them. The shared rime was highlighted in coloured pen, and training continued until the children could read the ten new words to criterion. Two control groups learned the same original word list, but were then given new words to learn that either shared onset-vowel units with this list (PIN, HOT), or that shared vowels only (RIB, GOT). The analogous portion of the spelling pattern was also highlighted in coloured pen for these groups, who were also trained to criterion.

Bruck and Treiman found that the rime-trained group learned to read the new words significantly more quickly than the other two groups. So rime analogies had a stronger effect on initial learning than onset-vowel or vowel analogies. However, in a test of retention, the rime group were significantly worse at remembering the pronunciations of the words that they had learned during training than the two control groups. They were also poorer at generalising from these words to new, unseen analogous nonsense words like 'nig' and 'dop'. The best generalisation was found for the vowel analogy group, who had taken longer to learn the training set.

Bruck and Treiman's interpretation of this result was that rime-based analogy training 'is not a panacea'. They pointed out that the rime-trained group forgot the rime-analogous words soon after learning them, and showed little generalisation to new words. However, the effectiveness of rime-based training has not really been tested by this study, because the rime-trained group learned the training list in significantly *fewer* training trials than the other two groups. This means that we cannot be sure that the retention effect is related to the type of training that the children received. Unless total training time is equated across different experimental treatments, it is impossible to assess the educational implications of training studies. As the rime-trained group actually received significantly *less* practice with the training words than the other two groups, this lack of practice could have caused the faster forgetting, and the lack of generalisation. The rime-trained group may have been disadvantaged in the longer term *because* they learned to read the training words so quickly by analogy.

An alternative interpretation of Bruck and Treiman's result is that, when rime-based training is too brief, a positive effect on reading will not be found. Children may need a lot of practice in using rime analogies before it will show up in their reading. It would be simple to check this 'lack of practice' interpretation of Bruck and Treiman's results by repeating their study, increasing the length of the training period, and equating the amount of practice across the different groups. Meanwhile, it is difficult to reconcile the results of their study with those reported by White and Cunningham (1990), who found a clear effect of rime-analogy training on reading. The children in White and Cunningham's study obviously got a lot of practice in using rime analogies, as they were trained for an entire year.

However, even a month's training in rime analogies may be suffi-cient to show a positive result in the classroom. This possibility is sug-gested by a classroom training study carried out in Canada by Peterson and Haines (1992). Like Bruck and Treiman, Peterson and Haines trained children to use rime analogies by providing individual teaching about ten key words. However, rather than using pairs of rhyming words to train analogy, Peterson and Haines used a 'word family' approach that was more similar to that used by White and Cunningham. The inclusion of more examples of analogous words as well as the use of a longer period of training may be important.

In Peterson and Haines' word family approach, a single key word was introduced in the context of five new rhyming words. The key word (e.g. BALL) would be introduced first of all, and the children would be shown how to segment the word into onset and rime ('b-all'). Another word from the family would then be introduced (e.g. HALL), and the children encouraged to decode this new word by also segmenting it into its onset and rime ('h-all'), and then comparing the similar rime spelling patterns ('all–all'). As training progressed, four more words were introduced in the same way (FALL, MALL, GALL, WALL), with the same segmentation and comparison of rimes. By the end of the month, all ten of the key words and their associated families had been trained.

Peterson and Haines found that the rime-trained group significant-ly out-performed a control group of children from the same class on a measure of reading new words by analogy. Analogy training improved other reading-related skills as well, such as word segmentation and letter–sound knowledge. Although this study is weakened by the use of an unseen control group, its positive result suggests that rime-anal-ogy training does benefit children's reading, and their reading-related skills, too. The depth of the training – the use of a number of analo-gous examples, as entailed in the 'family' approach, and the explicit instruction in segmenting the rime from the onset – may have been as important for this learning as the length of the training period itself.

The importance of explicitly teaching associated skills

Finally, analogy training per se is obviously limited in value if children do not know how to pronounce the *onsets* of analogous words, or how to *segment* and to *blend* sub-syllabic units. A child who learns how to pronounce BALL will be unable to read the word FALL by analogy unless that child also knows how to pronounce the initial 'f' in FALL, how to segment BALL into its onset and rime, and how to blend the new onset ('f') onto the shared rime ('all').

In practice, the knowledge of onsets is unlikely to pose a major problem. Most children *do* know the initial sounds in words once they start to learn to read, as these are the sounds first stressed by their teachers. They are also the sounds sometimes taught by their parents, and if children appear to be struggling to use analogies because they do not know individual onsets, this is easy to remedy. It is notable that none of the analogy training programmes discussed in the last section described how they set about teaching onsets to the children, and this is probably because the children taking part in these studies already knew the sounds that individual consonants make at the beginnings of words.

Segmentation and blending skills are less likely to be present in beginning readers. It is interesting to note that both of the successful training studies discussed above included some training in segmentation and blending (White and Cunningham, 1990; Peterson and Haines, 1992). This 'training' occurred naturally as the children learned how to put words into the correct word families, which required segmenting the rime from the onset, and blending new onsets onto the rime. Peterson and Haines also noted that the children who were better segmenters at the beginning of their study benefited more from the analogy training than the children who had poorer segmentation skills. They found that the relationship was a reciprocal one: after taking part in the analogy training, the children's segmentation skills improved.

Conclusions

Although many aspects of the theoretical and practical implications of reading by analogy remain to be investigated, some firm conclusions can be drawn from the research discussed in this chapter. On the theoretical side, it is clear that phonological knowledge underlies the early use of analogies in reading. Beginning readers largely restrict their use of analogy to spelling sequences corresponding to onsets or rimes. Theoretically, this suggests that children's early analysis of the orthography is founded in their phonological skills, particularly in their early sensitivity to the onset-rime division of syllables. As orthographic knowledge grows, this in turn refines their phonological skills, resulting in an interactive relationship between orthography and phonology throughout the process of learning to read and write.

On the practical side, these findings imply that rime-based analogy training should benefit children's reading. Although rime-analogy training does seem to improve reading ability, factors such as the length of the training provided, the level of the children's phonological skills and the number of analogous examples that they are taught all seem to affect the outcome of training studies. Explicit training in segmentation and blending, and in the pronunciation of onsets, may also be important. Research establishing whether some of these factors are more important than others, or whether a particular combination of these factors produces the strongest training effects, remains to be carried out. What is needed now are some careful pedagogical studies comparing the relative importance of these different variables, to enable the most effective pragmatic use of reading by analogy in the classroom.

References

Bradley, L. and Bryant, P.E. (1978). Difficulties in auditory organisation as a possible cause of reading backwardness. *Nature* **271**, 746–747.

Bradley, L. and Bryant, P.E. (1983). Categorising sounds and learning to read: A causal connection. *Nature* **310**, 419–421.

Bruce, D.J. (1964). The analysis of word sounds. *British Journal of Educational Psychology* **34**, 158–170.

Bruck, M. and Treiman, R. (1992). Learning to pronounce words: the limitations of analogies. *Reading Research Quarterly* **27**, 374–389.

Goswami, U. (1986). Children's use of analogy in learning to read: A developmental study. *Journal of Experimental Child Psychology* **42**, 73–83.

Goswami, U. (1988). Orthographic analogies and reading development. *Quarterly Journal of Experimental Psychology* **40A**, 239–268.

Goswami, U. (1990). A special link between rhyming skills and the use of orthographic analogies by beginning readers. *Journal of Child Psychology and Psychiatry* **31**, 301–311.

Goswami, U. (1992). *Analogical Reasoning in Children*. Hillsdale, NJ: Lawrence Erlbaum Associates.

Goswami, U. (1994). Towards an Interactive Analogy Model of Reading Development: Decoding vowel graphemes in beginning reading. *Journal of Experimental Child Psychology* in press.

Goswami, U. and Mead, F. (1992). Onset and rime awareness and analogies in reading. *Reading Research Quarterly* **27** (2), 152–162.

Liberman, I.Y., Shankweiler, D., Fischer, F.W. and Carter, B. (1974). Explicit syllable and phoneme segmentation in the young child. *Journal of Experimental Child Psychology* **18**, 201–212.

Lovett, M.W., Warren-Chaplin, P.M., Ransby, M.J. and Borden, S.L. (1990). Training the word recognition skills of dyslexic children: Treatment and transfer effects. *Journal of Educational Psychology* **82**, 769–780.

Peterson, M.E. and Haines, L.P. (1992). Orthographic analogy training with kindergarten children: Effects on analogy use, phonemic segmentation, and letter–sound knowledge. *Journal of Reading Behaviour* **24**, 109–127.

Stanback, M.L. (1992). Syllable and rime patterns for teaching reading: Analysis of a frequency-based vocabulary of 17,602 words. *Annals of Dyslexia* **42**, 196–221.

Stuart, M. and Coltheart, M. (1988). Does reading develop in a sequence of stages? *Cognition* **30**, 139–181.

Treiman, R. and Zukowski, A. (1991). Levels of Phonological Awareness. In S. Brady and D. Shankweiler (eds), *Phonological Processes in Literacy*. Hillsdale, NJ: Lawrence Erlbaum Associates.

White, T.G. and Cunningham, P.M. (1990). Teaching disadvantaged students to decode by analogy. Paper presented at the annual meeting of the American Educational Research Association, Boston, MA, April 1990.

Wimmer, H. and Goswami, U. (1994). The influence of orthographic consistency on reading development: Word recognition in English and German children. *Cognition* in press.

Wylie, R.E. and Durrell, D.D. (1970). Teaching vowels through phonograms. *Elementary English* 47, 787–791.

Chapter 3
Short-term Memory, Speech Rate and Phonological Awareness as Predictors of Learning to Read

SINÉ McDOUGALL and CHARLES HULME

Learning to read depends upon a number of underlying cognitive skills and considerable research effort has been devoted to identifying predictors of progress in learning to read. Of the wide variety of skills that have been studied, tests of children's phonological awareness (which assess the ability to reflect upon and manipulate the sound structure of spoken words) are among the best predictors of progress in learning to read (see Wagner and Torgesen, 1987; Goswami and Bryant, 1990, for reviews). However, systematic relationships have also been found between reading ability and other aspects of phono-logical processing which do not necessarily require conscious aware-ness. Verbal short-term memory tasks are a good example of such tasks and good readers typically perform better than poor readers on these tests (e.g. Mark et al., 1977; Mann, Liberman and Shankweiler, 1980; Katz, Healy and Shankweiler, 1983). Relatively little is known, however, about the interrelationships between measures of verbal short-term memory and other measures of phonological skill, particu-larly tasks assessing explicit phonological awareness. Awareness tasks typically have a memory component and it is quite possible that part of their predictive relationship with reading skill derives from their memory requirements.

Wagner and Torgesen (1987) proposed that there were three dis-tinct forms of phonological ability related to learning to read: phono-logical awareness, phonological recoding in lexical access (i.e. the

31

recoding of written symbols into a sound-based representational system) and phonetic recoding to maintain information in working memory. They argued that although there was evidence of some commonality among all three types of phonological ability, there were also reasons for distinguishing between them. They gave particular emphasis to the distinction between phonological awareness and phonological recoding in working memory, which were both seen as having separable predictive relationships with reading (see Goldstein, 1976; Mann and Liberman, 1984). This lends support to a distinction between measures of phonological ability that require awareness and those that do not.

Phonological Awareness and Learning to Read

The relationship between individual differences in children's reading ability and their performance on tests of phonological awareness has been well documented (see Wagner and Torgesen, 1987; Yopp, 1988; Goswami and Bryant, 1990, for reviews). Early studies examining this relationship employed a large number of experimental tasks to assess phonological awareness and it soon became apparent that the different cognitive requirements of the tasks might lead to a variety of predictive relationships with reading (Lewkowicz, 1980; Backman, 1983).

Stanovich and his colleagues (Stanovich, Cunningham and Cramer, 1984) examined the relationship between reading ability and several different phonological tasks with a variety of cognitive demands. These included tests of phoneme addition, deletion and substitution, as well as rhyme discrimination and production. They found that the phonological tasks had a large amount of common variance and a factor analysis revealed only one factor on which all the non-rhyming phonological tasks loaded highly. On the basis of these results, Stanovich argued that phonological awareness could be regarded as a unitary trait. Unfortunately this conclusion was limited by the fact that the children performed at ceiling on the rhyme tasks, so these were therefore omitted from the factor analysis. As a result differences in the predictive relationships between tasks involving awareness of rhyme and those requiring phoneme awareness cannot be ruled out.

When Yopp (1988) carried out a factor-analytical study examining the predictive validity of ten phonological awareness tasks, she also noted that most tests of phonological awareness were strongly correlated. However, a factor analysis of her data yielded two highly correlated factors. Five tasks, including phoneme blending and segmentation, loaded on one factor, whereas three others which involved phoneme deletion loaded on another. Tasks loading on the second factor appeared to be more difficult and 'required more steps to completion'. Yopp therefore suggested that these might involve a larger memory component than the other tasks. Two tasks which did not appear to load on either factor were auditory discrimination and rhyme. As these were the tasks children found easiest, this may well be the result of ceiling effects similar to those noted in Stanovich's study.

Goswami and Bryant (1990) have argued that differences between phonological tasks in their relationship to reading arise from a developmental progression in children's ability to recognise and manipulate word sounds. They propose that awareness of syllables, and the sub-syllabic units of onset and rime, arises early in development before children learn to read, and that awareness of these units is causally related to children's success in the early stages of learning to read (see Lenel and Cantor, 1981; Bradley and Bryant, 1983; Stuart and Coltheart, 1988). In contrast, they argue that awareness of phonemes as units of speech within words only develops later, possibly as a consequence of having learned to read an alphabetic script (MacLean, Bryant and Bradley, 1987; Bryant et al., 1989).

Short-term Memory and Learning to Read

Two possible roles for short-term memory in reading have been suggested. One is in text comprehension: a number of authors have suggested that, to understand a phrase or sentence, the reader must hold information about previous words to be able to relate this to words that are currently being identified (e.g. Kleiman, 1975; Daneman and Carpenter, 1980; Daneman, 1988). It might therefore be expected that children with comprehension difficulties would have poorer short-term memory skills than those with adequate comprehension skills. Empirical support for this proposal has been hard to find. No differences have been found in short-term memory span for digits or words when groups of good and poor comprehenders have been compared (Oakhill, Yuill and Parkin, 1986).

A recent study by Stothard and Hulme (1992) suggests that neither short-term nor working memory skills provide an adequate explanation of specific reading comprehension difficulties in children. They compared the short-term and working memory skills of poor comprehenders with chronological age controls. Short-term memory was assessed using digit span and working memory was assessed using the task developed by Daneman and Carpenter (1980), in which subjects are asked to recall the final word from a series of sentences in the correct order. Stothard and Hulme found no differences between the two groups on either measure and concluded that working memory processes were not a major cause of comprehension difficulties.

Another possible role for short-term memory in reading is in learning to identify single words. Baddeley (1986) suggested that short-term memory may act as a storage system when children are decoding unfamiliar words. When children apply grapheme–phoneme conversion rules to decode words, short-term memory may be used to hold the sequence of sounds in the word so that they can be blended together.

When children with decoding, rather than comprehension, difficulties are studied, consistent differences have been found between good and poor readers in memory for digits and letters (Shankweiler et al., 1979; Katz, Healy and Shankweiler, 1983), words (Mark et al., 1977) and sentences (Mann, Liberman and Shankweiler, 1980). These differences are specific to measures of verbal short-term memory span. Similar differences have not been found in memory for abstract shapes or nonsense drawings (Vellutino, 1979; Hulme, 1981; Katz, Shankweiler and Liberman, 1981).

Explanations of individual differences in memory span between good and poor readers is most often couched in terms of the working memory model proposed by Baddeley and Hitch (see Baddeley and Hitch, 1974; Baddeley, 1986). In this model working memory is composed of a central executive and two slave sub-systems: the visuospatial sketch pad (which is concerned with visual short-term memory) and the articulatory loop (which is concerned with verbal short-term memory). Differences in memory span between good and poor readers are usually explained in terms of the operation of the articulatory loop, which is a limited capacity system in which decaying traces may be refreshed by subvocal rehearsal. The number of items that can be maintained depends on how many can be refreshed before their traces have decayed beyond the point at which they can be recognised at retrieval. The capacity of the loop is estimated at between 1.5 and 2 seconds (Baddeley, Thomson and Buchanan, 1975; Hulme et al., 1984; Hitch, Halliday and Littler, 1989). Typically, recall is related to the number of items which may be subvocally rehearsed by subjects within that time. When words are longer, and therefore take longer to articulate, the number of items that can be rehearsed and so recalled will be smaller (e.g. Baddeley, Thomson and Buchanan, 1975). Further evidence that the articulatory loop makes use of a speech-based code is given by the finding that subjects have more difficulty in recalling consonants or words that are phonologically similar than those that are dissimilar (e.g. Conrad and Hull, 1964; Baddeley, 1966; Cowan et al., 1987; Henry, 1991).

The Articulatory Loop and Individual Differences in Reading

Research carried out by Shankweiler and his colleagues at the Haskins Laboratories has implicated the phonological loop in poor readers' short-term memory difficulties (e.g. Liberman et al., 1977; Shankweiler et al., 1979; Mann, Liberman and Shankweiler, 1980). Shankweiler et al. (1979) asked children who were either good, average or poor readers to recall lists of phonologically confusable (e.g. b, c, d, g) and non-confusable (e.g. h, k, q, w) letters. The better readers had better overall recall and were more sensitive to the effects of phonological confusability. Shankweiler and his colleagues therefore concluded that poor readers suffered from defective phonological coding in the articulatory loop.

Although these findings have been replicated (e.g. Olson et al., 1984; Brady, 1986; Rapala and Brady, 1990), other studies which have carefully controlled for the effects of task difficulty have not substantiated these findings (Hall et al., 1983; Johnston, Rugg and Scott, 1987; Holligan and Johnston, 1988). Johnston, Rugg and Scott (1987) determined the span length for each child and then used lists one item shorter than span for each individual. When this was done poor readers also showed the phonological confusability effect. Johnston and her colleagues suggested that, when list length was too long, poor readers switched to using non-phonological strategies and were therefore less susceptible when phonologically confusable items were presented. These findings make it more difficult to suggest that there is a direct link between phonological ability and the short-term memory problems of poor readers.

Speech Rate and Individual Differences in Reading

There is some limited evidence that the rate of processing in the phonological loop rather than the quality of processing limits span in children with reading difficulties. Speech rate provides a measure of the rate of processing within the phonological loop. The more quickly words can be encoded and rehearsed, the longer the sequence of items that can be remembered. A number of studies have shown that there is a systematic relationship between the rate at which words may be spoken and increases in memory span with age (Hulme et al., 1984; Hitch, Halliday and Littler, 1989; Hulme and Tordoff, 1989; Raine et al., 1991). For example, Hulme and Tordoff compared the memory span of 4, 7 and 10 year olds for one-, two- and three-syllable words. Not surprisingly there were considerable differences in memory span between groups. More significantly, however, differences in memory span between age groups were closely paralleled by increases in speech rate. One possibility that is considered further below is that the short-term memory problems of poor readers may derive from impairments in the rate at which they can articulate information they have to remember.

Long-term Memory Contributions to Memory Span

One further mechanism may be a candidate for explaining the relationship between memory span and reading. It is now clear that developmental increases in memory span are not entirely explicable in terms of increases in speech rate. For example, Henry and Millar (1991) presented 5 and 7 year olds with different sets of words which were equated for speed with which the children of different ages could articulate them. When this was done, differences in memory span between the age groups still persisted. Clearly, if changes in speech rate were the only determinant of developmental increases in memory span, this could not happen. If speech rate is the sole determinant of changes in span, then equating the rate at which children can articulate words should also equate memory span scores.

Recent studies of our own suggest that there are changes in a long-term memory contribution to memory span as children get older. Hulme, Maughan and Brown (1991) measured memory span for words and non-words of differing spoken durations. It was found that memory span for words was better than for non-words, even though the two sets of materials were equated for how quickly they could be spoken. It was argued that the poorer recall of the non-words was attributable to the absence of long-term memory representations for these items.

A subsequent study applied these findings to the study of age differences in memory span (Roodenrys, Hulme and Brown, 1993). Both younger and older children recalled words better than non-words (indicating that both benefited from a long-term memory component to memory span), but some of the age differences in memory span were independent of speech rate, suggesting that part of the age difference in memory span was attributable to differences in a long-term memory component. These findings raise the possibility that some of the differences in memory span between good and poor readers might be attributable to differences in the quality or accessibility of phonological representations in long-term memory.

Some evidence to support this idea comes from research carried out by Katz and Shankweiler (1985). They asked second grade children who were either good or poor readers to name five items over and over again as quickly as possible. They found a systematic relationship between children's reading and their performance on the rapid naming task when letters or words were used as stimuli, but not when pictures were presented. They concluded that poor readers did not have a general retrieval problem because this would have resulted in a difference between groups for both pictures and words, but suggested that poor readers had deficiencies either in the processing or quality of stored phonological information. This adds further weight to the suggestion that differences in memory span between good and poor readers might be the result of differences in the quality of long-term memory representations of speech.

Short-term Memory, Phonological Awareness and Reading

Given evidence that the relationship between measures of short-term memory and reading is mediated via phonology (either through the operation of the phonological loop or via long-term phonological representations), remarkably few studies have examined the relationships of short-term memory, phonological awareness and reading. Gathercole, Willis and Baddeley (1991) carried out a study to investigate whether short-term memory and rhyme awareness skills made common or dissociable contributions to reading in children of early school age. They argued that, if phonological memory and rhyme awareness tapped a common phonological skill, they would have similar patterns of association with reading scores.

Children in this study were either at the beginning of their first or second year in school (mean ages = 4;9 and 5;9 years, respectively). They were given a battery of tests which included measures of reading (the British Ability Scales (BAS) Single Word Reading Test – Elliot, 1983; and the Primary Reading Test – France, 1981), phonological awareness (the rhyme oddity detection task used by Bryant et al.,

1989) and short-term memory (non-word repetition and digit span), as well as measures of non-verbal intelligence and receptive vocabulary. The results suggested that measures of rhyme awareness and short-term memory were related to reading ability in different ways. Scores in both the short-term memory tests were significantly linked with both measures of reading in the 5-year-old group, but no link was found for the 4 year olds. Rhyme awareness scores, however, correlated significantly with performance in the Primary Reading Test, but not with performance in the BAS single word reading test.

On the basis of these results, Gathercole, Willis and Baddeley (1991) argue that short-term memory skills only become closely related to reading after a year of formal schooling, whereas rhyme awareness is linked to reading even when children have only just begun formal schooling. This line of argument ties in with the idea, put forward by Goswami and Bryant, that awareness of rhyme develops before formal schooling begins and is causally related to later success in learning to read. However, the results of the study by Gathercole and colleagues must be regarded with some caution because many of the children in the sample were unable to read. The 4-year-old group were essentially non-readers. Fifty-four out of a group of 57 failed to read any of the words in the BAS Single Word Reading Test and performed at chance on the Primary Reading Test (mean score = 4.34 out of a possible 16 when choosing one of four in a multiple-choice test). The results of statistical analyses in the 5-year-old group are perhaps slightly more reliable because they were scoring well above chance on the Primary Reading Test (mean score = 10.75), but nevertheless 17 children out of a sample of 51 failed to read any words on the single word reading test.

In a recent study of our own, there was an attempt to investigate the nature of the relationships among measures of phonological awareness, short-term memory and reading (McDougall et al., 1994). Sixty-nine children between the ages of 7;6 and 9;6 years were tested on measures of reading (BAS Single Word Reading Test), short-term memory (memory span for one-, two- and three-syllable words, speech rate and span for abstract forms) and phonological awareness (rhyme oddity detection and phoneme deletion), as well as a measure of intelligence (a short form of the Wechsler Intelligence Scale for Children – Revised – Wechsler, 1974). The sample was divided into three reading ability groups on the basis of the children's BAS Reading Test scores. There were 23 children in each of the low, average and high ability groups, and these groups were closely matched for chronological age.

In common with previous studies, no difference was found between reading ability groups in their memory for abstract shapes, although there were large differences between groups in memory span for words.

As can be seen from Figure 3.1, it was possible to plot a linear function for all three groups in which memory span for one-, two- and three-syllable words was related to speech rate. The figure shows that differences in memory span among the groups are roughly proportional to differences in the speed with which the words that are to

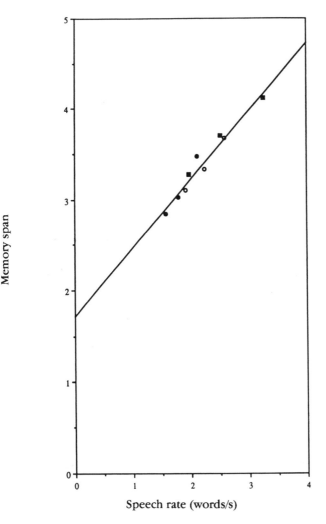

Figure 3.1 Memory span as a function of speech rate for long, medium and short words for the three reading ability groups: ●, low; ○, average; ■, high. (The three points for each reader group are for long, medium and short words respectively.) (Reproduced with permission from McDougall et al., 1994.)

be remembered can be articulated. In line with this, when the effects of speech rate differences between groups were controlled for statistically, differences in memory span were eliminated.

Data from this study are also relevant to the debate regarding the structure of the phonological skills that underpin children's reading. As discussed earlier, some have argued that phonological ability may be regarded as a single unitary trait (Stanovich, Cunningham and Cramer, 1984), whereas others have argued that different types of phonological task may tap distinct forms of phonological ability (Wagner and Torgesen, 1987; Yopp, 1988; Goswami and Bryant 1990). The present results support the idea that phonological skills are not unitary. Regression analyses showed that tests of phoneme and rhyme awareness both made independent contributions to predicting individual differences in reading ability (even after the effects of age and IQ had been controlled for).

The relative predictive relationships between short-term memory span and speech rate were also examined. Fixed order multiple regression analyses showed, surprisingly, that speech rate made an independent contribution to predicting reading even after the effects of short-term memory, phonological awareness and IQ had been controlled for. In contrast, once the effects of speech rate had been taken into account, short-term memory span had no residual effect on reading ability.

The question remains as to why speech rate, rather than span itself, predicts differences in single-word reading. Further studies are planned to investigate this. One possibility is that speech rate acts as an index of the speed and efficiency with which the phonological representation of words may be activated in memory. This may be critical in reading when a child needs to activate the phonological codes of words rapidly.

Conclusions

There is a massive amount of evidence showing that measures of phonological awareness are good predictors of the ease with which children learn to read. The recent studies reviewed make it hard to maintain the view that phonological skills are a unitary trait. Instead it seems as though different levels of phonological awareness make independent contributions to reading skill.

A further theoretical issue is to specify why phonological awareness tasks are such good predictors of reading ability. The studies reviewed certainly argue against the view that this is because of their memory requirements. In addition, however, we believe that awareness of phonological structure may not be as critical as the quality of underlying phonological representations and the processes that operate on them (c.f. Hulme and Snowling, 1992).

The findings from the study reviewed above also suggest that short-term memory per se may have much less to do with learning to read than has traditionally been supposed. Instead it appears that speech rate, which is intimately related to short-term memory skill, is a much better predictor of how easily children learn to read. We have speculated that the measure of speech rate used may provide one index of the speed of access to phonological information in memory. In this view the distinction between a factor tapped by measures of phonological awareness and one tapped by the speed of phonological processing (speech rate) may be more important than distinctions between different forms of phonological awareness which have been given prominence in studies in this area to date (c.f. Yopp, 1988; Goswami and Bryant, 1990).

References

Backman, J. (1983). The role of psycholinguistic skills in reading acquisition: A look at early readers. *Reading Research Quarterly*, **18**, 466–479.

Baddeley, A. D. (1966). Short-term memory for word sequences as a function of acoustic, semantic and formal similarity. *Quarterly Journal of Experimental Psychology*, **18**, 362–365.

Baddeley, A. D. (1986). *Working Memory*. Oxford: Oxford University Press.

Baddeley, A. D. and Hitch, G. (1974). Working memory. *In* G. H. Bower (ed.), *The Psychology of Learning and Motivation*, Vol. 8, pp. 47–90. New York: Academic Press.

Baddeley, A. D.. Thomson, N. and Buchanan, M. (1975). Word length and the structure of short-term memory. *Journal of Verbal Learning and Verbal Behavior*, **14**, 575–589.

Baddeley, A. D., Logie, R., Nimmo-Smith, I. and Brereton, N. (1985). Components of fluent reading. *Journal of Memory and Language*, **24**, 119–131.

Bradley, L. and Bryant, P. E. (1983). Categorising sounds and learning to read – a causal connection. *Nature*, **301**, 419–521.

Brady, S. (1986). Short-term memory, phonological processing and reading ability. *Annals of Dyslexia* **36**, 138–153.

Bryant, P. E., Bradley, L., MacLean, M. and Crossland, J. (1989). Nursery rhymes, phonological skills and reading. *Journal of Child Language*, **16**, 407–428.

Conrad, R. and Hull, A. J. (1964). Information, acoustic confusion and memory span. *British Journal of Psychology*, **55**, 429–432.

Cowan, N., Cartwright, C. Winterowd, C. and Sherk, M. (1987). An adult model of pre-school children's speech memory. *Memory and Cognition*, **15**, 511–517.

Daneman, M. (1988). Reading and working memory. In J. R. Beech and A.M. Colley (eds), *Cognitive Approaches to Reading*. Chichester: Wiley.

Daneman, M. and Carpenter, P.A. (1980). Individual differences in working memory and reading. *Journal of Verbal Learning and Verbal Behaviour*, **19**, 450–466.

Elliot, C.D. (1983). *British Ability Scales*. Windsor: NFER-Nelson.

France, N. (1981). *Primary Reading Test* (revised edition). Windsor: NFER-Nelson.

Gathercole, S. E., Willis, C. and Baddeley, A. D. (1991). Differentiating phonological memory and awareness of rhyme: Reading and vocabulary development in children. *British Journal of Psychology*, **82**, 387–406.

Goldstein, D. M. (1976). Cognitive–linguistic functioning and learning to read in pre-schoolers. *Journal of Educational Psychology*, **68**, 680–688.

Goswami, U. and Bryant, P. (1990). *Phonological Skills and Learning to Read*. London: Lawrence Erlbaum Associates.

Hall, J., Wilson, K., Humphreys, M., Tinzman, M. and Bowyer, P. (1983). Phonemic similarity effects in good vs. poor readers. *Memory and Cognition*, **11**, 520–527.

Henry, L. A. (1991). The effects of word length and phonemic similarity in young children's short-term memory. *Quarterly Journal of Experimental Psychology*, **43A**, 35–52.

Henry, L. A. and Millar S. (1991). Memory span increase with age: A test of two hypotheses. *Journal of Experimental Child Psychology*, **51**, 459–484.

Hitch, G. J., Halliday, M. S. and Littler, J. E. (1989). Item identification time and rehearsal as predictors of memory span in children. *Quarterly Journal of Experimental Psychology*, **41A**, 321–338.

Holligan, C. and Johnston, R. S. (1988). The use of phonological information by good and poor readers in memory and reading tasks. *Memory and Cognition*, **16**, 522–542.

Hulme, C. (1981). *Reading Retardation and Multi-sensory Teaching*. London: Routledge & Kegan Paul.

Hulme, C. and Snowling, M. (1992). Deficits in output phonology: a cause of reading failure? *Cognitive Neuropsychology*, **9**, 47–72.

Hulme, C. and Tordoff, V. (1989). Working memory development: The effects of speech rate, word length and acoustic similarity on serial recall. *Journal of Experimental Child Psychology*, **47**, 72–87.

Hulme, C., Maughan, S. and Brown, G. D. A. (1991). Memory for familiar and unfamiliar words: Evidence for a long-term memory contribution to short-term memory span. *Journal of Memory and Language*, **30**, 685–701.

Hulme, C., Thomson, N., Muir, C. and Lawrence, A. (1984). Speech rate and the development of short-term memory. *Journal of Experimental Child Psychology*, **38**, 241–253.

Johnston, R. S., Rugg, M. and Scott, S. (1987). Phonological similarity effects in memory span and development reading disorders: The nature of the relationship. *British Journal of Psychology*, **78**, 205–211.

Katz, R. B. and Shankweiler, D. (1985). Repetitive naming and the detection of word retrieval deficits in the beginning reader. *Cortex*, **21**, 617–625.

Katz, R. B., Healy, A. F. and Shankweiler, D. (1983). Phonetic coding and order memory in relation to reading proficiency: A comparison of short-term memory for temporal and spatial order information. *Applied Psycholinguistics*, **4**, 229–250.

Katz, R. B., Shankweiler, D. and Liberman, I. Y. (1981). Memory for item order and phonetic recoding in the beginning readers. *Journal of Experimental Child Psychology*, **32**, 474–484.

Kleiman, G.M. (1975). Speech recoding in reading. *Journal of Verbal Learning and Verbal Behaviour,* 24, 323–339.

Lenel, J.C. and Cantor, J.H. (1981). Rhyme recognition and phonemic perception in young children. *Journal of Psycholinguistic Research,* 10, 57–68.

Lewkowicz, N. (1980). Phonemic awareness training: What to teach and how to teach it. *Journal of Educational Psychology,* 72, 686–700.

Liberman, I.Y., Shankweiler, D., Liberman, A.M., Fowler, C. and Fischer, F.W. (1977). Phonetic segmentation and recoding in the beginning reader. In A.S. Reber and D.L. Scarborough (eds), *Toward a Psychology of Reading: The Proceedings of the CUNY Conferences,* pp. 207–225. Hillsdale, NJ: Lawrence Erlbaum Associates.

McDougall, S., Hulme, C., Ellis, A. and Monk, A. (1994). Learning to read: The role of short-term memory and phonological skills. *Journal of Experimental Child Psychology,* in press.

MacLean, M., Bryant, P.E. and Bradley, L. (1987). Rhymes, nursery rhymes and reading in early childhood. *Merrill-Palmer Quarterly,* 33, 255–282.

Mann, V.A., Liberman, I.Y. and Shankweiler, D. (1980). Children's memory for sentences and word strings in relation to reading ability. *Memory and Cognition,* 8, 329–335.

Mark, L.S., Shankweiler, D., Liberman, I.Y. and Fowler, C.A. (1977). Phonetic recoding and reading difficulty in beginning readers. *Memory and Cognition,* 5, 623–629.

Oakhill, J., Yuill, N. and Parkin, A. (1986). On the nature of the difference between skilled and less skilled comprehenders. *Journal of Research in Reading,* 9, 80–91.

Olson, R.K., Davidson, B.J., Kliegl, R. and Davies, S.E. (1984). Development of phonetic memory in disabled and normal readers. *Journal of Experimental Child Psychology,* 37, 187–206.

Raine, A., Hulme, C., Chadderton, H. and Bailey, P. (1991). Verbal short-term memory span in speech-disordered children: Implications for articulatory coding in short-term memory. *Child Development,* 62, 415–423.

Rapala, M. M. and Brady, S. (1990). Reading ability and short-term memory: The role of phonological processing. *Reading and Writing,* 2, 1–25.

Roodenrys, S., Hulme, C and Brown, G.D.A. (1993). The development of short-term memory span: Separable effects of speech rate and long-term memory. *Journal of Experimental Child Psychology,* 56, 431–442.

Shankweiler, D., Liberman, I.Y., Mark, L.S. and Fowler, C.A. (1979). The speech code and learning to read. *Journal of Experimental Psychology: Human Learning and Memory,* 5, 531–545.

Stanovich, K.E., Cunningham, A.E. and Cramer, B. (1984). Assessing phonological awareness in kindergarten children: Issues of task comparability. *Journal of Experimental Child Psychology,* 38, 175–190.

Stothard, S.E. and Hulme, C. (1992). Reading comprehension difficulties in children: The role of language comprehension and working memory skills. *Reading and Writing,* 4, 254–255.

Stuart, M. and Coltheart, M. (1988). Does reading develop in a sequence of stages? *Cognition,* 30, 139–181.

Vellutino, F.R. (1979). *Dyslexia: Theory and Research.* Cambridge, MA: MIT Press.

Wagner, R.K. and Torgesen, J.K. (1987). The nature of phonological processing and its causal role in the acquisition of reading skills. *Psychological Bulletin*, **101**, 192–212.

Wechsler, D. (1974). *Wechsler Intelligence Scale for Children – Revised*. New York: The Psychological Corporation.

Yopp, H.K. (1988). The validity and reliability of phonemic awareness tests. *Reading Research Quarterly*, **13**(2), 159–177.

Chapter 4
Influence of Phonological Awareness and Letter Knowledge on Beginning Reading and Spelling Development

VALERIE MUTER

It is well documented that phonological awareness and knowledge of letter names are very strong predictors of early reading progress (see Adams, 1990, for a review). Phonological awareness refers to a child's awareness of the speech sounds within words: the realisation that words can be broken down into sequences of constituent sound segments. Early large-scale studies of beginning readers in the USA found pre-readers' letter knowledge to be the best predictor of first grade reading, followed by their ability to discriminate phonemes auditorally, with mental age coming in third (Bond and Dykstra, 1967; Chall, 1967). These findings held up irrespective of the teaching method employed (Bond and Dykstra, 1967). This chapter describes the results of a longitudinal study in which 38 British children were followed from nursery school through their first 2 years at school. It focuses on the nature of phonological awareness, its interaction with letter knowledge, and its contribution to beginning reading and spelling.

Phonological Awareness and Beginning Reading

Correlational and longitudinal research has established that phonological awareness, even when assessed in pre-schoolers, is a powerful predictor of progress in beginning reading. Adams (1990) divides tasks that measure phonological awareness into four main types:

1. Tasks of syllable and phoneme *segmentation* in which the child identifies, taps or counts the constituent syllables or phonemes of presented words, e.g. for the word 'cat', the child taps three times to indicate the three constituent phonemes within the word.

2. *Sound-blending* tasks require the child to put together strings of phonemes provided by the examiner, e.g. 'c – a – t' blends to yield 'CAT'.

3. *Rhyming* tasks typically require the child to detect a rhyming word embedded within a sequence of other non-rhyming words. Alternatively, these might require the production of rhyming responses when given a stimulus word, e.g. in a rhyme production task, the child produces rhyming responses such as 'mat, fat, sat' for the stimulus word 'CAT'.

4. *Phoneme manipulation* tasks require the child to add, delete or transpose syllables and phonemes within words, e.g. in an initial consonant deletion task, 'cat' without the 'c' says 'at'.

Although all the measures of phonological awareness described above will predict reading and spelling success, some tasks are nevertheless better predictors than others. Adams (1990) draws attention to the fact that, in general, the skills which are more difficult and acquired later (such as phoneme segmentation and manipulation) yield stronger predictions of reading development than the earlier acquired skills (such as nursery rhyme knowledge, syllable segmentation and sound blending). It could be the case that different phonological awareness skills are relevant to the reading process at different points in its development. Thus, phoneme segmentation and manipulation skills, being closer in form to the skills demanded by the reading process, are initially the more influential.

Although phonological awareness clearly exerts a profound influence over subsequent reading development, this does not imply that the direction is necessarily one-way. Indeed, there is good evidence that learning to read affects the development of phonological awareness, especially of the more advanced skills of phoneme segmentation and manipulation (Alegria, Pignot and Morais, 1982). Liberman et al. (1974) demonstrated that, although most pre-schoolers can segment words into syllables, very few can readily segment them into phonemes. The more sophisticated stage of phoneme segmentation is not reached until the child has received formal reading instruction. Children appear to require exposure to letter–sound relationships before they can proceed further to advanced phonological awareness. The available evidence suggests that there is a two-way interactive process between phonological awareness and learning to read. As Bryant and Goswami (1987) point out, it may be that some forms of phonological awareness are causes of reading, whereas others are caused, or at any rate influenced, by exposure to print.

Phonological awareness skills have been studied in dyslexic, as well as normal, children. Snowling, Stackhouse and Rack (1986) found, in their study of seven dyslexic children, reading at either the 7- or 10-year level, that all the children were significantly worse than younger children of equivalent reading age on tests of rhyming and phoneme segmentation. Rohl and Tunmer (1988) demonstrated that children who are poor spellers find it harder to tap out phonemes than younger children with a comparable spelling age. Finally, Bruck and Treiman (1988) showed that 10 year olds with a reading age of only 7 years had greater difficulty on a phoneme deletion test than normal 7 year olds. Thus, one probable source of reading difficulty in dyslexic children is their inability to acquire phonological awareness skills sufficient to support the development of early literacy development.

Phonological Awareness – Its Nature and Development

Although there are many different types of phonological awareness task, it might be argued that they all measure essentially the same single global skill. Alternatively, phonological awareness may comprise a number of constituent subskills, each of which plays a different role in early literacy development.

Stanovich, Cunningham and Cramer (1984) gave ten different phonological awareness tasks to kindergarten children: rhyme detection and production, detection of same initial and final consonant, phoneme deletion, two tests of detection of different initial consonants, detection of final consonants, supplying of initial consonants and substituting initial consonants. They found that the *non-rhyming* tests were highly intercorrelated. It might be argued that the conclusions of Stanovich, Cunningham and Cramer are weakened by the finding that many of the children in nursery school whom they studied were at ceiling on the rhyming tests (Bryant and Goswami, 1987). Nevertheless, a factor analysis revealed only one factor on which all the non-rhyming tests loaded highly. Stanovich and colleagues reported that these measures were all moderately related to later reading ability and, when employed in sets, proved to be very strong predictors. Wagner and Torgeson's (1987) principal components' analysis of Lundberg, Olofsson and Wall's (1980) data also yielded just one factor.

In contrast, Yopp (1988) uncovered two factors from a principal components' analysis (with oblique rotation) of 10 phonological awareness tests given to 96 kindergarten children. The tests of phoneme blending, segmentation, counting and isolation loaded highly on one factor, whereas the phoneme deletion tests loaded highly on a second factor. The two factors were highly correlated, however, and appeared to reflect two levels of difficulty rather than two qualitatively different kinds of skill. The first factor, *simple phonemic awareness*, required only one cognitive operation – the segmentation, blending or isolation of a given sound followed by a response. The second factor, *compound phonemic awareness*, involved two operations, and placed a heavier burden on memory; the respondent performed an operation, such as isolating a given sound, then held the resulting sound in memory while performing a further operation (phoneme deletion or manipulation tasks). Both factors accounted for a significant proportion of the variance in a non-word reading task. Rhyming ability was only minimally involved in these two factors, which led Yopp to conclude 'rhyme tasks may tap a different underlying ability than other tests of phonemic awareness' (p. 172).

On the basis of these findings, Yopp recommended caution about reading research which draws its conclusions about phonological awareness from rhyming tasks. However, Goswami and Bryant (1990) did not share this view. They argued that segmentation, deletion and similar tasks are measures of phonemic awareness, whereas rhyming tests are sensitive, not to individual phonemes within words, but to onset-rime units within words. The onset of a single syllable word is its initial consonant or consonant cluster, whereas the rime is the vowel and final consonant (s). So, tests of phoneme awareness tap the phonemic structure of the word, e.g. 'c – a – t', whereas tests of rhyming access its onset-rime boundary, e.g. 'c – at'. Thus, according to Goswami and Bryant (1990), rhyming and segmentation skills should exert quite different influences over reading and spelling development.

Sara Taylor and I studied the development of phonological awareness in 38 4-year-old children over a 2-year period. The children were recruited while in their last term at nursery school. They ranged in age from 3;10 to 4;9 years, with a mean age of 4;3 years; they were all of normal intelligence (mean Wechsler Preschool and Primary Scale of Intelligence IQ = 114.67 – Wechsler, 1989). We first established that none of the children could read at the outset of the study, and any child reading even one word correctly from the British Ability Scales Word Reading Test (Elliot, 1983) was excluded from the sample.

All the children underwent testing at three equidistant points in time over a 2-year period, initially at nursery school and then during each of their first 2 years of infant schooling. They were given four tests of phonological awareness while at nursery; there were two tests of rhyme, one of rhyme detection and one of rhyme production. In the detection test, the children had to say which of three words (e.g. fish, gun, hat) rhymed with or 'sounded like' the stimulus word (e.g. CAT) for each of 10 items. In the rhyme-production test, the children were given 10 seconds to produce words that rhymed with each of two stimulus words (day and bell), both words and non-words being permissible responses. The third task was one of phoneme segmentation, based on a test devised by Morag Stuart (Stuart and Coltheart, 1988) and comprising eight items. The child was requested to 'finish off' the final phoneme of a single-syllable word for which the examiner supplied, with picture accompaniment, the first part of the word, e.g. 'here is a picture of a ca–' (CAT) to which the child responded 't'. For the final test, one of phoneme deletion, the child was requested to delete the initial single consonant phoneme of a single syllable word in a series of 10 items, e.g. 'CAT' without the 'c' says – –, the correct response being 'at'. All four phonological awareness tasks were repeated, with the addition of the Sound Blending Task from the Illinois Test of Psycholinguistic Abilities (Kirk, McCarthy and Kirk, 1968), during the children's first and second year at infant school. In the sound-blending task, the child joined together a string of phonemes supplied by the examiner, using a range of single-syllable words, multisyllable words and non-words.

The results of our study demonstrated that phonological awareness shows a clear developmental progression between ages 4 and 6 years, as children proceed from nursery through their first 2 years of formal schooling. In accord with the results of previous studies (summarised by Adams, 1990), rhyme detection turned out to be the easiest task during the nursery year, followed by phoneme segmentation, then rhyme production and, finally, phoneme deletion, which proved very difficult indeed. The children's scores on all the phonological measures steadily improved during the course of the following 2 years, although on none of them did the mean score reach 'ceiling'. It might be anticipated that if the study had continued for a further year, the mean scores on the rhyme detection and segmentation tests would almost certainly have reached ceiling, whereas the scores on the blending and deletion tests might have fallen just short of this upper limit. These results provide further evidence for the view that the more advanced stages of phonological awareness (e.g. phoneme segmentation and manipulation) are unlikely to be attained by most children until they have received exposure to formal reading instruction. This, in turn, supports the view that the ability to segment and manipulate phonemes in speech may arise, at least in part, from the experience of learning to read and to spell (Bryant and Goswami, 1987; Adams, 1990).

The children's scores on each of the phonological awareness tasks were entered into a series of principal components' analyses. These were conducted separately for each of the 3 years of the study. Two independent (uncorrelated) factors emerged: one was termed a 'segmentation factor' and was the factor on which the phoneme segmentation, deletion and blending tests loaded most highly; the other was interpreted as a 'rhyming factor' because the rhyme detection and production tests loaded most highly on this factor. The phonological awareness tests and their loadings on the rhyming and segmentation factors are presented in Table 4.1. This study appears to be the first to demonstrate the existence of two essentially independent skills underlying early phonological awareness. The results are in line with Goswami and Bryant's (1990) model of early reading development, which assumes that rhyming ability and phoneme awareness constitute separate and distinct subskills within the phonological domain. In their model, rhyming reflects children's awareness of onset-rime boundaries within words. They proceed to argue that onset-rime awareness forms a basis for children's ability to make use of analogical strategies in reading and spelling. In a series of elegant experimental studies, Goswami has demonstrated that young children can use a clue spelling like 'beak' to help them read new words such as 'weak' and 'peak' which share the clue word's rime (see Goswami and Bryant, 1992, for a review). In Goswami and Bryant's model, tests of phoneme deletion and segmentation reflect children's awareness of the smaller phonemic units within words which they use, not so much in early reading, but certainly in the 'sounding out' of words they are asked to spell.

Table 4.1 Summary of the principal components analyses: loadings of the phonological awareness tests on the derived factors, rhyming and segmentation

Test	Segmentation			Rhyming		
	Year 1	Year 2	Year 3	Year 1	Year 2	Year 3
Phoneme segmentation	0.81	0.84	0.91	0.20	−0.01	−0.02
Phoneme deletion	0.86	0.77	0.60	−0.01	0.26	0.64
Sound blending		0.69	0.72		0.40	0.50
Rhyme detection	0.32	0.29	0.16	0.82	0.75	0.84
Rhyme production	−0.06	0.06	0.07	0.91	0.90	0.85

Training Studies and the Phonological Linkage Hypothesis

Correlational and longitudinal studies of phonological awareness and literacy development have been complemented by training studies in which phonological skills (or, less frequently, letter names) have been taught to children on the assumption that this will lead to an improvement in their reading and spelling achievement.

Three of the earliest large-scale studies of phonological awareness training and reading (Bradley and Bryant, 1983; Olofsson and Lundberg, 1985; Lundberg, Frost and Petersen, 1988) produced rather disappointing results. In each study, young children were systematically trained on phonological awareness tasks, and their subsequent performance on measures of reading and spelling compared with that of children in specified control groups. In the Olofsson and Lundberg (1985) study, the only reliable improvement was recorded ~~...elling~~. A follow-up of the children a year later showed no lasting ~~...~~ reading or spelling. Bradley and Bryant (1983) found that ~~...egorisation~~ training alone produced no significant improvements over a semantic training control condition. However, when sound-categorisation training was combined with experience of (plastic) alphabetic letters this did produce significant improvements in reading. Lundberg, Frost and Petersen (1988) found that their training programme significantly improved the subjects' phonological awareness as well as their reading and spelling on follow-up. It should, however, be pointed out that the authors define the statistical significance of the improvement as 'only marginal' ($p < 0.10$). Consequently, none of these well-controlled large-scale studies had established an unequivocal link between the development of phonological awareness and subsequent improvements in reading.

In these training studies, the authors aimed for a sharp separation of the independent variable, phonological awareness, and the dependent or outcome variable – reading; in other words, the training in phonological awareness did not involve reading directly. Indeed, Bryant and Goswami (1987) consider this to be a fundamental requirement of training studies of this sort. Yet, clearly, the required outcome of the training studies – a demonstrable improvement in reading – had not been forthcoming. A similar situation existed in respect of training in letter name knowledge. It has been seen that pre-schoolers' knowledge of letter names is a powerful predictor of reading achievement a year later. However, there is good evidence to show that training in letter names does not give children any appreciable reading advantage (Adams, 1990). Perhaps, as Wagner and

Torgesen (1987) point out, it is very difficult to train phonological skills in isolation from other components of a literacy programme.

More recent training studies have shown that it may not be viable to separate phonological awareness training from within the context of reading instruction if meaningful improvements are to be produced in children's performance on literacy tasks. Ball and Blackman (1988) found that 5 year olds receiving instruction in word segmentation, letter names and sounds, and sound categorisation obtained higher scores on tests of phoneme segmentation and reading than children subjected to general language-enhancement exercises, together with the learning of letter names and sounds. Cunningham (1990) showed that nursery school and first grade children given phoneme-awareness training and reading instruction which were explicitly and actively linked scored significantly higher on tests of phonemic awareness and reading than children having phonic 'skill and drill' training.

Hatcher, Hulme and Ellis (1994; see Chapter 10) have pointed out that the results of training studies conducted over the last 10 years have failed to demonstrate a straightforward causal relationship between phonological awareness and subsequent improvements in reading. Rather, the available evidence supports an alternative view that they term the 'phonological linkage hypothesis'. According to this perspective, training in phonological skills which is isolated from reading and spelling may be less effective than training which forms explicit links between children's underlying phonological skills and their experiences in learning to read. Hatcher, Hulme and Ellis tested this hypothesis directly by carrying out a training study in which 128 poor readers aged 7 years were allocated to one of four groups matched for age, IQ and reading age. The 'reading + phonology' group received phonological awareness training, reading experience and activities that linked the two components. The 'phonology alone' group experienced phonological awareness training, but had no explicit reading instruction. The 'reading alone' group read books, had multisensory training and learned letter names (but had no phonological training). A control group received conventional classroom instruction. The children were subjected to 40 sessions of individual instruction over a 20-week period. At post-test, the 'reading + phonology' group scored significantly higher than the other groups on measures of reading; these improvements were sustained at follow-up 9 months later (at least for the reading comprehension measure). The effects were specific to reading: there were no differences between the groups on their arithmetic scores. The beneficial effects of the 'reading + phonology' intervention were not purely mediated by changes in phonological skill. Larger improvements in phonological skills post-test were obtained for the 'phonology alone' group than for the 'reading + phonology' group. It is thus evident that phonological processes influence reading through their interaction with other reading-relevant skills.

Experimental training studies have helped to make more explicit the interaction of phonological awareness with other reading components. Byrne and Fielding-Barnsley (1989) studied the acquisition of the alphabetic principle in pre-literate children aged 3–5 years. They defined this principle as 'a usable knowledge of the fact that phonemes can be represented by letters, such that whenever a particular phoneme occurs in a word, and in whatever position, it can be represented by the same letter' (p. 313). The children were first taught how to read the words MAT and SAT; they were then asked to decide whether the printed word MOW should be pronounced as 'mow' or 'sow'. Reliable performance on this transfer task was achieved only by those children who could phonemically segment the speech items, identify the initial sound segments and had learned the graphic symbols for the sounds 'm' and 's'. Thus, phoneme awareness *and* grapheme–phoneme knowledge are needed in combination for successful acquisition of the alphabetic principle.

Phonological Awareness, Letter Knowledge and Literacy Development – A Longitudinal Perspective

The longitudinal study of phonological awareness conducted by Sara Taylor and me had suggested the existence of two relatively independent subskills: rhyming and segmentation. In addition to the phonological awareness tests given at nursery and infant schools, we also monitored the children's development of letter naming knowledge, reading and spelling during the 2 years of the study. The children's ability to identify randomly presented letters by name was assessed at nursery and during each of the first 2 years at infants school. In the first and second year of infant school, the author gave the children tests of single word reading (British Ability Scale, Word Reading Test), prose reading (Neale Analysis of Reading Ability – Revised – Neale, 1989) and spelling (Schonell Spelling Test – Schonell and Schonell, 1956). All of the tasks were administered individually to the children.

The results were analysed using a statistical technique called *path analysis*. Path analysis is an extension of multiple regression, and allows the charting of the relationships between the reading-related measures from nursery through the first and then the second year at school. In the resultant path diagrams, the standardised path coefficients denote the strength of the relationship for a given path. The measures entered into the path analyses were: IQ, factor scores for rhyming and segmentation (as derived by the principal components' analyses), letter-name knowledge, reading and spelling. The raw score for each variable was converted into a *z* score; the purpose of 'centring' the scores in this way was to ensure comparability of measurement scales across all of the variables for all the analyses. Each year span of the study is considered in turn, i.e. from nursery through to first year infants, and from first year through to second year infants.

Nursery to first year infants

The first question that we asked was: what are the relative contributions of rhyming and segmentation skills to reading and spelling during the first year of learning to read and spell? Our path analyses demonstrated that segmentation made a highly significant contribution to early reading and spelling skills, whereas rhyming did not (Figure 4.1). The path diagrams in Figure 4.1 show the significant standardised path coefficients (β weights) for the paths between IQ and reading, and between segmentation and reading (and the corresponding paths for spelling). Rhyming failed to make a significant

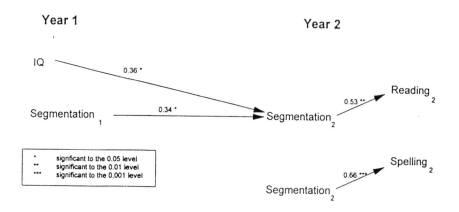

Figure 4.1 Path diagrams showing the contributions of IQ and segmentation to reading and spelling during the first year of the study.

contribution to either reading ($\beta = -0.20$, not significant or NS) or to spelling ($\beta = 0.12$, NS). The differential effects of rhyming and segmentation skills on literacy development in the first year provided further evidence for the distinction between these two phonological skills. The process appeared to be one in which IQ and pre-school segmentation ability both contributed to segmentation skills in the following year, which, in turn, drove reading and spelling progress during the first year at school. The effect of IQ on reading was not direct. Rather it exerted its influence through segmentation ability; brighter children found segmenting words into phonemes easier than less bright children, and it was this skill in segmentation that promoted reading development. It may seem incongruous that IQ did not play a greater role in early literacy development. However, this is in accord with the results of previous studies which have indicated that IQ comes in third, after phonological awareness and letter knowledge, in the prediction of early literacy skills (Bond and Dykstra, 1967; Chall, 1967). This is not to say, of course, that IQ need not contribute to later reading development, as contextual and comprehension factors come to play an increasingly important role.

The second question concerned the effects of letter name knowledge on early reading and spelling development. In particular, does knowledge of letter names interact with segmentation skills to facilitate literacy development? The relationships among segmentation, letter knowledge, and reading and spelling are shown in the path diagrams of Figure 4.2. In keeping with the findings of other studies (Bond and Dykstra, 1967; Chall, 1967), letter name knowledge

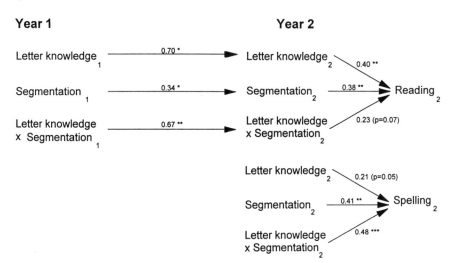

Figure 4.2 Path diagrams showing the contributions of letter knowledge, segmentation and the product term to reading and spelling during the first year of the study

proved a powerful contributor to reading and spelling processes during the first year of infant school. Segmentation and letter knowledge made separate and specific contributions to both early reading and spelling, with an *additional* significant contribution from the product term, 'Letter knowledge x Segmentation', which reflected the interaction of the two component skills. The product term exerted a small additional influence on reading, and a massive effect on spelling.

It seemed probable that this study was capturing most of the children at that point in their literacy development when they were beginning to acquire the alphabetic principle, i.e. the knowledge that particular phonemes in words are represented by particular letters (Byrne and Fielding-Barnsley, 1989). According to Ehri (1992), this level is achieved when children have had sufficient exposure to letters presented in graphemic form, and after they have attained a level of phonological awareness which enables them to split words into their component sounds. However, it seems unlikely that arriving at this developmental stage is simply a question of the children achieving phonological awareness and graphemic knowledge in an additive fashion. Recent training studies show that children make most progress in reading when phonological awareness training is combined in a meaningful way with the learning of letter names and sounds. It is this combination which is reflected in the product term, Letter knowledge x Segmentation. Phonological awareness training and teaching letter–sound relationships may help improve children's reading, but, when they are taught in combination, the effect on progress is significantly enhanced. The especially pronounced effect of the product term in spelling (as opposed to the more modest influences in reading) is consistent with the view that the alphabetic approach has more salience for early spelling than reading (Bradley and Bryant, 1983; Frith, 1985). The clear demonstration of positive contributions from segmentation and letter knowledge to early literacy progress and, more importantly, the additional influence of the interacting or potentiating effect of these two skills supports the phonological linkage hypothesis (Hatcher, Hulme and Ellis, 1994). Thus, to optimise progress in reading, it is necessary to teach children in such a way that explicit links are formed between children's underlying phonological awareness and their experiences in learning to read. The extent to which linkage has occurred, as measured by the additional variance accounted for by the product term in this study, predicts success in early reading and, more particularly, spelling development.

Second year infants

Turning to the second year of learning to read and spell, phonological awareness skills showed markedly different effects on reading and spelling in the last year of the study. Neither rhyming nor segmentation skills made a contribution to the children's reading scores during their second year at infant school. However, the children's reading vocabulary of the previous year exerted a powerful influence over their reading development in the last year of the study (Figure 4.3). Thus, the children studied seemed in some way to be using their existing vocabulary base, in a manner which was independent of their phonological awareness, to develop further reading skills.

The interpretation of these findings is speculative. It could be that the children had entered a 'consolidation' phase after establishing the alphabetic principle during their first year or so of learning to read. Alternatively, these results might reflect the development of a sight reading vocabulary through visual–phonological connections, along the lines described by Ehri (1992). In Ehri's view, children set up connections between sequences of letters in printed words and the phonemes that represent them. The connections are formed out of the reader's knowledge of sound–letter correspondences and of orthographic regularities abstracted from his or her reading experiences. Children use these connections which have been set up in memory to access the pronunciations of words. This process is faster than one involving repeated use of translation rules, and does not rely so heavily on phonemic awareness, but builds instead on the child's reading experience.

The path analysis showed that the major contributors to reading progress in the last year of the study were reading vocabulary from

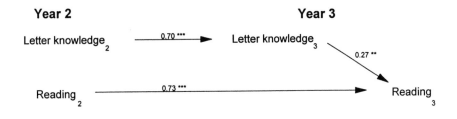

Figure 4.3 Path diagram showing the contributions of earlier reading skill and letter knowledge to reading in the second year of the study

the previous year and concurrent letter knowledge. These results are consistent with Ehri's view that the child is continuing to take note of sound–letter correspondences and using his or her established reading lexicon to draw inferences about orthographic regularities. These two processes in combination then fuel further reading development but without a phonological component; had it played a role this would have been reflected in significant contributions to final year reading from segmentation, possibly rhyming, and the Letter knowledge x Segmentation product term.

In the final year of the longitudinal study, we included an experiment looking at the relationship between children's phonological awareness and their ability to make analogical inferences in reading (Muter, Snowling and Taylor, 1994). Like Goswami, the author found that children trained to criterion on a series of clue words were able to read more words that shared spelling patterns with the clue words than control words. However, this effect was substantially reduced when the clue word was not exposed post-test. We found that the analogy effect correlated significantly with reading performance for the children who did *not* have the clue exposed post-test. It is proposed that, for these children, training on the clue word may have primed their pre-existing lexical knowledge of words that were orthographically similar. Thus, analogical strategies come into force after children have had the opportunity to build up a reading sight vocabulary on which to base their analogical inferences. Although rhyming ability did not contribute to reading skill, as measured by the standardised tests employed in the longitudinal study, we were able to demonstrate a significant and special relationship between rhyming and analogising at age 6. The findings of the longitudinal study and the analogy experiment favour an interpretation of children first using knowledge of sound-to-letter relationships to read and, later, with increasing awareness of orthographic regularities and rhyme, using analogies.

In contrast to the findings in reading, phonological awareness continued to exert a powerful influence on spelling throughout the first 2 years at infant school. Not only did segmentation persist in its contribution to spelling, but rhyming also entered the picture (Figure 4.4). Segmentation ability contributed to first year spelling in its own right and in interactive combination with letter knowledge. In the following year, segmentation skills continued to play an important role in spelling but the product term was no longer an additional influence. It seemed as though, once the alphabetic principle had been established during the first year at school, the children proceeded to a subsequent stage in which segmentation skills continued to exert

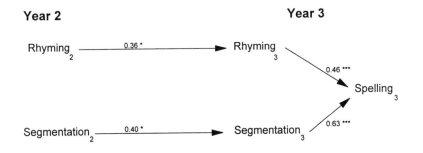

Figure 4.4 Path diagram showing the contributions of rhyming and segmentation to spelling during the second year of the study

an effect but not in relation to simple letter–sound knowledge. Rhyming as a contributory skill did not become a viable force until the final year of the study. The children's rhyming ability in that year was significantly related to their rhyming competence in the previous year. Concurrent rhyming then contributed to final year spelling. Although not directly assessed in this study, it may be the case that rhyming and segmentation contribute to quite different aspects of the spelling process. In line with the Goswami and Bryant model, it could be hypothesised that rhyming skills promote children's awareness of onset-rime boundaries within words which may, in turn, influence their use of analogy in spelling. In contrast, segmentation abilities promote children's awareness of phonemes within words which then facilitate their ability to make use of phoneme–grapheme principles in spelling. The present finding would support the view that children apply such correspondences in their early spelling attempts, but then later on begin to take note of larger segments in words, probably of analogy/onset-rime units.

Conclusions and Implications for Assessment and Teaching

Our longitudinal study led us to propose a model of early literacy development. First, phonological awareness comprises two independent subcomponents, specifically phoneme segmentation and rhyming. These skills exert differential influences over early reading and spelling development. Segmentation (but not rhyming) ability had a powerful effect on the first year of learning to read and spell, and so, to a roughly equal extent, did letter knowledge. In line with

Byrne and Fielding-Barnsley (1989), therefore, a minimal level of phonemic awareness and knowledge of at least some sound-to-letter correspondences leads to the acquisition of the alphabetic principle, and this, in turn, propels children through the early phase of literacy development. However, there is the separate and additional influence of a 'product term' which reflects the interaction of segmentation ability and letter knowledge. This is thought to be a direct measure of the linkage component described in the phonological linkage hypothesis (Hatcher, Hulme and Ellis, 1994), whereby children make more progress in reading and spelling when phonological awareness is combined in a meaningful way with literacy experiences.

Reading and spelling were affected by different cognitive processes during the second year at school. The results for reading appeared to capture the consolidation of a sight-reading vocabulary very much along the lines proposed by Ehri (1992). Once children have established the alphabetic principle, they have less need to apply phoneme-to-grapheme translation rules. Rather they use their improvements in knowledge of sound-to-letter relationships and their increasing awareness of orthographic regularities to read words by visual–phonological connections. Spelling, however, appears to remain phonologically and phonemically bound, with both segmentation and rhyming influencing the second year of learning to spell. It may be that children's segmentation abilities promote their phonemic awareness as they 'sound out' words they are asked to spell. Rhyming, which emerges as a later influence, might concentrate children's attention to the onset-rime boundaries of words, eventually promoting the adoption of analogical principles for words that share the same rime.

It is evident from the present and previous studies that phonological awareness skills and knowledge of letter names are powerful predictors of reading success. Their potential as screening instruments is considerable. The administration of tests of phonological awareness, particularly those that assess segmentation skills, and of letter–name knowledge to children in nursery or the first year of school is a relatively simple and cost-effective way of reliably identifying children at risk for reading problems. Early identification and treatment of reading failure are obviously desirable goals in a successful education system. The findings from recent training studies and our own longitudinal study suggest that phonological awareness training which is linked in a meaningful way to children's experience of print promotes their development of effective early reading strategies. The implications for the successful teaching of reading within the classroom, particularly for those children to whom reading does not come naturally and easily (e.g. dyslexic children) are obvious. Dyslexic children tend to have poor phonological awareness. Teaching schemes which specifically train these skills, and link the children's improved perception of speech sounds within words to their graphemic representation, are an important constituent of an effective remedial programme for dyslexic children.

Acknowledgements

The research described in this chapter was funded by a grant from the Leverhulme Trust (F427C) to Dr Faraneh Vargha-Khadem. Appreciation is expressed to Dr Vargha-Khadem for her advice and support throughout the project, and to Dr Jim Stevenson for his assistance with statistical analysis.

References

Adams, M.J. (1990). *Beginning to Read – Thinking and Learning about Print*. Cambridge, MA: MIT Press.

Alegria, J., Pignot, E. and Morais, J. (1982). Phonetic analysis of speech and memory codes in beginning readers. *Memory and Cognition*, 10, 451–456.

Ball, E.W. and Blackman, B.A. (1988). Phoneme segmentation training: Effect on reading readiness. *Annals of Dyslexia*, 38, 208–225.

Bond, G.L. and Dykstra, R. (1967). The cooperative research programme in first grade reading instruction. *Reading Research Quarterly*, 2, 5–142.

Bradley, L. and Bryant, P.E. (1983). Categorising sounds and learning to read – a causal connection. *Nature*, 301, 419–521.

Bruck, M. and Treiman, R. (1990). Phonological awareness and spelling in normal children and dyslexics: The case of initial consonant clusters. *Journal of Experimental Child Psychology*, 50, 156–178.

Bryant, P.E. and Bradley, L. (1983). Psychological strategies and the development of reading and writing. In M. Martlew (Ed.), *The Psychology of Written Language: Developmental and Educational Perspectives*, pp. 163–178. Chichester: John Wiley.

Bryant, P.E. and Goswami, U. (1987). Phonological awareness and learning to read. In J. Beech and A. Colley (Eds), *Cognitive Approaches to Reading*, pp. 213–243. Chichester: Wiley.

Byrne, B. and Fielding-Barnsley, R. (1989). Phonemic awareness and letter knowledge in the child's acquisition of the alphabetic principle. *Journal of Educational Psychology*, 82, 805–812.

Chall, J.S. (1967). *Learning to Read: The Great Debate*. New York: McGraw-Hill.

Cunningham, A.E. (1990). Explicit versus implicit instruction in phonemic awareness. *Journal of Experimental Child Psychology*, 50, 429–444.

Elliot, C.D. (1983). *British Ability Scales*. Windsor: NFER-Nelson.

Ehri, L.C. (1992). Reconceptualising the development of sight word reading and its relationhip to recoding. In P.B. Gough, L.C. Ehri and R. Treiman (Eds), *Reading Acquisition*, pp. 107–143. Hillsdale, NJ: Lawrence Erlbaum Associates.

Frith, U. (1985). Beneath the surface of developmental dyslexia. In K. Patterson, M. Coltheart and J. Marshall (Eds), *Surface Dyslexia*, pp. 301–330. London: Lawrence Erlbaum Associates.

Goswami, U. and Bryant, P.E. (1990). *Phonological Skills and Learning to Read*. London: Lawrence Erlbaum Associates.

Goswami, U. and Bryant, P.E. (1992). Rhyme, analogy and children's reading. In P.B. Gough, L.C. Ehri and R. Treiman (Eds), *Reading Acquisition*, pp. 49–63. Hillsdale, NJ: Lawrence Erlbaum Associates.

Hatcher, P., Hulme, C. and Ellis, A.W. (1994). Ameliorating reading failure by integrating the teaching of reading and phonological skills: The phonological Linkage Hypothesis. *Child Development*, 65, 41–57.

Kirk, S.A., McCarthy, J.J. and Kirk, W.D. (1968). *Illinois Test of Psycholinguistic Abilities*. Urbana, IL: University of Illinois Press.

Liberman, I.Y., Shankweiler, D., Fischer, F.W. and Carter, B. (1974). Reading and awareness of linguistic segments. *Journal of Experimental Child Psychology*, 18, 201–212.

Lundberg, I., Frost, J. and Petersen, O-P. (1988). Effects of an extensive programme for stimulating phonological awareness in pre-school children. *Reading Research Quarterly*, 23, 264–284.

Lundberg, I., Olofsson, A. and Wall, S. (1980). Reading and spelling skills in the first school years predicted from phonemic awareness skills in kindergarten. *Scandinavian Journal of Psychology*, 21, 159–173.

Muter, V., Snowling, M. and Taylor, S. (1994). Orthographic analogies and phonological awareness: their role and significance in early reading development. *Journal of Child Psychology and Psychiatry*, in press.

Neale, M.D. with Christophers, U. and Whetton, C. (1989). *Neale Analysis of Reading Ability – Revised British Edition*. Windsor: NFER-Nelson.

Olofsson, A. and Lundberg, I. (1985). Evaluation of long-term effects of phonemic awareness training in kindergarten: Illustrations of some methodological problems in evaluation research. *Scandinavian Journal of Psychology*, 26, 21–34.

Rohl, M. and Tunmer, W.E. (1988). Phonemic segmentation skill and spelling acquisition. *Applied Psycholinguistics*, 9, 335–350.

Snowling, M.J., Stackhouse, J. and Rack, J. (1986). Phonological dyslexia and dysgraphia – a developmental analysis. *Cognitive Neuropsychology*, 3, 309–339.

Stanovich, K.E., Cunningham, A.E. and Cramer, B.B. (1984). Assessing phonological awareness in kindergarten children: Issues of task comparability. *Journal of Experimental Child Psychology*, 38, 175–190.

Stuart, M. and Coltheart, M. (1988). Does reading develop in a sequence of stages? *Cognition*, 30, 139–181.

Schonell, F.J. and Schonell, F.E. (1956). *Diagnostic and Attainment Testing: Including a Manual of Tests, Their Nature, Use, Recording and Interpretation*. London: Oliver & Boyd.

Wagner, R.K. and Torgesen, J.K. (1987). The nature of phonological processing and its causal role in the acquistion of reading skills. *Psychological Bulletin*, 101, 192–212.

Wechsler, D. (1967). *Wechsler Preschool and Primary Scale of Intelligence*. San Antonio: The Psychological Corporation.

Yopp, H.K. (1988). The validity and reliability of phonemic awareness tests. *Reading Research Quarterly*, 13 (2), 159–177.

Part II
The Nature and Causes of
Reading Difficulties

Chapter 5
Variability in Dyslexia

PHILIP SEYMOUR

An important, if unresolved, topic within the study of dyslexia concerns the possible variability of the condition (Ellis, 1985). Some people take the view that dyslexia reflects a single pattern of malfunction, perhaps resulting from a single cause. Others believe that there are qualitatively distinct varieties of dyslexia which may be associated with differing causes. The issue has significant implications for methodology, the kinds of theories which are constructed and the remedial approaches which might be recommended.

The first viewpoint states that dyslexia is a unified homogeneous condition. This view sanctions a methodology in which it is legitimate to average results obtained from members of a dyslexic sample and compare them statistically with averaged results obtained from members of a control sample (Vellutino, 1979). A theoretical goal is to show that the malfunction of the developing reading process follows a recurrent pattern which is consistently associated with a 'core deficit', such as a problem of phonological processing (Stanovich, 1988). The practical implication is that a common programme of remediation, probably emphasising the phonological basis of literacy, should be appropriate for all cases.

The second viewpoint sees dyslexia as variable or heterogeneous. If so, the practice of averaging results over cases will come to appear inappropriate. What is required is some method of examining cases individually and assigning them to subgroups which exhibit a common pattern of malfunction (Seymour, 1986). A theoretical scheme will need to explain how the reading process can break down in different ways and whether differing causes are implicated. Remediation may involve the construction of alternative programmes which are suitable for cases showing particular characteristics.

In recent years there has been increasing interest in the application of the methods of cognitive psychology, psycholinguistics and cognitive neuropsychology to the study of childhood dyslexia. The contribution of these approaches consists mainly in:

1. The formulation of an analytical method which might be used to verify the existence of the underlying processes and to monitor their availability at different stages of normal or impaired development.
2. The presentation of a theoretical framework which could be used to guide research and to inform the interpretation of results.

A goal of this chapter is to assess the implications of cognitive research and theory for the issue of variability in dyslexia.

Cognitive Theory

We know that an illiterate person may possess fully normal capabilities in the areas of perception and action, and in the reception, production and comprehension of spoken language. The component which makes the difference between literacy and illiteracy is a specialised mental mechanism, which may be referred to as the 'orthographic processor'; this mediates between the visual input from the written page and the already established processes of speech and understanding. A theory of literacy acquisition is, in effect, a theory about the formation of this specialised 'orthographic processor'.

The general distinction which is intended here was clearly stated by Gough and Tunmer (1986), who outlined a 'simple' model of reading, such that:

$$R = D \times C$$

where R refers to success in 'reading with comprehension', D refers to 'decoding' ability, and C refers to 'listening comprehension' ability. In the present discussion the 'orthographic processor' may be equated with D, a process of visual word recognition which is cognitively distinct from meaning and comprehension. According to Gough, the construction of the 'orthographic processor' involves a process akin to cryptanalysis – using this a child comes to internalise the complex cipher by which letters are related to speech in written English. The understanding of the cipher depends, among other things, on the perception of the segmental structure of spoken words. Once formed, it supports competence in both reading and spelling.

The important point here is that the cognitive system is held to contain a specialised orthographic process, D, and a set of other processes, including comprehension, which are non-orthographic in function. According to the 'simple view', varieties of reading disability can be defined in terms of the relationship between the orthographic process, D, and the comprehension process, C. If these are represented as adequate $(+)$ or inadequate $(-)$ a 2 x 2 classification of the form shown in Table 5.1 can be derived. This suggests distinctions between: (1) 'dyslexia', defined as poor 'decoding' and good comprehension; (2) 'hyperlexia' (good decoding and poor comprehension); and (3) the 'garden variety' poor reader, who is impaired in both decoding and comprehension. However, the distinction between 'dyslexic' and 'garden variety' poor readers relates only to the non-orthographic comprehension process. The two groups are equated in terms of their orthographic malfunction, or the effect on D, the internalised orthographic cipher.

Table 5.1 Gough and Tunmer's (1986) classification of reading difficulties in terms of the adequacy of orthographic decoding and listening comprehension

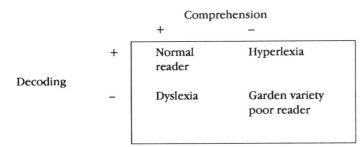

		Comprehension	
		+	−
Decoding	+	Normal reader	Hyperlexia
	−	Dyslexia	Garden variety poor reader

On these grounds, it can be suggested that Gough's theory is consistent with the unified or homogeneous definition of dyslexia. It proposes a structure for the mental system (a 'cognitive architecture') in which an internally undifferentiated 'orthographic processor' is viewed as being distinct from other mental functions. It also proposes a developmental progression which proceeds from an early stage of visual cue reading towards the internalisation of the orthographic cipher (see Gough and Hillinger, 1980; Ehri, 1992, for more detailed accounts of this progression). Finally, it suggests that the primary cause of the problem is an inability to relate 'ciphertext' (arrays of letters) to 'plaintext' (sequences of phonemes), perhaps on account of a lack of definition of the components making up the plaintext.

A theoretical scheme which was compatible with a variable heterogeneous account of dyslexia would need to differ from Gough's account by suggesting that the 'orthographic system' was made up of a number of components which might have distinct developmental histories or be vulnerable to disruption by different causes. The work of

Boder (1973) provides an early example of such a scheme. She proposed the existence of visual and auditory processes in reading and spelling which might be selectively impaired, producing the contrasting patterns of 'dysphonetic dyslexia' and 'dyseidetic dyslexia'. In more recent cognitive research, it has become clear that the possible subdivision of the 'orthographic system' can be stated in terms of two main sets of distinctions. One of these concerns the difference between the recognition processes required for reading and the production processes required for spelling. It is possible that independently vulnerable orthographic systems underlie reading and spelling. The second relates to the distinction between familiar and unfamiliar forms. There has been a general acknowledgement that the orthographic system must necessarily embody two kinds of competence, which can be referred to as:

1. A morphographic capability for identification and production of specific lexical items (words or morphemes).
2. A phonographic capability for dealing with unfamiliar forms in terms of their component letters and sounds.

These two aspects might also be supported by separately vulnerable systems.

These comments lead to the suggestion that an internally differentiated 'orthographic system' might contain four components. Examples of such proposals have been formulated by Ellis and Young (1988) and Morton (1989). Morton argued that reading development involved the construction of separate systems for morpheme recognition and alphabetic letter–sound translation. Spelling development, by analogy, depended on the establishment of a process of sound–letter translation and of a morphologically structured store of word forms.

The effect of this proposal is to complicate Gough's 'simple' model by proposing that D, the embodiment of the 'orthographic cipher', is made up of four elements, such that:

$$D = I(M) + I(P) + O(M) + O(P)$$

where I is an input process (reading) and O is an output process (spelling) and (M) and (P) are the morphographic and phonographic functions respectively. Variations in dyslexic pattern will arise to an extent that reflects the separate vulnerability of these processes. If each component was allowed to vary in adequacy of implementation, a large number of differing patterns might be observed. However, in a developmental context, it seems more likely that some components will be 'coupled', tending to vary together because of dependence on one another or on some common causal factor. Thus, Boder (1973) referred to reading/spelling patterns, so that:

$$D = [I(M) + O(M)] + [I(P) + O(P)]$$

implying that morphographic or phonographic impairments will affect both input and output.

Frith (1985) outlined a developmental framework which was expressed in terms of three strategies, designated as 'logographic', 'alphabetic' and 'orthographic', which were held to emerge sequentially in reading and spelling. The first 'logographic' process appears to be analogous to 'visual cue' reading in the schemes of Gough and Hillinger (1980) and Ehri (1992), and is thought to provide a goal of direct word recognition but not to survive as a functioning system (Morton, 1989). The critical step is held to be the adoption of the 'alphabetic' strategy, which involves the use of letter–sound correspondences in spelling and then in reading (components $O(P)$ and $I(P)$), and which is dependent for its development on awareness of the phonemic structure of speech. If development is 'arrested' at this point the subsequent establishment of the 'orthographic' processes in reading and spelling – $I(M)$ and $O(M)$ – will be inhibited. The implication is that a phonological process, P, lies at the origin of a causal sequence:

$$P \rightarrow [O(P) \rightarrow I(P) \rightarrow I(M) \rightarrow O(M)]$$

in which all four components are effectively 'coupled'. Hence, Frith's model, though apparently differentiated, ends by predicting a unified form of 'classic' developmental dyslexia, as in Gough's 'simple' model.

Frith (1985) suggested that there was one additional category of disorder which could be distinguished from 'classic' dyslexia. The reference here is to a special difficulty in spelling. Frith (1980) noted that the relationship between reading (I) and spelling (O) took three forms: type A: $I+O+$ (both adequate); type B: $I+O-$ (good reading but impaired spelling); and type C: $I-O-$ (both impaired). A characteristic of the type B pattern was that spelling appeared phonetically plausible but morphographically incorrect. This pattern implies that $O(M)$ may be impaired even though the other three functions have developed normally.

Evidence of Variability

In this section consideration is given to the evidence for variability of dyslexia. Questions can be posed concerning methodological issues:

1. What behavioural measures should be considered?
2. In which way should the data be treated?

There is now fairly general agreement that a contrast between familiar words and unfamiliar non-words is of fundamental importance. The morphographic capability can be studied through performance on tasks involving reading or writing of specific words. The phonographic aspect has been defined in terms of ability to read or write unfamiliar non-words. Reading aloud and writing to dictation tasks are usually employed, although there are other possibilities (e.g. the phonological and orthographic decision procedures used by Olson et al., 1985).

One approach to data presentation involves correlational and factorial analyses which aim to identify the dimensions of variation that are characteristic of a sample of cases (Mitterer, 1982; Bryant and Impey, 1986; Olson et al., 1990). The disadvantage of this approach is that the detail of individual case variations is discarded. An alternative approach involves the construction of detailed descriptions of individual cases who are held to exemplify particular patterns, often equated with the variations which have been observed in cases of 'acquired dyslexia' (Marshall, 1987). The disadvantage of this approach is that it provides no information about the incidence or distribution of the patterns.

Ellis (1985) suggested that the variation in dyslexia might be expressed in terms of the location of cases on a surface defined by dimensions of (1) whole word reading (the morphographic aspect), and (2) non-word reading (the phonographic aspect). In this type of analysis the variations in dyslexia are associated with the regions of the two-dimensional space which are occupied by individuals (see also Castles and Coltheart, 1993). Seymour and Evans (1993) plotted the locations of the individual members of a series of primary-school-aged dyslexic cases on a scattergraph defined by percentage error for reading lower frequency words of varying complexity and regularity against percentage error for reading non-words of comparable orthographic structure. An idealised version of the outcome is shown in Figure 5.1a. This indicates that (virtually) all cases fell in the lower triangle of the graph, representing a higher rate of error for non-words than for words, but that they were scattered widely across this region. The scatter reflects a variation in the severity of the impairment (distance from the origin of the graph) and also in the degree of discrepancy between word reading and non-word reading. To capture this latter aspect, the occupied area was bisected into two regions, referred to as the 'upper quadrant' and the 'lower quadrant'. Cases

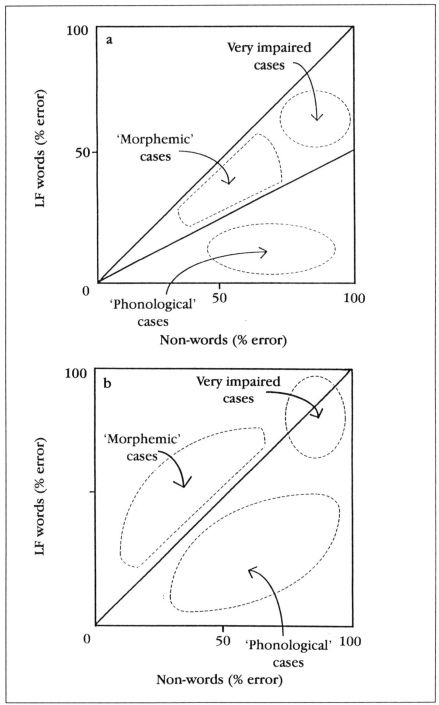

Figure 5.1 Schematic representation of the location of cases for (a) reading words and non-words and (b) spelling words and non-words in the studies reported by Seymour and Evans (1993).

falling in the upper quadrant have similar error rates in word and non-word reading; those in the lower quadrant display a discrepant pattern in which error rates for non-words are disproportionately higher than error rates for structurally comparable words.

Seymour and Evans (1992) undertook individual cognitive investigations of the reading processes of each member of the series, using error rate, error type and reaction time (RT) as indicators of process. These studies suggested that the 'upper quadrant' cases might reasonably be viewed as two subgroups:

1. A group of 'very impaired' individuals who could read hardly any words or non-words.
2. A remaining group of individuals who displayed many of the features of 'morphemic dyslexia' as described by Seymour and MacGregor (1984) and Seymour (1986).

This condition is defined as a primary impairment of the morphographic (word recognition) process, the $I(M)$ function in the present discussion. It is associated with recurrent features such as similarity of error rates and reaction times in word and non-word reading, evidence of serial processing, and sensitivity to word frequency and orthographic regularity. These features have been summarised and illustrated in Figure 5.2.

The cases falling in the 'lower quadrant' were found to exhibit the features of 'phonological dyslexia'. This is defined as a special difficulty affecting the phonographic (letter–sound translation) process, $I(P)$, which is reflected in the disproportionate difficulty in reading unfamiliar non-words. The individual cognitive analyses suggested the presence of two distinct reaction time patterns. Some cases, referred to as 'fast non-word readers', responded rapidly but inaccurately to non-words. Other cases, the 'slow non-word readers', made laborious responses which resulted in distinctively different reaction time distributions for words and non-words. These characteristics have been summarised and illustrated in Figure 5.3.

Seymour and Evans (1994) reported a similar analysis for spelling the words and non-words by the members of this sample. The general appearance of the scattergraph is shown in Figure 5.1b. The cases were distributed about equally either side of the main diagonal and were classifiable as 'above diagonal', indicating higher rates of error for word spelling than for non-word spelling, or 'below diagonal', indicating higher error rates for non-words than for words. Thus, the analysis of the spelling data indicates a variation in the direction of the lexicality effect – the word/non-word difference. This can be interpreted as a variation in the balance of adequacy in the morphographic

Reading process

- Raised error rate in word reading, especially lower frequency items
- Strong effect of regularity
- Some errors are regularisations
- Error rate for non-words similar to error rate for words
- Slow dispersed reaction time distribution of similar appearance for words and non-words (a)
- Strong effect of word length on reaction time (b)

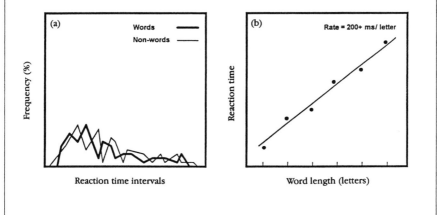

Spelling process

- Reversed lexicality effect in spelling (more errors on lower frequency words than non-words)
- Strong effect of regularity on spelling accuracy
- Some spelling errors may be phonetically plausible
- Confusions over spelling of heterographic homophones

Figure 5.2 Summary of the characteristics of morphemic dyslexia: primary impairment of morphographic (word recognition) process.

and phonographic spelling functions, $O(M)$ and $O(P)$.

According to the 'coupled' theory of Boder (1973), there should be a co-variation in the balance of the morphographic and phonographic functions in reading and spelling. In terms of Figure 5.1 this implies that 'upper quadrant' reading cases should be found in the 'above diagonal' region for spelling, and vice versa. Seymour and Evans (1994) reported that there was indeed a strong relationship between the two regional classifications. It was, in addition, true that the sample contained a number of cases who appeared to be

Reading process

- Error rate in non-word reading substantially higher than error rate for structurally comparable words
- Reaction times may be fast in attempts at both words and non-words (a)
- Reaction times may be fast for words but slow and laboured for non-words, producing strikingly discrepant patterns (b)

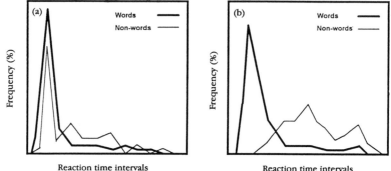

Spelling process
- Positive lexicality effect (more errors on non-words than lower frequency words)
- Effect of regularity
- Errors may appear dysphonetic

Phonological processes
- Difficulties with tasks involving retention and manipulation of speech segments

Figure 5.3 Summary of the characteristics of phonological dyslexia: primary impairment of the phonographic (letter–sound) process

impaired in spelling but not in reading, corresponding to the type B pattern of Frith (1980).

The notion of 'coupled' processes implies that the variations in reading and spelling should be similar for the morphographic and phonographic measures. As a check on this, the error scores for reading and spelling non-words were plotted as a scattergraph (Figure 5.4). The scatter shows a high correlation ($r = +0.826, p < 0.01$) and a tendency for the great majority of cases to lie on or slightly below the main diagonal (representing equivalent error rates for words and non-words). There were, nevertheless, a few cases who appeared especially disadvantaged in reading (above-diagonal outliers) and a few others who were disadvantaged in spelling (below-diagonal outliers). These deviations reflect an imbalance in the proportions of non-words which were spelled but not read ($R–S+$) or read but not spelled ($R+S–$). The imbalance was assessed individually by calculating a χ^2 for a comparison between a 50:50 distribution and the actual frequencies of $R–S+$ and $R+S–$ items (using the non-words which were common to the reading and spelling assessments). The bias in favour of spelling was significant in only one instance, case LT. The general trend in the data was for $R+S–$ to exceed $R–S+$, i.e. for non-words to be read better than they were spelled. This effect was significant overall according to a Wilcoxon test (with $n = 42$, $W = 591.5$, $p < 0.005$), and individually, at $p < 0.01$ or better, for seven cases (GR, MS, GRD, GD, GP, RFC and IS).

To examine the same issue for the morphographic aspect, the scatter of cases for reading and spelling the lower frequency words was

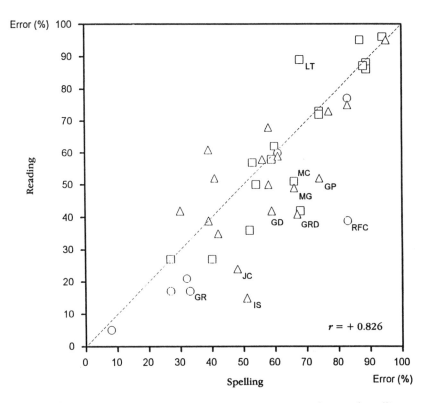

Figure 5.4 Scatter of cases for error rates (per cent) in reading and spelling non-words. Pattern: □, morphemic, △, phonological, ○, type B speller. (From Seymour and Evans, 1993)

plotted (Figure 5.5). An interesting departure from a closely correlated pattern is evident. The 'upper quadrant' cases occupy a vertical region on the extreme right of the scattergraph. This means that the series reflects a variation in the adequacy of the morphographic reading process, $I(M)$, combined with an extreme impairment of the morphographic spelling process, $O(M)$. The 'lower quadrant' cases occupy a horizontal strip in the lower region of the graph. This reflects a variation in the adequacy of morphographic spelling, $O(M)$, combined with relative efficiency in word recognition, $I(M)$.

The analysis suggests that the nature of the link between reading and spelling differs for 'morphemic' and 'phonological' cases. In morphemic dyslexia it appears that the primary impairment affects word recognition, $I(M)$, producing the variation on this dimension, and that this has a large secondary effect on the possibility of storage of orthographic patterns or word-specific information needed for conventionally accurate spelling. For phonological dyslexia it seems possible that the phonological impairment is damaging for the formation

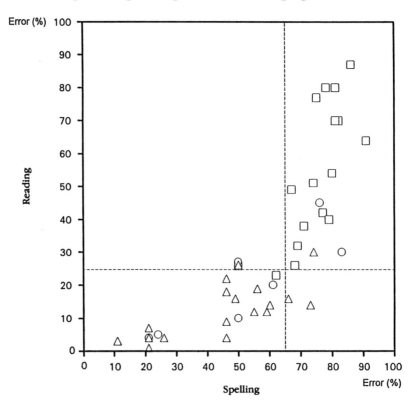

Figure 5.5 Scatter of cases for error rates (per cent) in reading and spelling low frequency words. The symbols used have the same meaning as in Figure 5.4. (From Seymour and Evans, 1993)

of a spelling system, thus affecting both $O(P)$ and $O(M)$, but that the consequences for word recognition in reading, process $I(M)$, are relatively less severe.

Implications for Theory

Going back to a consideration of the implications of variability for the explanation of dyslexia within a cognitive theory of literacy acquisition, the variation is, on the face of it, incompatible with theories which envisage the formation of a single 'orthographic system' (e.g. Gough and Tunmer, 1986). This conclusion also applies to more highly specified models, such as the connectionist simulation of reading acquisition described by Seidenberg and McClelland (1989). The architecture of their model included a single pathway linking orthographic elements to phonemic elements via a set of 'hidden units'. The model was subjected to a training procedure and learned to connect printed words of varying frequency and regularity to their pronunciations. Seidenberg and McClelland made the important claim that the internalisation of a word vocabulary generalised to the reading of unfamiliar non-words. In the terms of the present discussion, this means that the morphographic and phonographic aspects of written English might well be captured within a single network. Rather similar conclusions have been reached from connectionist models of sound–print connections in spelling (Brown, Loosemore and Watson, 1994).

In these simulations, 'dyslexia' can be induced by limiting the resources (units or connections) which are available to support the learning process. One possibility is that alterations in the location of the resource limitation – e.g. the orthographic units, or the hidden units, or the phonemic units – might produce differing outcomes which correspond to the morphemic and phonological patterns (Seidenberg, 1992). Another possibility is that networks which are required to deal simultaneously with generalisation and storage of specifics might vary in suitability for one function or the other, depending perhaps on the size of the set of available hidden units. This could produce outcomes in which the balance of adequacy in the morphographic and phonographic functions appeared to vary. Further simulations will be necessary if these possibilities are to be properly evaluated.

The data are compatible with the more differentiated models, such as that of Morton (1989), in which distinct morphographic and phonographic systems are postulated. It could be that the factors affecting the development of each type of system differ somewhat. As already noted, some relaxation of the developmental postulates of the theory would be required. Thus, it might be suggested that influences operating within the alphabetic domain – $I(P) \leftrightarrow O(P)$ – and within the orthographic domain – $I(M) \leftrightarrow O(M)$ – are relatively more significant than influences operating between domains. Frith's (1985) concept of the 'pacemaker' effects is consistent with a unidirectional version of this suggestion, where $O(P) \rightarrow I(P)$ and $I(M) \rightarrow O(M)$. The problem with the theory is that only one source of impairment is identified, notably a 'phonological awareness' of speech segments. It is easy to see how this could affect the phonographic processes. What is missing is some other factor, perhaps associated with the logographic processes, which might directly affect the morphographic developments.

Ehri (1992) has proposed a theory of word reading development in which phonographic processing is integrated into the lexical (morphographic) route. Although Ehri was critical of the two-channel model, it does appear from her discussion that she envisages a 'decoding' process which is applied at the first encounter with an unfamiliar word (or non-word) and which is presumably functionally distinct from the process of 'sight word' reading of familiar words. According to her theory, repetition of the decoding operation results in the formation of a phonologically based access path for a word, which, for a mature reader, will be founded on links between component graphemes and phonemes. Thus, the theory provides an account of the way in which alphabetic knowledge may contribute directly to the morphographic process (see Stuart and Coltheart, 1988, for a not dissimilar proposal).

There is no direct discussion of the issue of variability in dyslexia in Ehri (1992). However, her model could be adapted to address this issue if, for example, some children had a disorder affecting implementation of the decoding process, resulting in a phonological dyslexia, whereas others were unable to integrate grapheme–phoneme links into access routes for sight words, resulting in a morphemic dyslexia.

An alternative position is the 'dual foundation' model of Seymour (1990, 1993). A schematic representation of this theory is shown in Figure 5.6. It is assumed that the more advanced levels of reading depend on the formation of a central structure, called the 'orthographic framework', which develops from a basic 'core' to incorporate increasingly complex structures. This framework encodes both the general properties of letter–sound association (the 'orthographic cipher') and lexical specifics, as proposed by Seidenberg and McClelland (1989). A difference between this scheme and the connectionist model is that the organisation of the orthographic framework is assumed to be dominated by phonological categories, especially those that relate to the hierarchical structure of the syllable. Of most direct relevance to the present discussion is the proposal that orthographic development depends on inputs from the logographic and alphabetic 'foundation' processes. These processes may be independently vulnerable to disturbance. An effect on either one will impair the development of an orthographic framework, though in somewhat different ways, producing outcomes which correspond to the 'phonological' and 'morphemic' patterns.

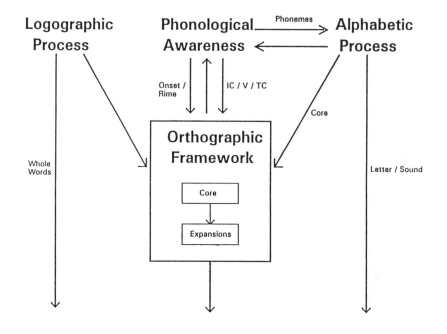

Figure 5.6 Schematic representation of the 'dual foundation' model of orthographic development. (From Seymour, 1993)

Evidence of 'Foundation' Impairments

Expectations arising out of the 'dual foundation' model are the following:

1. Distinct logographic and alphabetic processes should be discernible in early reading.
2. The processes may be selectively impaired.

The evaluation of this hypothesis will require detailed longitudinal studies of early reading development in cases of dyslexia.

Investigations of this kind are currently in progress in Dundee and will be reported fully in due course. The experience so far gained suggests that children with reading ages below about 6;7 years typically show incomplete development of the foundation processes. In these studies the logographic foundation has been assessed by asking children to read high-frequency words of irregular spelling which occur in a number of popular reading schemes. Where words cannot be recognised they are taught using standard whole word methods, including pairing with associated pictures. A logographic impairment is inferred if a child experiences extreme difficulty in acquiring a small sight vocabulary and if reading appears to be dominated by sequential processing and letter sounding. The alphabetic foundation has been defined in terms of ability to associate the letters with their dominant 'sounds', and to apply this knowledge in reading or writing C–V–C non-words. An alphabetic impairment is inferred if a child has extreme problems in learning to tackle the simple unfamiliar forms. Preliminary inspection of results contributed by 'foundation' cases supports the conclusion that some children exhibit a special difficulty in acquiring a logographic vocabulary, whereas others have major difficulties in sequential application of letter–sound knowledge.

As an illustration of the second – alphabetic – category a brief reference is made to results obtained from work with an 8-year-old girl of average or above intelligence and a reading age of about 6 years, who is referred to as case AB. Her reading of the high-frequency words was typically logographic, with errors all consisting of refusals or word substitutions, such as green – 'garden', ball – 'bell', father – 'frightened'. After a few teaching sessions, in which she fitted the words into pictorial scenarios of her own creation, she learned to recognise all 40 items from the vocabulary without difficulty. At the same time, although aware of most letter–sound associations, she was unable to read or write the simple non-words. Initially, these items were attempted without sounding and a proportion of responses were word substitutions. A substantial pedagogic effort was required to establish a systematic decoding procedure for dealing with the unfamiliar C–V–C forms. This included association of the C–V–Cs with people or creatures, colour coding of the initial consonant, vowel and terminal consonant units, and linkage with a family of 'phoneme puppets'. After prolonged effort she succeeded in reading 18 of 24 non-words and spelling 15 of 24.

In other cases the acquisition of a sight vocabulary has appeared to create special difficulties. For example, a girl, referred to as EK, was first seen at the age of 7;5 years, when she was found to be of average ability but to be unable to read any of the words on the Schonell list. She was also unable to recognise any words from the lists used to assess the logographic foundation. During the next 18 months efforts were made to establish the alphabetic foundation and also to teach the 40 words as a sight vocabulary. EK was unable to remember the words from one session to the next. Post-test she was able to identify only 10 words, almost always with support by sounding of letters.

A second example is provided by LK, also aged 7;5 years and of average ability, but with evidence of dysgraphic writing. Initial responses to the logographic assessment lists were very slow, accompanied by sounding, with correct responses on only 5 of 40 words. Teaching was directed towards extension of the sight vocabulary, involving introduction of only a few words at a time, association with pictures and learning from flash cards. Progress was very slow and LK persisted in attempting to sound out words which had already been taught. A check applied after 8 weeks yielded 17 of 40 correct responses. This had risen to 24 of 40 after a further six sessions. At this time, LK did not 'sound' letters audibly but could be seen to move his lips. The errors appeared phonetically motivated, e.g. high – 'hig', green – 'gren'. After further weeks of teaching he was able to read 30 of 40 words. He was unable to recognise items which were briefly presented by flashcard or on the computer screen.

When these longitudinal studies have been completed and analysed, it will be possible to determine whether logographic and alphabetic impairments can be distinguished at the foundation level of development, and whether they are indeed the precursors of the morphemic and phonological patterns which have been identified at the more advanced 'orthographic' levels.

Implications for Remediation

From a practical standpoint, the issue of variability in dyslexia is of importance mainly because different underlying patterns of dysfunction might require specially adapted approaches to remediation. This was indeed proposed by Boder (1973) who suggested that remediation might usefully focus on the stronger rather than on the weaker of the two hypothesised processes. It may be worth while to consider briefly whether the contemporary theoretical viewpoint, with its contrasts between 'foundation' and more advanced development, and between the 'phonographic' and 'morphographic' aspects of orthographic processing, leads to any obvious recommendations.

The current research at Dundee is based around the 'dual foundation' model sketched in Figure 5.6. The model includes the foundation processes which have been described. It also contains hypotheses regarding the content of the 'core' and advanced levels of structure contained in the 'orthographic framework' (Seymour, 1990; Seymour, Bunce and Evans, 1992). The pedagogic implication of the model depends on the level of development which has been reached. For 'foundation' cases it has appeared relevant to address the weaker function, as illustrated in the examples. At the more advanced 'orthographic' levels, the requirement is to build up a structural framework which can accommodate both generalities and specific items associated with a given level. Although differing in detail, the objectives appear comparable for morphemic and phonological cases, both of whom lack a normally formed framework (see Seymour and Bunce, 1994).

Conclusion

The aim of this chapter has been to discuss the issue of variability in dyslexia from the standpoint of cognitive psychology. It was argued that the possibility of variation raises questions relating to methodology, theory and remedial practice.

Methodology

The preferred research method is one which reveals the overall distribution of cases while at the same time allowing for a focus on the characteristics of individuals. A case series approach, using scatter charts to show the overall appearance of a sample, together with detailed cognitive assessments of the individuals, is recommended. The heart of the method involves the contrast between familiar words and unfamiliar non-words, because this defines the morphographic and phonographic dimensions that underlie the plot of the scatter of cases and the process analyses of the individuals.

Theory

The implications of the variability for theory are not yet fully clear. However, it seems likely that an adequate theoretical scheme must refer to the developmental progression as well as to the structure of the processing system, and that it must allow for some measure of independence in effects on the morphographic and phonographic aspects of reading development. The 'dual foundation' model (Figure

5.6) is proposed as a scheme which incorporates the widely acknowledged acceptance of phonological processes as a common influence
on orthographic development but which allows for alternative
sources of dysfunction in the two foundation processes.

Remediation

Dyslexic children differ from normal readers in terms of the course of
orthographic development. For normal children, the provision of
encouragement of the foundation processes, together with adequate
experience of texts and speech, seems sufficient to initiate a process
of internalisation of the 'orthographic cipher'. This does not happen
in dyslexia. Accordingly, remediation involves an attempt to establish
the orthographic structure in an explicit step-by-step fashion. It is
suggested that this task applies equally for all cases, irrespective of
the underlying pattern, but that the detail of its implementation may
vary. At a foundation level, where two separate functions are hypothesised, it will usually be necessary to attempt to establish both processes before proceeding to the orthographic framework, although the
emphasis in teaching will vary depending which function is more
severely affected.

References

Boder, E. (1973). Developmental dyslexia: A diagnostic approach based on three
    atypical reading-spelling patterns. *Developmental Medicine and Child
    Neurology*, **15**, 663–687.
Brown, G.D.A., Loosemore, R.P.W. and Watson, F.L. (1994). Normal and dyslexic
    spelling: A connectionist approach. *Cognition*, in press.
Bryant, P. and Impey, L. (1986). The similarities between normal readers and devel-
    opmental and acquired dyslexics. *Cognition*, 24, 121–137.
Castles, A. and Coltheart, M. (1993). Varieties of developmental dyslexia.
    Cognition, 47, 149–180.
Ehri, L.C. (1992). Reconceptualising the development of sight word reading and its
    relationship to recoding. In P.B.Gough, L.C.Ehri and R.Treiman (eds), *Reading
    Acquisition*. Hillsdale, NJ: Lawrence Erlbaum Associates.
Ellis, A.W. (1985). The cognitive neuropsychology of developmental (and acquired)
    dyslexia. *Cognitive Neuropsychology*, 2, 169–205.
Ellis, A.W. and Young, A.W. (1988). *Human Cognitive Neuropsychology*. London:
    Lawrence Erlbaum Associates.
Frith, U. (1980). Unexpected spelling problems. In U. Frith (ed.), *Cognitive
    Processes in Spelling*. London: Academic Press.
Frith, U. (1985). Beneath the surface of developmental dyslexia. In K.E.Patterson,
    J.C.Marshall and M.Coltheart (eds), *Surface Dyslexia: Neuropsychological and
    Cognitive Analyses of Phonological Reading*. London: Lawrence Erlbaum
    Associates.

Gough, P.B. and Hillinger, M.L. (1980). Learning to read: An unnatural act. *Bulletin of the Orton Society*, 30, 179–196.

Gough, P.B. and Tunmer, W.E. (1986). Decoding, reading, and reading disability. *Remedial and Special Education*, 7, 6–10.

Marshall, J.C. (1987). The cultural and biological context of written languages: Their acquisition, deployment and breakdown. In J.Beech and A.Colley (eds), *Cognitive Approaches to Reading*. Chichester: Wiley.

Mitterer, J.O. (1982). There are at least two kinds of poor readers: Whole word poor readers and decoding poor readers. *Canadian Journal of Psychology*, 36, 445–461.

Morton, J. (1989). An information processing account of reading acquisition. In A.M.Galaburda (ed.), *From Reading to Neurons*. Cambridge, MA: MIT Press.

Olson, R.K., Kleigl, R., Davidson, B.J. and Foltz, G. (1985). Individual and developmental differences in reading disability. In G.E.MacKinnon and T.G.Waller (eds), *Reading Research: Advances in Theory and Practice*, Vol. 4. Orlando, FL: Academic Press.

Olson, R., Wise, B., Connors, F. and Rack, J. (1990). Organisation, heritability, and remediation of component word recognition and language skills in disabled readers. In T.H.Carr and B.A.Levy (eds), *Reading and its Development: Component Skills Approaches*. London: Academic Press.

Seidenberg, M.S. and McClelland, J.L. (1989). A distributed, developmental model of word recognition and naming. *Psychological Review*, 96, 523–568.

Seidenberg, M.S. (1992). Dyslexia in a computational model of word recognition in reading. In P.B.Gough, L.C.Ehri and R.Treiman (eds), *Reading Acquisition*. Hillsdale, NJ: Lawrence Erlbaum Associates.

Seymour, P.H.K. (1986). *Cognitive Analysis of Dyslexia*. London: Routledge & Kegan Paul.

Seymour, P.H.K. (1990). Developmental dyslexia. In M.W.Eysenck (ed.), *Cognitive Psychology: An International Review*. Chichester: Wiley.

Seymour, P.H.K. (1993). Un modele du developpement orthographique a double fondation. In J-P. Jaffre, L.Sprenger-Charolles and M.Fayol (eds), *Lecture-ecriture: Acquisition. Les Actes de la Villette*. Paris: Nathan Pedagogie.

Seymour, P.H.K. and Bunce, F. (1994). Application of cognitive models to remediation in cases of developmental dyslexia. In M.J.Riddoch and G.W.Humphreys (eds), *Cognitive Neuropsychology and Cognitive Rehabilitation*, in press. Hove: Lawrence Erlbaum Associates.

Seymour, P.H.K. and Evans, H.M. (1992). Beginning reading without semantics: A cognitive study of hyperlexia. *Cognitive Neuropsychology*, 9, 89–122.

Seymour, P.H.K. and Evans, H.M. (1993). The visual (orthographic) processor and developmental dyslexia. In D.Willows, R.Kruk and E.Corcos (eds), *Visual Processes in Reading and Reading Disabilities*. Hillsdale, NJ: Lawrence Erlbaum Associates.

Seymour, P.H.K. and Evans, H.M. (1994). Sources of constraint and individual variations in normal and impaired spelling. In G.D.A.Brown and N.C.Ellis (eds), *Handbook of Normal and Impaired Spelling Development: Theory, Processes and Interventions*. Chichester: Wiley.

Seymour, P.H.K. and MacGregor, C.J. (1984). Developmental dyslexia: A cognitive experimental analysis of phonological, morphemic and visual impairments. *Cognitive Neuropsychology*, 1, 43–82.

Seymour, P.H.K., Bunce, F. and Evans, H.M. (1992). A framework for orthographic assessment and remediation. In C.Sterling and C.Robson (eds), *Psychology, Spelling and Education*. Clevedon: Multilingual Matters.

Stanovich, K.E. (1988). Explaining the difference between dyslexic and garden-variety poor readers: The phonological-core variable-difference model. *Journal of Learning Disabilities*, **21**, 590–604.

Stuart, M. and Coltheart, M. (1988). Does reading develop in a sequence of stages? *Cognition*, **30**, 139–181.

Vellutino, F.R. (1979). *Dyslexia*. Cambridge, MA: MIT Press.

Chapter 6
Phonological Constraints on Learning to Read: Evidence from Single-case Studies of Reading Difficulty

MARGARET SNOWLING, NATA GOULANDRIS and
JOY STACKHOUSE

The Development of Literacy: A Brief Review

For most children, learning to read involves integrating a system for processing written language with one that already exists for processing spoken language. When learning to read in an alphabetic script such as English, children have to learn that printed words convey meanings, that the graphemes of printed words map on to speech segments at the phonemic level and that there are irregularities in these mappings. They do this only gradually. In addition, when reading text, children have to integrate the meanings of words within phrases and sentences using knowledge of syntax and semantics.

The most appropriate framework within which to investigate developmental disorders of reading and spelling is within the context of theories dealing with the normal development of literacy skills. There are now a number of versions of 'stage' theories of reading development (e.g. Frith, 1985; Morton, 1989; Seymour, Bunce and Evans, 1989; Ehri, 1990). These theories view the child as passing through a series of stages or phases before becoming fully literate. In the initial stage it is widely held that reading is visually based and proceeds by the use of partial cues. At this stage the child has no strategies for deciphering unfamiliar printed words (other than by visual approximation to known words) and spelling is restricted to a few words learned by rote. The next stage, according to most theories, is when the child begins to decode using knowledge of the mappings between letters and sounds. Spelling using sound–letter correspondences also becomes possible at this stage. In the final stages of literacy development, reading and writing are automatic processes, the mappings between print and sound being at the phonemic level (Ehri, 1992).

There is currently debate about the status of stage models of reading (Stuart and Coltheart, 1988; Wimmer and Hummer, 1990). There is agreement, however, that phonological awareness is one of the best predictors of reading achievement, even when the substantial effect of IQ is controlled (see Goswami and Bryant, 1990, for a review). Some of the strongest evidence for this claim comes from longitudinal and training studies which show that children who perform well on phonological processing tasks go on to become good readers, and that training in phonological awareness promotes the development of literacy (Bryant and Bradley, 1985; see Chapters 9–11). The corollary of this is that phonological deficits are characteristic of dyslexia in children (Hulme and Snowling, 1992a).

Dyslexia and Learning to Read

Studies have shown that, on average, groups of dyslexic readers have difficulties on tests of phonological awareness, phonological short-term memory, verbal repetition and verbal naming (see Snowling, 1991, for a review). In addition, a great many experience deficits in non-word reading indicating problems with the application of phonological reading strategies (Rack, Snowling and Olson, 1992). The strength and consistency of the evidence are such that Stanovich (1990) has argued that dyslexia can be considered to be a core phonological deficit. Data consistent with the phonological deficit hypothesis come from a series of single case-studies exploring reading and associated cognitive deficits of dyslexic individuals (e.g. Campbell and Butterworth, 1985; Snowling, Stackhouse and Rack, 1986; Funnell and Davidson, 1989). Such studies, however, have also highlighted the fact that there is considerable variation among dyslexic readers (Seymour, 1986; see Chapter 5). Any adequate theory of dyslexia must take account not only of the consistent pattern of deficit in phonological processing which has been reported, but also of the cases of dyslexic readers who do not appear to have phonological deficits, for example, the dyslexic student, JAS, who has been described elsewhere (Goulandris and Snowling, 1991).

Surprisingly, given that dyslexia is a developmental disorder, rather little is known about the development of dyslexic children over time. In particular, we know very litttle about how a dyslexic child's cognitive skills might predispose him or her to a particular pattern of reading and spelling development. Yet these are important questions.

Answers to such questions might bring us closer to understanding the causes of dyslexia and also to isolating prognostic indicators.

One of our studies has tracked the development of a dyslexic boy, JM, for some 8 years. When first seen, JM was 8 years old and, although a boy of superior intelligence, he had only just begun to read and spell. At this stage in his development, he was what could be described as a 'logographic' reader – he could read words but not new or unfamiliar words (non-words) and his spelling was dysphonetic, e.g. he spelled CAP → gad, POLISH → bols and REFRESHMENT → refent. Snowling and Hulme (1989) reported that 4 years after this initial assessment, JM had progressed by roughly half the average rate in his literacy development. Moreover, his reading and spelling profile had not changed; he still had significant difficulty in non-word reading and his spelling was still dysphonetic. Thus, JM showed a stable reading and spelling profile. Although he had learned to read, he seemed to have done so by relying on visual strategies.

Snowling, Stackhouse and Rack (1986) and Snowling and Hulme (1989) suggested that a cause of JM's dyslexia could be found in his phonological system. JM was next tested when he was 13 years old (Hulme and Snowing, 1992b). On this occasion, he was administered a series of tests of phonological processing which placed differential emphasis on phonological input and phonological output processing.

First, to test whether JM's auditory processing of speech input was intact, he was presented with a difficult discrimination task. Twenty pairs of identical non-words (e.g. clird–clird, bannifer–bannifer) and 20 pairs of non-words differing by a single phoneme (e.g. thickery–shickery, bift–baft) were presented auditorily for same–different judgements. These non-words were the stimuli used by Gathercole and Baddeley (1989) to assess phonological memory and were subsequently used for repetition in this study. JM's performance was virtually perfect – he discriminated 38 of 40 items correctly.

JM's excellent performance in the auditory discrimination test ruled out a peripheral auditory-processing problem. To determine whether JM could access the phonological representations of spoken words, he was presented with a lexical decision task in which he had to respond 'Yes' if he heard a word and 'No' if he heard a non-word. The stimuli were all single syllables and the non-words differed from the words by a single phoneme, making the decisions difficult, e.g. dog–tog, grouse–crouse, friend–thrend. Altogether 48 words and 48 non-words were presented, half of each set being presented with noise masking. The use of masking was not central to this study and can be ignored for present purposes. JM made 18 out of 24 correct 'Yes' responses without masking and 17 out of 24 when stimuli were presented with a noise mask. His performance was within the range of normal reading age-matched controls who made, on average, 17.1 and 16.7 correct responses. It can be concluded that JM's ability to access the lexical representations of spoken words was at least as good as would be expected given his reading skills.

Next, JM was asked to repeat the Gathercole and Baddeley (1989) non-words which he had previously discriminated adequately. He repeated 25 of 40 correctly. This score was below the level of younger reading age-matched controls who repeated on average 35.5 of 40 correctly. This finding suggested that JM had problems assembling new speech output codes. It is important to note that the repetition and discrimination tasks were of equivalent levels of difficulty for normal control children. Unlike the reading age-matched controls, JM had much greater difficulty with the repetition than the discrimination task. JM, while performing at the top of the normal range for the discrimination task, was outside the range of normal controls when asked to repeat these same stimuli. These data provide powerful evidence for a differential deficit in JM.

To assess output phonological processing further, JM was asked to repeat 36 single-syllable non-words from the same corpus as those used in the lexical decision task. He also repeated the 36 words from which they were derived. He made 10 errors when repeating the words and 13 when repeating the non-words. His error rate was significantly higher than that of reading age-matched controls, and indeed outside the normal range of scores for both word and non-word repetition. As his ability to make lexical decisions regarding items in this same set of stimuli was equal to that of reading age-matched controls, these data confirmed that his deficit was at the level of output phonology. He had difficulty both in retrieving output phonology for words he knew and in assembling new articulatory codes for output when repeating non-words.

The finding of selective deficits at the level of output phonology in JM led us to hypothesise that output phonological representations play an important role in learning to read (Hulme and Snowling, 1992b). Specifically, the authors proposed that children use output phonology when mapping the letters in printed words onto the sound structure of spoken words. JM lacked stable output representations and therefore it was argued that his acquisition of a visual word recognition system had been delayed. Furthermore, he had been unable to abstract and use letter–sound rules to facilitate his reading because of his output difficulties.

If the hypothesis that learning to read depends upon the adequacy of output phonological representations is correct, then it should be possible to find other children who, like JM, have deficits in output phonology and have failed to read in a qualitatively similar way. Moreover, the severity of the phonological deficit experienced by such children, and possibly its nature, should predict the severity of the reading and spelling disorder.

Here data are presented from one dyslexic child, MB, from a group of 24 that the authors have been studying over a 2-year period of time (M. Snowling, N. Goulandris and N. Defty, unpublished data). MB, like JM, had deficits in output phonology. Contrary to hypothesis, however, his reading and spelling development had been somewhat different. We will discuss his case in detail and offer suggestions to account for the subtle differences between his literacy skills and those of JM.

The Case of MB

MB was first seen when he was 12;8 years of age. His WISC-R Full-Scale IQ was found to be 96 and there was no discrepancy between his verbal and performance skills. MB had specific reading difficulties; his reading age on the British Ability Scales Word Reading Test (Elliot, 1983) was 8;6 years, some 4 years below expectation. His reading comprehension was somewhat better and measured at 10;1 years on the Neale Analysis of Reading Ability (Neale, 1989). MB also experienced spelling problems and his spelling age, as measured by the Vernon Test (Vernon, 1977), was 8 years.

MB had been slow to speak and he had received speech and language therapy from 2 years of age. He attended a language unit for a year before transferring to an opportunity class in which he received intensive help. Following a period of education in a school for children with moderate learning difficulties, he was placed in a school specialising in the teaching of dyslexic children, which was where he was being educated when we saw him.

At 12 years of age, MB's language skills were within the normal range. On the vocabulary subtest of WISC-R (Wechsler, 1974) in which words have to be defined, he gained a scaled score of 9 which is average, and on the British Picture Vocabulary Scale (Dunn et al., 1982), a test of receptive vocabulary in which spoken words have to be matched to pictures, he attained an age-appropriate score at the 42nd centile. Although MB's vocabulary development was normal, it should be noted that he had specific difficulties with naming. His errors included naming a koala bear as 'lives in America' and a stethoscope as 'heliscope'. JM also had word-finding difficulties in the absence of vocabulary deficits.

An assessment of MB's phonological processing skills also revealed similarities to JM. He made very few errors on a rhyme detection task in which he had to decide whether the names of pairs of pictured objects rhymed or not. It is relevant, however, that his responses were slow. Moreover, he had great difficulty with a task in which he was required to produce rhyming words to a target. For example, in response to CLOWN, he produced 'sound, found, clown, shed, cloud, sound'. In response to STAR, he produced 'car, far, clock, shark, stars, store, stallion'. Generally, he produced fewer rhyming items than would be expected given his age, and he tended to lose track and to produce phonologically incorrect responses. MB also had difficulty on a test of sound categorisation requiring rhyme detection. Here he had to say which was the 'odd one out' of four auditorily presented items, for example, SUN, GUN, *RUB*, FUN (Bradley and Bryant, 1983). He made 5 out of 16 errors on this test, a score outside the normal range for children of similar reading skill.

Finally, MB had severe difficulty on tests of verbal repetition. On a test in which he was asked to repeat a series of words and matched non-words, his scores fell well below expectation for both his age and reading age. He also had great difficulty repeating the 40 non-words devised by Gathercole and Baddeley (1989). He repeated only 30 of these correctly – a score in the same range as that of JM. A similar pattern of reading and spelling performance to JM was therefore anticipated.

Phonological Processing Deficits, Reading and Spelling

When assessed at 12 years of age, MB read a matched set of regular words, such as GRILL, TASK, MARKET and irregular words, such as FLOOD, DOVE, POLICE. Generally, young children read regular words better than irregular because these are amenable to sound analysis (a phonic approach). MB showed this pattern of performance and read 27 regular words compared with 18 irregular words. JM, however, had done equally well on both sets of words suggesting that his reading was visually based. In addition, many of MB's attempts at irregular words were regularisations, e.g. he read SWORD as [swɔd] and SWAN as [swæn]. JM had never made these phonologically based errors.

MB was next administered a much larger set of regular and irregular words devised by Seymour (1986). He read an equal number of regular and irregular high-frequency words correctly, but he showed a significant regularity effect for low-frequency words reading 25 regular words correctly compared to 14 irregular words. The time taken by MB to read the words was also recorded. He took significantly longer to read low-frequency words which were regular in their orthography (1243 ms) than matched irregular words (1139 ms) suggesting that he was doing so by the laborious application of letter–sound rules.

MB's reading was therefore unlike that of JM. Although JM read regular and irregular words equally well and his reading errors were visually based, MB showed an advantage for regular words and his reading errors were regularisations, indicating that he was able to use letter–sound rules. These data led us to expect that, unlike JM, MB would be able to read non-words at a level commensurate with his reading age.

To investigate non-word reading, MB was asked to read 10 simple non-words e.g. TIG, ZUK and 22 complex non-words including one-syllable items such as TRESH and two-syllable items such as JENTER and KEPSTUD. He read 8 of 10 simple items and 18 of 22 complex items correctly. His performance was within the normal range of children of similar reading age to himself. These data confirmed that MB was able to use letter–sound rules in his reading.

To assess MB's ability to use phonological strategies to spell words, he was asked to write the simple and complex non-words which he had previously read. He was successful in spelling the simple non-words but only managed to spell 27% of the complex items correctly . His errors included TEGWOP → tekwop; ROMSIG → romsick. His performance compared unfavourably with the average for normal readers of similar reading skill who spelled 65% correctly.

Further evidence for MB's difficulty with phonological spelling strategies came from a qualitative analysis of his spelling errors. He attempted 40 words ranging in length from one to four syllables (after Snowling, Stackhouse and Rack, 1986). He spelled 19 of 40 correctly but, more significantly, 57% of his spelling errors were dysphonetic. For example, he spelled FINGER → thinger, CIGARETTE → securte, ADVENTURE → affench and POLITICIAN → potishone. At a similar stage in his development, JM's tendency to spell in this dysphonetic way was more marked than that of MB (some 75–85% of JM's errors were non-phonetic).

Thus, contrary to prediction, MB did not show the same pattern of reading impairment as JM although he had similar problems with spelling. In reading, MB made more effective use of letter–sound rules than JM – he could use these to read non-words and also to decode words with regular orthographic structure. However, although MB could use phonology in reading, he was less proficient in its use for spelling. In spelling MB had some difficulties with the transcription of non-words and his spelling errors tended to be dysphonetic.

MB was seen 2 years after the first assessment to review his progress and determine whether there had been qualitative changes in his reading and spelling strategies. It was clear that there had been little change in his language and phonological processing skills. He again obtained a scaled score of 9 on the WISC-R Vocabulary Subtest and his performance in naming remained poor. His verbal short-term memory was impaired (he gained a scaled score of 6 on the WISC-R Digit Span subtest) and he had persisting difficulties on tests of sound categorisation and rhyme production. His word repetition had improved to within the normal range of performance but he still had obvious difficulty with non-word repetition.

When assessed at follow-up, MB was 14;9 years. His reading age as measured by the British Ability Scales Word Reading Test (previously 8;6 years) was now 11;7 years and his reading comprehension (formerly 10;1 years) was 12;10 years. Thus, MB had made very good progress in the intervening 24 months; his reading had progressed at more than one and a half times the normal rate. MB's spelling development had been less good. At follow-up, he obtained a spelling age of 9;8 years.

The sets of matched regular and irregular words were again presented to MB for reading. This time he scored 19 of 31 on the irregular words and 30 of 31 on the regular items. Although we must interpret the score for regular word reading cautiously because of the possible ceiling effects, it is important to note that his reading of irregular words had not improved over the 2-year period. Similar data were obtained when once again MB read the low-frequency regular and irregular words from the set compiled by Seymour (1986). On this occasion he read 23 regular and 17 irregular words correctly and, once again, it took him longer on average to read the regular (1183 ms) than the irregular words (1037 ms). Thus, MB's reading development seems to have been supported by the development and use of phonological reading strategies. His word recognition skills, as evidenced by irregular word reading, had not, however, improved to a significant extent.

MB was asked to read the simple and complex non-words which he had read on a previous occasion. Effectively his scores had remained unchanged, which is perhaps a little surprising but might indicate a ceiling effect. Moreover, MB now showed some difficulty on other non-word reading tasks. He was asked to read a set of non-words derived from irregular words by changing the first letter (e.g. PLOOD, KISCUIT). His performance on this set of non-words containing 'inconsistent' spelling patterns was one standard deviation below the average for his reading level. Moreover, when asked to read complex two-syllable non-words, such as HINSHINK, his performance was outside the normal range.

The picture that emerged from testing MB when he was 14 years of age was that, although he could decode simple single-syllable non-words accurately he had difficulty in using complex letter–sound rules. He had made good progress during 2 years but his skill in reading irregular words had not increased. These data present a puzzling picture. It seems that MB had sufficient phonological reading skill to support the development of reading. However, there had not been a corresponding increase in his sight vocabulary. His reliance on phonological reading skills put him at a disadvantage when reading irregular words and his lack of knowledge of the spelling patterns embodied in these had a detrimental 'knock-on' effect on his reading of non-words based on them.

The spelling tests administered to MB were also repeated at follow-up. His non-word spelling remained weak and, still, some 40% of the errors which he made when spelling words were dysphonetic. For example, he spelled GEOGRAPHY → goegogh, POLITICIAN → polution, PUPPY → pupper, TULIP → trolip. Like JM, his rate of spelling progress was less good than his reading development and he had great difficulty with the use of phonological spelling strategies.

What Causes Individual Differences in Dyslexia?

In the 2 years in which we followed MB, some interesting similarities were observed between his performance and that of JM. MB and JM were broadly similar in terms of their cognitive profile. Both children had difficulties on tasks requiring phonological processing. They also had difficulties with object naming and impairments of verbal short-term memory. In addition, both children had difficulties at the level of output phonology. It was therefore surprising that MB's literacy skills were only broadly similar to those of JM. A particularly notable difference was that MB was able to use letter–sound rules in reading whereas JM was not. Both children had serious difficulties, nevertheless, with the application of sound-to-letter rules for spelling.

What might be the cause of these subtle differences in the reading skills of JM and MB? One obvious difference between the two boys was in their general intellectual ability. JM's general language skills were much better than those of MB and, indeed, his verbal IQ exceeded that of MB by some 20 points. It is possible that this IQ advantage enabled JM to use semantic context more effectively than MB during reading. Such use of semantic context in the face of weak decoding skills could promote the acquisition of a sight vocabulary and so increase JM's knowledge of irregular words over that of MB.

An alternative hypothesis is that JM had better visual memory skills than MB, presenting him with the ability to learn irregular words by their visual appearance. This explanation is not so likely because MB's visual memory was in fact quite good – he scored at the 95th centile on the British Ability Scales, Test of Recall of Designs, a test in which abstract figures have to reproduced following a 5-second delay.

Thus, although it is plausible that JM had developed a sight vocabulary more effectively than MB by relying upon a combination of visual and semantic skills (c.f. Hulme and Snowling, 1992b), this explanation can only go part of the way to explaining the differences between the two developmental dyslexic children. One difference which this explanation does not come close to explaining is MB's ability to use letter–sound rules in comparison to JM's inordinate inability to do so. Our initial hypothesis had been that difficulties with phonological reading strategies were the outcome of problems at the level of output phonology. However, MB and JM did equally badly on such measures. This lack of a difference brings us to a major shortcoming of quantitative measures of phonological processing. In quantitative terms, JM's deficit in tests of phonological output processing was no more severe than that of MB. However, if his responses, e.g. on verbal repetition tasks, were examined qualitatively, some major differences were revealed.

A phonological analysis of JM's speech production errors compared with a similar analysis for MB (at the second time of test) revealed that JM's errors were much more severe. JM's responses were generally further from target than those of MB, more of his errors contained multiple substitutions, there was inconsistency in his responding and considerable dysfluency in his planning of speech output. To give just two examples: when asked to repeat 'fenneriser', JM's response was [fɛn?(.)fəhɛ?(.)f.fənɛn :(.)fənɛnifsfõ]; MB's response was 'venneriser'. When asked to repeat 'glistering' JM's response was [kl(.)glistɹin(.)glistəɹin]; MB's was [glistrin].

We decided to classify the errors that the dyslexic children made when required to repeat the Gathercole and Baddeley (1989) non-words in the following way: responses in which there were several consecutive attempts at the target were regarded as planning errors, e.g. 'fenneriser' → [fɛn? (.)fəhɛ?(.)f.fənɛn :(.)fənɛnifsfð]. As these were serious errors, they were given an error score of 2. Similarly, multiple substitutions, e.g. 'empliforvent' → [empəfɔmənt], blonterstaping → [plɔntəsːtefin] were regarded as serious and scored as 2 errors each. Single substitution errors were regarded as far less serious, e.g. 'fenneriser' → [vɛnəɹisə], 'tafflest' → [təfləs.]; such errors were given a score of 1.

Although JM and MB had made a similar number of errors overall on this test, the distributions of their scores across these three error classes difffered. JM made six planning errors, six multiple substitutions and four single substitutions. MB, on the other hand, made three planning errors, zero multiple substitutions and ten single substitutions. The total error scores using the more sensitive scoring system outlined above were 28 for JM and 16 for MB. Thus, these data confirmed that JM's output phonology was more seriously impaired than that of MB.

Interestingly, the disorder within JM's phonological system, compared to that of MB, also seemed to cause more difficulties for his spelling production. It will be recalled that, although MB and JM both showed a tendency to make dysphonetic spelling errors, the tendency was much more marked in the case of JM. Indeed, JM's spelling errors have been the focus of a number of investigations linking deficits in output phonology with deficits in the use of phonological spelling strategies (e.g. Snowling et al., 1992).

Thus, the detailed investigation of MB, a dyslexic boy with deficits in phonological processing, has led us to refine hypotheses about the association between underlying difficulties of phonological processing and reading and spelling development. In particular, comparison of MB with JM has suggested that his relatively less severe impairments of output phonology have afforded him the benefit of the use of letter–sound rules for reading, albeit at a later stage of development than otherwise expected. The use of such rules seems to be denied dyslexic children who have more severe difficulties with output phonology. It follows that children with marked speech difficulties (at the level of output phonology) should have considerable difficulty in learning to read and spell.

Learning to Read and Spell with a Phonological Disorder

To test this idea, Stackhouse and Snowling (1992a) examined two children who had serious speech difficulties typical of the condition known as developmental verbal dyspraxia. Criteria for this condition include clumsiness, incoordination of the vocal tract, groping for articulatory postures and inconsistent articulatory output (see Stackhouse and Snowling, 1992b for a review). One of these children, Michael, will be described here.

Although of average intelligence, Michael's speech had been unintelligible during his early school life. In addition, he had a history of fluctuating hearing loss although during the course of this study his hearing was within normal limits. Michael was tested during two time periods. At the beginning of the study he was aged 10;7 years and, at follow-up, 4 years later, he was 14;5 years. During this time he was educated in a language unit where he received daily speech and language therapy, and reading and spelling tuition. In spite of this assistance, Michael made very little progress with his literacy skills. When first assessed his reading age was 7;7 years (Schonell Graded Word Reading Test – Schonell and Schonell, 1956) and 4 years later it was 7;8 years. Spelling measured at 6;8 years (Schonell Graded Word Spelling Test – Schonell and Schonell, 1956) at the first time of test and had increased to 7;9 years 4 years later.

To quantify the extent of Michael's phonological processing difficulties, he was administered tests tapping auditory discrimination, auditory lexical decision, sound categorisation, rhyme detection and rhyme production at the two points in time. Michael had more difficulty than reading-age-matched controls on all of these tasks at the first time of testing and, of course, he also had severe speech production difficulties. Thus, he had problems affecting both input and output phonology as well as phonological awareness. His difficulties were noticeably more severe and more pervasive than those of JM. Some 4 years later, when tested on the same tests, he performed within the normal range for reading-age-matched controls in auditory lexical decision. However, it should be noted that the normal controls were up to 7 years his junior and this therefore in no way reflected a competent performance.

To investigate Michael's reading and spelling development at the first time of test, he was asked to give the names and sounds of the letters of the alphabet. His letter–name knowledge was good but he had difficulty both in producing and in writing letter–sounds. To investigate his use of lexical and phonological reading strategies, he read 31 regular, irregular and non-words used in the authors previous studies. In each case 19 were of one syllable (e.g. 'lime', 'flood', 'plood') and 12 were of two syllables (e.g. 'butter', 'biscuit', 'kiskuit'). Both rule-based and exceptional pronunciations of the non-words were counted as correct. The normal readers showed a clear regularity effect with these stimuli, suggesting they were making use of phonological reading strategies. At the first time of test, Michael performed towards the lower end of the normal range and did not show a regularity effect. In addition, he failed to read any of the non-words correctly.

Over 50% of Michael's reading errors were lexicalisations (e.g. PINT → 'paint', FLOOD → 'foot', DRUG → 'drum', GRILL → 'glue', LIME → 'lemon'). The next highest proportion of errors, some 35%, were completely unsuccessful attempts to read words by sound. Only two regularisations were recorded. This was fewer than the number made by a control group of 7 year olds who made 19% regularisations on one-syllable words and 6% on two-syllable words (Snowling, Stackhouse and Rack, 1986). When tackling non-words, most of Michael's errors were again lexicalisations (e.g. GARKET → 'garden', ISLANK → 'island', TATCH → 'tissue', HIGN → 'hide'). However, some 34% were completely unsuccessful sound attempts.

Four years later, Michael's reading performance was similar to that of very much younger, reading age-matched controls and he showed a regularity effect. However, he persisted in making predominantly word-errors (62%). Once again two regularisations were recorded. By this stage, Michael could read non-words to some extent, although here too most of his errors, some 56%, were lexicalisations (e.g. RASK → 'risk', SWAD → 'swam', KISCUIT → 'kissed').

Thus, as predicted by our hypothesis, Michael had severe reading difficulties in association with his phonological problems. To investigate his spelling, he was asked to spell the one-, two- and three-syllable words which had also been give to JM and MB. At the first time of testing, Michael's spelling was poorer than expected considering his reading age. At the 4-year follow-up his spelling was as accurate as that of the comparison group. Again, it should be stressed that these children were some 7 years his junior. Moreover, Michael made very serious spelling errors which were not characteristic of the normal group. Only a minority of his spelling errors resembled the mistakes made by young normal children; these were spellings of LIP → lepp, BANK → back, KITTEN → keten. Most of his errors were dysphonetic. For example, he spelled BUMP → borr, TRAP → thew, SACK → satk, INSTRUCTED → nisokder.

At the first time of test, Michael transcribed the initial consonant correctly 90% of the time and maintained the syllable structure of the words on 45% of occasions. At the second test, he transcribed initial sounds perfectly but had inordinate difficulty in representing the other sounds. There were just three semi-phonetic spelling errors (BUMP → bup, PUPPY → pupe, POLISH → plish). Once again, most of his errors were dysphonetic and the proportion of these far exceeded that seen in normal readers.

Observation of Michael while he was spelling, together with an analysis of his errors, suggested that he was attempting to spell words sound by sound. Although this was a strategy fostered by teaching it was generally unsuccessful. His difficulties were plausibly related to severe problems with segmentation processes. For example, he would often only attempt the first and last sound in a two-syllable word (e.g. TULIP → tottper, PACKET → pater) and three-syllable words were frequently reduced (e.g. CONTENTED → kitr, REFRESH-MENT → lophet). Although these responses at first appeared bizarre, a consistent pattern emerged. Michael was able to identify initial and final sounds, but not sounds embedded within the words. He exaggerated his articulation, particularly of the final consonants to include a schwa, and hence the letter corresponding to the sound plus 'er' was often written down.

It seems highly likely that aberrant speech processes were affecting and intruding on Michael's attempts to spell by ear. Michael's speech could be quite unintelligible and a number of abnormal speech processes were present. Of central interest was the finding that these speech difficulties appeared to be recapitulated in Michael's spelling errors. For instance, there was a tendency for intrusive sounds to be included (e.g. SACK → satk, PUPPY → pats) and for consonant changes involving stops (POLISH → porter). Clusters such as [sp], [spl], [tr] and [str] were an added complication for Michael. His spelling TRAP → thewenmt may be the result of attempting to segment the initial cluster /tr/. Thus the *the* marks the added aspiration which was present when forcing a /t/, the *we* is the result of Michael labialising /r/ sounds to /w/ in his speech, and the last three letters, *nmt*, were attempts at /p/ being mistimed and resulting in changes of manner and place.

Michael's spellings of three syllable words were also interpretable in relation to his speech difficulties. He spelled CIGARETTE → satersatarhaelerar. This error can be deciphered with the knowledge that he made repeated attempts to segment and spell parts of the word. This 'searching' behaviour when spelling has a parallel in dyspraxic speech, namely articulatory searching or 'groping'. The error CIGA-RETTE → satersatarhaelerar provided another illustration of this phenomenon. Here Michael first attempted to transcribe the first and the last syllable twice (*cig* → sa., *ette* → ter, *cig* → sa, *ette* → t). He then attempted the middle syllable (*gar*) four times – ar hael er ari. Similarly, UMBRELLA → rberherrelrarlsrlles can be interpreted as repeated attempts to get the second syllable (*brel*) – r be rhe rre –

one attempt at the final syllable (*la*) – l̩, – two more attempts at the second syllable – ra r – and so forth. Analyses of these errors are by necessity subjective. However, the important point is that, although on first examination they appear bizarre, knowledge of Michael's speech difficulties provides a way of interpreting them. Close examination of his responses suggested that they reflected attempts to use a 'sound-by-sound' spelling strategy which was compromised by severe segmentation and speech difficulties.

At follow-up, Michael's non-phonetic errors were not as perseverative as the examples analysed above. However, he still reduced syllables (e.g. CIGARETTE → sicerk, MEMBERSHIP → minship, UMBRELLA → urmpt), and made intrusion and substitution errors (FINGER → fling, BANK → bark). This time a strategy of spelling by word components was observed to some extent. Thus, he spelled CATALOGUE → catlong, ADVENTURE → addever, REFRESHMENT → readfashmet. It had been noted that JM used this strategy to some extent also; for example, when he was 12 years old he spelled UNIFORM → youofrom, WILDERNESS → wilonset, APPRENTICE → apartent and TOMATO → tomanto.

Thus, at the outset of this study, Michael had severe difficulties with speech production, accompanied by problems with input phonology and phonological awareness. At 10 years of age, although of average intelligence, he had only just begun to learn to read and write. In reading he relied exclusively upon a small sight vocabulary, his knowledge of letter–sound rules was imperfect and he was unable to read non-words. In addition, his use of phonological spelling strategies was grossly deficient. Between the first and the second time of testing, Michael's speech had improved. He had also improved on tests of phonological awareness (possibly as the result of speech and language therapy) but continued to have difficulty with rhyme production. In addition, he had demonstrable difficulty on a test of sound blending in which single-syllable words containing clusters (e.g. ramp, pram) had to be synthesised from component sounds.

Michael showed only a marginal improvement in reading and spelling as measured by standardised tests. He had in fact progressed by less than one year in four. Qualitatively, Michael still used primarily lexical reading strategies, although he showed a regularity effect and his tendency to apply letter–sound rules unsuccessfully was reduced. Turning to spelling, improvements in word spelling were not matched by an increase in the ability to spell non-words. Moreover, a preponderance of serious non-phonetic spelling errors confirmed that phonological spelling strategies were grossly impaired. Michael's spelling errors seemed plausibly related to his residual speech errors.

Thus, after 4 years of remediation, Michael remained unable to use phonological reading and spelling strategies. He had been fairly resistant to intensive speech and language therapy and a phonic teaching regime. Even though he had been taught letter–sound translation rules, he was unable to apply these in reading and spelling because his phonological system was too impaired to support the acquisition of literacy along normal lines.

Conclusions

This chapter has focused on the reading difficulties of three children: JM and MB were both developmental dyslexic children and had relatively severe reading and spelling difficulties. Michael had a primary speech disorder which affected intelligibility, and associated problems with literacy.

In spite of differences in aetiology, all three children had phonological processing deficits which included problems with phonological awareness and in output phonology. Arguably, they differed both in the extent and severity of their phonological processing difficulties. In comparison to JM and Michael, MB's phonological difficulties were mild but they were still significant relative to reading age-matched controls. JM had difficulties on the same range of phonological tasks as MB. However, an analysis of the errors he made on a test of nonword repetition indicated that his processing difficulties were more severe. Finally, Michael had pervasive phonological difficulties that affected both input and output processing.

The relative severity of the phonological processing difficulties of MB, JM and Michael correlated with relative differences in the severity of their reading and spelling impairments. It is not possible to make strict comparisons between the three children because they differed, not only in phonological ability, but also more generally in verbal IQ and educational placement. Nevertheless, it is interesting to note that the relative severity of the three children's processing difficulties was paralleled by a relative difference in their progress over time. They also differed in the same orderly fashion in the level of proficiency that they eventually achieved in non-word reading (a good indicator of decoding skill) and in phonetic spelling (Table 6.1).

Taken together these findings have led us to refine our hypothesis that learning to read depends upon the integrity of output phonological representations. To this hypothesis should be added the rider that individual differences in dyslexia are the consequence of variation in the severity of phonological processing deficits. We suggest that when phonological processing skills are severely

Table 6.1 Reading and spelling progress of three children with deficits in output phonology

| | Phonological processing (no. of errors in non-word repetition*) | Progress (achievement ratio†) | | Outcome | |
		Reading	Spelling	Non-word reading (%)	Phonetic spelling (%)
MB	16	1.67	0.83	77.4	60
JM	28	0.72	0.58	25.5	22
Michael	Severely impaired	0	0.28	22.2	20

*Maximum = 80.
†Normal progress = 1.

impaired, the development of phonological or alphabetic reading and spelling strategies is compromised. The dyslexic profile that results has been described as developmental phonological dyslexia and is best exemplified here by JM. When phonological processing skills are weak but not severely impaired, phonological reading and spelling strategies can develop, albeit slowly. It could be argued that this was the case for MB who was certainly able to use phonology in reading, if not perfectly in his spelling.

If this hypothesis is correct, then it might be possible to account for the considerable variation seen between dyslexic children at the behavioural level in terms of an underlying cognitive deficit which is shared between them. The deficit would be in phonological processing. It would not be necessary to invoke alternative theories, e.g. involving visual processing deficits, to account for the failure to acquire a sight vocabulary in cases of so-called 'surface' or 'morphemic' dyslexia (see Chapter 5). Indeed the hypothesis that we currently favour is that differences between the reading strategies of individual dyslexic children is the result of variations in the severity of their underlying phonological deficits in interaction with individual differences in cognitive capacities. A child like JM who had strong visual and semantic skills was able to follow a developmental pathway in learning to read which would be denied to another child similarly lacking phonological expertise, who also had visual or semantic deficits. A child with a relatively mild phonological disorder may learn to read using phonology, but will only do so slowly if an alternative compensatory pathway is not available.

Acknowledgements

This research was supported by grant G8801538 from the Medical Research Council to the first author. We thank JM, MB and Michael for their willing participation and Bill Wells for his advice on the classification of speech errors.

References

Bradley, L. and Bryant, P.E. (1983). Categorising sound and learning to read. *Nature*, **301**, 419–421.

Bryant, P.E. and Bradley, L. (1985). *Children's Reading Problems*. Oxford: Blackwell.

Campbell, R. and Butterworth, B. (1985). Phonological dyslexia and dysgraphia in a highly literate subject: a developmental case with associated deficits of phonemic processing and awareness. *Quarterly Journal of Experimental Psychology*, **37A**, 435–475.

Dunn, L.M., Dunn, L.M., Whetton, C. and Pintilie, D. (1982). *British Picture Vocabulary Scale*. Windsor: NFER-Nelson.

Ehri, L. (1990). The development of reading and spelling in children: an overview. In M. Snowling, and M. Thomson (eds), *Dyslexia: Integrating Theory and Practice*, pp. 63–79. London: Whurr.

Ehri, L.C. (1992). Reconceptualizing the development of sight word reading and its relationship to recoding. In P.B. Gough, L.C. Ehri and R. Treiman (eds), *Reading Acquisition*, pp. 107–144. Hillsdale, NJ: Lawrence Erlbaum Associates.

Elliot, C.D. (1983). *British Ability Scales*. Windsor: NFER-Nelson.

Frith, U. (1985). Beneath the surface of developmental dyslexia. In K.E. Patterson, J.C. Marshall and M. Coltheart (eds), *Surface Dyslexia*. London: Routledge & Kegan Paul.

Funnell, E. and Davison, M (1989). Lexical capture: a developmental disorder of reading and spelling. *Quarterly Journal of Experimental Psychology*, **41A**, 471–488.

Gathercole, S.E. and Baddeley, A.D. (1989). Evaluation of the role of phonological STM in the development of vocabulary in children: a longitudinal study. *Journal of Memory and Language*, **28**, 200–213

Goswami, U. and Bryant, P.E. (1990). *Phonological Skills and Learning to Read*. London: Lawrence Erlbaum Associates.

Goulandris, A. and Snowling, M. (1991). Visual memory deficits: A plausible cause of developmental dyslexia? Evidence from a single case study. *Cognitive Neuropsychology*, **8**, 127–154.

Hulme, C. and Snowling, M (1992a). Phonological deficits in dyslexia: a 'sound' reappraisal of the verbal deficit hypothesis. In N.N. Singh and I.L. Beale (eds), *Learning Disabilities: Nature, Theory and Treatment*. New York: Springer-Verlag.

Hulme, C. and Snowling, M. (1992b). Deficits in output phonology: an explanation of reading failure?. *Cognitive Neuropsychology*, **9**, 47–72.

Morton, J. (1989). An information-processing account of reading acquisition. In A. Galaburda (ed.), *From Reading to Neurons*, pp. 43–66. Cambridge, MA: MIT Press.

Neale, M.D. with Christophers, U. and Whetton, C. (1989). *Neale Analysis of Reading Ability – Revised British Edition*. Windsor: NFER-Nelson.

Rack, J., Snowling, M. and Olson, R. (1992). The non-word reading deficit in dyslexia: a review. *Reading Research Quarterly*, 27, 28–53.

Schonell, F.J. and Schonell, F.E. (1956). *Diagnostic and Attainment Testing: Including a Manual of Tests, Their Nature, Use, Recording and Interpretation*. London: Oliver & Boyd.

Seymour, P.H.K. (1986). *Cognitive Analysis of Dyslexia*. London: Routledge & Kegan Paul.

Seymour, P.H.K., Bunce, F. and Evans, H.M. (1990). A framework for orthographic assessment and remediation. In C.M. Sterling and C. Robson (eds), *Psychology, Spelling and Education*, pp. 224–249. Clevedon: Multilingual Matters.

Snowling, M. and Hulme, C. (1989). A longitudinal case study of developmental phonological dyslexia. *Cognitive Neuropsychology*, 6, 379–401.

Snowling, M., Stackhouse, J. and Rack, J. (1986). Phonological dyslexia and dysgraphia: a developmental analysis. *Cognitive Neuropsychology*, 3, 309–339.

Snowling, M. , Hulme, C., Wells, B. and Goulandris, N. (1992). Continuities between speech and spelling in a case of developmental dyslexia. *Reading and Writing*, 4, 19–31.

Stackhouse, J. and Snowling, M. (1992a). Barriers to literacy development in two cases of developmental verbal dyspraxia. *Cognitive Neuropsychology*, 9, 273–299.

Stackhouse, J. and Snowling, M. (1992b). Developmental verbal dyspraxia: a developmental perspective. *European Journal of Disorders of Communication*, 27, 35–54.

Stanovich, K.E. (1990). The theoretical and practical consequences of discrepancy definitions of dyslexia. In M. Snowling and M. Thomson (eds), *Dyslexia: Integrating Theory and Practice*, pp. 125–143. London: Whurr.

Stuart, M. and Coltheart, M. (1988). Does reading develop in a sequence of stages? *Cognition*, 30, 139–181.

Vernon, P.E. (1977). *Vernon Graded Word Spelling Test*. Seven Oaks: Hodder & Stoughton.

Wechsler, D. (1974). *Wechsler Intelligence Scale for children – Revised*. New York: Psychological Corporation.

Wimmer, H. and Hummer, P. (1990). How German-speaking first graders read and spell? Doubts on the importance of the logographic stage. *Applied Psycholinguistics*, 11, 349–368.

Chapter 7
Phonological Errors in the Spelling of Taught Dyslexic Children

MARY KIBEL and T.R.MILES

The word 'dyslexia', as used in this chapter, refers to the group of difficulties which have been described by Hinshelwood (1917), Orton (1937, 1989), Hallgren (1950), Critchley (1970), Naidoo (1972), Thomson (1991a), Miles (1993), and many others. These difficulties show themselves in lateness in learning to read, persistent difficulty with spelling, and in a general slowness in processing symbolic information.

There is reason to think that the central problem for dyslexic children lies in the area of phonology, i.e. in the representation of speech sounds (Tallal, 1980; Snowling et al., 1986; Catts, 1989). There is clear evidence of a link between phonological awareness and reading ability (Liberman et al., 1974; Sweeney and Rourke, 1978; Baron et al., 1980; Stanovich, Cunningham and Cramer, 1984), and in addition it has been shown in a number of studies that, if phonological skills are trained, then both reading and spelling will improve (see Chapters 9–11).

These findings open up new possibilities for the teacher. When dyslexic children begin their course of training there are often very obvious phonological difficulties. Some of the younger ones cannot isolate beginning and final sounds in words and have to be taught to do so. Others need to be helped to become aware of the differences between the short vowels, for instance, or to notice the sounds that make up the consonant blends. However, such awareness can quite easily be taught, and most dyslexic children move comfortably on to tackle the more advanced spellings which make up the main body of their course.

There is evidence, however, that in the case of dyslexic children phonological difficulties persist and continue to affect performance in a variety of subtle ways (Snowling, 1980; Rack, 1985). This was the basic idea which prompted the present research. On the surface, the dyslexic children who were studied had developed phonological awareness and were able to use a phonic strategy in spelling. It was possible, however, that the phonological difficulty remained and that it continued to affect their performance in ways that were less obvious.

At the outset it was not entirely clear what questions should be asked; it was therefore decided in the first place to carry out an exploratory study, not with clearly defined goals but simply in order to check on dyslexic children's ability to perceive and label speech sounds.

Exploratory Study

Children were selected for the study by the following criteria:

1. Their spelling age on the Schonell S1 Spelling Test (Schonell and Schonell, 1952) had to be at least 2 years behind their chronological age.
2. They had to have at least five positive indicators on the Bangor Dyslexia Test (Miles, 1982).
3. They had to have had at least 6 months of individual tuition by a teacher trained in a method that was structured, multisensory and phonic.
4. In the opinion of their teacher their knowledge of the grapheme–phoneme correspondences for short vowels and consonants had to be secure and easy to use.

All the children were attending normal schools and most were of at least average intelligence. To test their ability to segment and transcribe speech sounds, lists of words and non-words were prepared of varying degrees of complexity which they were required to spell. All the words could be correctly spelled by using short vowel and consonant sounds only, with no other spelling knowledge needed.

Words and non-words of five levels of complexity were used, as follows:

Level 1:   CVC, e.g. TAP, LOG; san, nim
Level 2:   CCVC, e.g. PLOT, TRIP; scap, crin
Level 3:   CVCC, e.g. SILK, DUMP; belk, pold
Level 4:   CCVCC, e.g. TRUST, CRAMP; climp, trilt
Level 5:   CCCVC, e.g. THROB, SPLIT; spleg, stron.

There were thus five sets of words and five sets of non-words. The words were dictated one at a time for spelling and were followed by a short sentence to make the meaning clear. In the case of the non-words, the children were told that these were made-up words but that they were like real words. Each non-word had to be repeated by the child so that the tester (MK) could be sure that it had been heard correctly.

The important requirement was to devise a method of scoring which would indicate phonological awareness rather than spelling knowledge as such. A response was therefore scored as correct if *each phoneme* was represented, regardless of whether the spelling was actually correct. Thus 'silk' would be scored as correct if the child wrote 'silk', 'silc', 'silck', 'sillck', etc.

Every phoneme error was counted. This allowed for the possibility of there being more than one error per word. For example, SILK → sik was scored as one error ('l' omitted); SILK → selk was scored as one error ('e' for 'i'); SILK → sek was scored as two errors ('l' omitted and 'e' for 'i')

Most sets contained 20 words, but as the study was only exploratory no attempt was made to ensure that each child completed every set and the number of scripts studied was based solely on availability. As a result the numbers of words and non-words attempted at each level are somewhat uneven.

The results of the exploratory study are summarised in Table 7.1 which gives the number of words and non-words attempted, together with the number and percentage of errors.

It is plain from inspection of this table that the children made more errors in spelling non-words than words. However, observation of the children suggested that they adopted the same strategy for spelling the non-words which they used for spelling difficult words. The fact the children here coped relatively well with spelling non-words appears to be at variance with the results reported by Jorm (1981) and Frith (1980). The most probable explanation is that the children in the present study had received an unusually large amount of training in the use of phonic strategies. If the children in the Frith and Jorm studies had been similarly trained, it is possible that they would have achieved greater success. Also, in the present study, the non-words were only one syllable in length, whereas Frith's test included more complicated words such as 'usterand' and 'rekind'. It is possible that if polysyllabic non-words had been used in the present study the children would have had greater difficulty. As a result of the similar pattern in the data for words and non-words, it was decided not to include non-words in any later testing.

Table 7.1 Number of word and non-word spellings attempted and number and percentage of errors (exploratory study)

Level	No. of spellings attempted	No. of errors	Percentage errors
Level 1 (CVC)			
Words	90	6	7
Non-words	80	8	10
Level 2 (CCVC)			
Words	342	44	13
Non-words	252	45	18
Level 3 (CVCC)			
Words	266	27	10
Non-words	154	34	22
Level 4 (CCVCC)			
Words	340	57	17
Non-words	110	44	40
Level 5 (CCCVC)			
Words	91	41	45
Non-words	49	22	45
Totals	1129	328	

In addition the exploratory study produced a number of useful pointers. On the surface, all the children were competent in their phonological skills; in particular they could deal comfortably with short vowels and consonant blends. Yet it seemed that this knowledge was still vulnerable: children with spelling ages as high as 9 years sometimes made phonological errors in regular one-syllable words. It was also noticed that if children were afterwards asked to re-spell their incorrect words they tended to get them right. Thus it seems that their phonological skills were not yet automatised. Instances where children were completely unaware of phonemes were rare: with a little prodding they usually found that they could 'hear' the sounds in question. It seems, therefore, that to the concept of 'phonological awareness' should be added the concept of 'phonological instability', and that among dyslexic children there is a long period of uncertainty before phonological awareness is fully secure.

A further point of interest was the nature of the errors themselves. There were many misrepresented vowel sounds, for example MEND was written as 'mand', or RISK as 'resk'. Consonants were also misrepresented, for example 'sofd' for SOFT and 'grop' for CROP. In addition, consonant clusters were frequently reduced: thus HELP might be written as 'hep' or 'stip' for STRIP. There were also a small number of letter misplacements and of extra letters added.

It will be seen from Table 7.1 that the total number of errors was 328. Table 7.2 gives details of how these errors can be broken down into the above groups. Percentages of the total number of errors are given in brackets.

Errors in which 'b' and 'd' were confused have been classified separately: they are both visually and auditorily confusing, and the reasons for error may well be complex. Substitutions of 'ed' for 't' have not been included; this is because children are regularly taught that the suffix 'ed' sometimes has a 't' sound, and this substitution may therefore not be a phonological error at all but the result of spelling knowledge wrongly applied.

The misrepresentations of consonants and vowels were of particular interest. When the scripts were examined it soon became clear that the errors were not just accidental slips. They tended to fall into regularly occurring categories and these appeared to have a basis in speech. For example, in the case of consonants there was a clear tendency for confusions to arise between the voiced and unvoiced members of a pair, e.g. c/g, p/b, t/d, and between phonemes that are differentiated late in the acquisition of speech, e.g. th/f, r/w. There was also a distinctive non-randomness about the vowel errors (see below). It was found, in the case of consonants, that the errors were liable to go 'in either direction'; thus 'p' was written as 'b' six times and 'b' was written as 'p' five times. In contrast, in the case of vowels the errors tended to be 'in one direction only'; thus 'e' was written as 'a' 23 times but 'a' was written as 'e' only once.

This result confirmed our initial idea that phonological difficulties continue to affect the way in which dyslexic children spell. It was decided that it would be useful to treat errors which involved failure to represent speech sounds accurately ('phonological errors') as a distinctive group. As a result of the exploratory study, therefore, it was decided to investigate speech-based errors further by means of a more systematic investigation.

Table 7.2 Classification of spelling errors (exploratory study)

Type of error	No. of occurrences	%
Misrepresented consonants	74	22.56
Misrepresented vowels	76	23.17
Cluster reductions	121	36.89
Misplaced consonants	13	3.96
b–d confusion	16	4.88
Other	28	8.54
Total	328	

Two studies will be reported. The purposes of study 1 were, first, to check whether the suggestion made in the exploratory study, that phonological errors become more frequent as word complexity increases, would be confirmed, and, second, to explore further whether phonological errors have a basis in speech. The purpose of study 2 was to discover if normal spellers make similar errors to dyslexic children.

Study 1

Various modifications were made to the original test. In particular words containing the letters 'z' and 'j' were included; the number of words in each set was systematised, and each child completed the same number of sets. Because of the possibility that the results might be influenced by MK's personal style or accent, a second tester, who has a background in linguistics and phonetics, tested some of the children and made an independent classification of the errors.

Twenty-nine dyslexic children took part in the study. They fulfilled the same criteria as the children in the exploratory study. Their spelling ages ranged from 7;0 years to 10;5 years; their chronological ages were between 9 and 15 years. Seven of them had taken part in the exploratory study.

The basic method was the same as that used in the exploratory study: the children were asked to spell regular words of five different levels of complexity.

At each level from 1 to 4 (CVC, CCVC, CVCC, and CCVCC), 20 words were used; at level 5 (CCCVC) 10 words were used. This disparity was unavoidable because words with three-letter blends are quite small in number and a list containing more than ten would have been repetitive and tiresome for the children. The short vowels were equally balanced in sets 1 to 4, although it was not possible to balance them in set 5. All the consonants were included, and each appeared on at least three occasions. The children took the tests in consecutive weeks over a 6-week period. The words were read out one at a time and were followed by a short sentence to make the meaning clear. Details of the words used and of all relevant misspellings are given in Appendix I.

Table 7.3 shows the number and percentage of errors at the five different levels of complexity.

Inspection of this table shows that there were very few errors in the CVC words and that the order of difficulty was CVC, CCVC, CCVCC, CVCC and CCCVC. Thus three-letter clusters presented the

Table 7.3 Study 1: number and percentage of errors at the five different levels of complexity

Type of word	No. of words	No. of scripts	Opportunities for error	No. of errors	%
CVC	20	29	580	51	8.79
CCVC	20	29	580	194	33.44
CVCC	20	29	580	278	47.93
CCVCC	20	29	580	249	42.93
CCCVC	10	29	290	192	66.21
Totals	90	145	2610	964	

greatest difficulty, whereas two-letter clusters at the end of a word presented marginally more difficulty than two-letter clusters at the beginning of a word. The fact that the CVCC pattern included some extra difficult words such as BULB and VALVE may account for the relatively high number of errors among CVCC words. (The words VALVE, FILTH and WIDTH were classified as CVCC because the study was concerned with the children's ability to represent phonemes, not with their ability to represent letters.)

What is of particular interest is that these children had been taught – and could say with no difficulty – the sounds made by individual letters. It seems therefore that this knowledge cannot necessarily be applied when words become more complex.

The classification of errors was the same as that used in the exploratory study (see Table 7.2). Table 7.4 shows the number and percentage of each kind of error, with the percentages in the exploratory study given as well.

Table 7.4 Study 1: number and percentage of errors of different types

Type of error	Occurrences No.	(%)	Exploratory study (%)
Misrepresented consonants	204	(21.16)	23.17
Misrepresented vowels	250	(25.93)	22.56
Cluster reductions	399	(41.39)	36.89
Misplaced consonants	24	(2.49)	3.96
b–d confusions	21	(2.18)	4.88
Other	66	(6.85)	8.54
Total	964		

The error patterns which occurred in the exploratory study re-occurred in this study in a remarkably similar form. The main ones were cluster reductions, misrepresented consonants and misrepresented vowels. These accounted for 82.7% of the errors in the exploratory study and for 88.6% of the errors in study 1. Thus, it is probable that these error patterns are not accidental ones but that they form a normal part of the spelling development of dyslexic children.

Table 7.5 gives details of the substitutions. The figures refer to the number of times that particular letters were confused in the corpus of errors. It can again be seen that the substitutions could take place 'in either direction'; thus there were 11 substitutions of 'g' for 'c' and 7 substitutions of 'c' for 'g'.

It remains to consider how these errors might be related to speech. The continuity between speech and spelling has been well documented by Read (1971, 1986) in analyses of the invented spellings of a group of pre-readers. For example, these children often spelled /tr/ with the letters CH. This error is understandable given that when /t/ is producd before /r/, it is affricated, producing a sound that is phonetically similar to /tʃ / (which is usually spelled CH).

Table 7.5 Consonant errors: number of substitutions made across words

Error	Number	Total	Error	Number	Total
b → p	4	6	l → w	3	4
p → b	2		w → l	1	
c → g	11	18	r → w	2	8
g → c	7		w → r	6	
c → t	2	4	th → v	4	5
t → c	2		v → th	1	
d → t	1	11	v → f	9	9
t → d	10		f → v	0	
f → th	28	98	z → s	11	11
th → f	70		s → z	0	
l → r	5	9	st → sh	2	2
r → l	4		sh → st	0	
m → n	4	8	dr → jr	3	3
n → m	4				

The following substitutions occurred once only: t → s, t → p, r → y, th → s, l → p, f → h, n → t, p → s.

Therefore spelling TRUCK → chuc reveals a sophisticated appreciation of phonology. In addition, pre-readers tend to make spelling errors as a result of phonemic confusions, particularly voicing errors in the same way as the dyslexic children in this study. Treiman (1993) has also presented data from normal first-grade children showing that they are susceptible to similar phonemic errors in their spelling. Furthermore, consonant reduction errors such as spelling TREE → tee are also common in this group. Treiman suggests that, because children are unable to analyse clusters such as /tr/ into separate phonemes when spelling, they are likely to represent them with only one letter. Marcel (1980) has also pointed out that cluster reductions are common in the speech of young children, for example, saying GREEN → 'geen'. He suggests it is possible that children who reduce clusters in spelling are analysing speech in the manner of children at an earlier stage of phonological development. He also shows that the vulnerable phonemes predicted in terms of the articulation of speech are, in fact, the ones omitted in children's spelling.

In the case of consonant and vowel errors it was decided to examine them in terms of 'distinctive features'. Linguists have developed classification systems for phonemes that are based on how they are articulated. Consonants are classified according to whether they are voiced or unvoiced, by the manner of production (e.g. stops, fricatives, nasals), and by the place of production (e.g. labial, alveolar, palatal).

In the case of consonants, it is possible, following Roach (1983, p. 52), to distinguish four types of error pairs:

1. In the case of some pairs, namely b/p, c/g, d/t, f/v and s/z, both sounds are articulated in the same place and in the same manner. These will be referred to as the *place and manner* group.
2. In some cases, namely l/n, m/b, n/t and t/s, there is the same place of articulation but not the same manner. These will be referred to as the *place only* group.
3. In some cases, namely d/g, p/c, p/g, th/s, c/t, m/n and r/y, both members of the pair are articulated in the same manner but not in the same place. These will be referred to as the *manner only* group.
4. If the members of a confused pair are similar in neither place nor manner of articulation, this will be referred to as the *neither* group.

Table 7.6 gives the totals of the consonant substitutions found in the exploratory study and in study 1, broken down into these four

Table 7.6 Consonant confusions classified according to shared articulatory features: exploratory study and study 1

Place and manner	b/p	c/g	d/t	f/v	s/z			
	17	32	14	9	11			
Place only	l/n	m/b	n/t	t/s				
	4	1	2	1				
Manner only	d/g	p/c	p/g	th/s	c/t	m/n	r/y	p/t	f/h
	2	3	2	1	6	13	1	7	1
Neither	l/p	m/d	n/g	n/p	p/			
	1	1	1	1	1			

groupings. The members of each pair have been 'pooled' irrespective of the direction of the substitution; thus 'p/b' includes both substitutions of 'b' for 'p' and substitutions of 'p' for 'b'. Certain errors have been omitted from the analysis because it is felt that they are caused by other factors. These include errors that derive from distinctions which are made late in the acquisition of speech (th/f, th/v and w/r). Also it was unclear how to classify the l/r and l/w errors because, in these consonants, the articulation is imprecise. Several such errors occurred and it is possible that the imprecision is what causes the confusion.

It is clear that most consonant errors which the children made are related in some way to the articulation of speech and that 'sharing' a distinctive feature increases the likelihood of confusion. Although interpretation of this post hoc analysis must proceed cautiously, it seemed that consonants in the *place and manner* group were the most likely to be confused. The phonemes represented by these letters differ only in voicing. Read (1971) has shown that in the 'invented' spellings of young precocious spellers, such voicing errors are common. Read has interpreted such voicing errors in terms of the low degree of salience of voicing in the phonological system of young children. Those that were similar in either *place only* or *manner only* were less likely to be confused, but they were more vulnerable than consonants that had no link at all. Only five errors occurred in the *neither* group.

It may therefore be suggested that consonant phonemes with no distinctive feature in common are unlikely to be confused, and that sharing a distinctive feature increases the likelihood of error and contributes to a phoneme's instability.

Table 7.7 gives a list of all the vowel substitutions found in the first four levels of study 1. (Those at level 5 have not been included

Table 7.7 Vowel errors: number of substitutions made in individual words, levels 1 to 4 (omissions and additions not included)

Error	Total	Error	Total	
a → e	5	o → a	5	
a → i	1	o → e	0	
a → o	7	o → i	0	
a → u	3	o → u	2	
e → a	60	u → a	38	
e → i	4	u → e	3	
e → o	2	u → i	0	
e → u	0	u → o	32	
i → a	4			
i → e	62			
i → o	0			
i → u	0			

because the possibility for error was not the same for the different vowels, see p.110.)

It will be seen that vowels, unlike consonants, tended to produce errors in one direction only; thus there were 60 substitutions of 'a' for 'e' but only 5 substitutions of 'e' for 'a'. With regard to a possible basis in speech, Roach (1983) has described the articulation of vowels according to the conventional criteria of 'open/closed' and 'back/front'. The 'open/closed' dimension refers to the position of the tongue relative to the roof of the mouth. The 'back/front' description indicates the part of the mouth in which the vowel is formed.

It is interesting to speculate on the possibilities. The two most secure vowels, 'a' and 'o', are the two most open vowels, and it may therefore be true in general that openness favours stability. The error patterns i → e, e → a, u → o, and u → a also show the effect of openness, because each defaults to an adjoining vowel in the general direction towards *open*. Thus the 'i' moves to the 'e', the 'u' is equally affected by 'a' and 'o', and the 'e' defaults to 'a'. The 'u' is perhaps nearer to the 'e' in terms of openness, but the 'e' shares the front dimension with the 'a' as an additional link.

If we make the prediction that errors tend to be from 'closed' to the nearest 'open' vowel and not from 'open' to the nearest closed, this predicts that:

1. i → e will be more frequent than e → i
2. e → a will be more frequent than a → e
3. u → a will be more frequent than a → u
4. u → o will be more frequent than o → u

5. There will be fewer errors with the fully open vowels, 'a' and 'o', than with the rest.

It is clear from Table 7.8 that all of these five predictions are fulfilled.

Table 7.8 Vowel error pairs classified according to articulatory features

i → e	62	e → i	4
e → a	60	a → e	5
u → a	38	a → u	3
u → o	32	o → u	2

Misrepresentations of a and o: 23.
Misrepresentations of e, i and u: 205.

The suggestion is not that articulation is the *only* factor at work in producing these consonant and vowel substitutions. For instance the error-pairs m/n and b/p could be visually confusing as well as sharing a distinctive feature; it is possible that the e/a and i/e errors could be influenced by letter-names because the sound of each is similar to the name of its partner.

Overall, however, it seems likely that the main categories of error, namely cluster reductions and misrepresented consonants and vowels, are related in some way to the articulation of speech and can therefore properly be called 'speech-based'.

Study 2

The purpose of this study was to discover whether similar phonological errors are also found in normal readers. The dyslexic subjects were those who had taken part in study 1. To ensure that the controls were all normal spellers the following selection criteria were specified:

1. No child would be included whose spelling age was more than 6 months below his or her chronological age.
2. To exclude unusually *good* spellers, no child would be included whose spelling age was 6 months or more above his or her spelling age.
3. No child would be included who had received specialist help.
4. To avoid giving formal tests to very young children, no child would be included whose age was 7;4 years or less.

All the children aged 7;4 years and upwards in two primary schools were given the Schonell S1 Spelling Test (Schonell and

Schonell, 1952). It was possible as a result to find 21 'matches' for the dyslexic children. Those for whom 'matches' could not be found were excluded from the study.

A new spelling test was constructed comprising 30 words. All were of one syllable and were of similar structure (CVC to CCCVC) to the previous ones. Details of the individual words are given in Appendix II. Table 7.9 gives details of the ages and number of phonological errors made by each matched pair of dyslexic and normal spellers in spelling the list of 30 words. The dyslexic children here were aged between 9;6 and 15;2 years and, in each case, their spelling age was 2 years or more below their chronological age. The control children were aged between 7;4 and 11;5 years and, in each case, their spelling age was within 6 months of their chronological age.

It is plain from Table 7.9 that the dyslexic children made many more phonological errors than the non-dyslexic children ($p < 0.01$, Wilcoxon matched pairs test). The highest numbers of errors among the latter were eight and seven (subjects 2 and 3), whereas the dyslexic children with the eight lowest spelling ages (numbers 1–8) all

Table 7.9 Number of errors made by 21 dyslexic children and 21 controls of the same spelling age

Spelling age (years)	Dyslexics		Non-dyslexics	
	Case no.	No. of errors	Case no.	No. of errors
7;4	1	18	1	0
7;5	2	17	2	8
7;6	3	13	3	7
7;8	4	10	4	4
7;8	5	10	5	2
8;0	6	34	6	5
8;1	7	13	7	0
8;1	8	20	8	3
8;4	9	5	9	1
8;8	10	9	10	0
9;1	11	1	11	2
9;1	12	6	12	4
9;3	13	7	13	1
9;4	14	6	14	0
9;9	15	1	15	0
10;0	16	1	16	0
10;2	17	1	17	1
10;5	18	3	18	0
10;6	19	4	19	0
10;9	20	0	20	0
11;5	21	3	21	0

made 10 errors or more. Only one dyslexic child (number 20) was error-free compared with 10 non-dyslexic children, whereas among the non-dyslexic children with spelling ages of 9;3 years and over, only two errors were made *in toto*.

The delay before dyslexic children acquire secure phonological skills can also be illustrated as follows (Tables 7.10 and 7.11). If we take the five dyslexic children with the highest spelling ages (10;2–11;5 years, cases 17–21) and total their errors, it is necessary to move back to spelling ages of 8;1–9;1 to match this total in the non-dyslexic spellers. It should be remembered that the comparison is between specially taught dyslexic children and control children who had had no special teaching. Even with this teaching the dyslexic children appear to be about 2 years delayed in the acquisition of secure phonological skills.

The combined effect of these results is to show that phonological

Table 7.10 Illustration of delay on the part of the dyslexic children in acquiring phonological skills: spelling ages of five dyslexic children (10;2–11;5 years) with the corresponding spelling ages of non-dyslexic children for a similar number of phonological errors

Spelling age (years)	Case no. (dyslexic)	No. of errors	Spelling age (years)	Case no. (non-dyslexic)	No. of errors
10;2	17	1	8;1	7	3
10;5	18	3	8;4	9	1
10;6	19	4	8;8	10	0
10;9	20	0	9;1	11	2
11;5	21	3	9;1	12	4
Total		11			10

Table 7.11 Illustration of delay on the part of dyslexic children in acquiring phonological skills: spelling ages of five dyslexic children (8;4–9;3 years) with the corresponding spelling ages of non-dyslexic children for a similar number of phonological errors

Spelling age (years)	Case no. (dyslexic)	No. of errors	Spelling age (years)	Case no. (non-dyslexic)	No. of errors
8;4	9	5	7;5	2	8
8;8	10	9	7;6	3	7
9;1	11	1	7;8	4	4
9;1	12	6	7;8	5	2
9;3	13	7	8;0	6	5
Total		28			26

errors tend to persist in dyslexic children when non-dyslexic ones of the same spelling age no longer make them. In the process of learning to spell, non-dyslexics do, indeed, make phonological errors but it seems that they readily grow out of them. Very few can be expected in children over the age of 9;6 years, whereas they are found in taught dyslexic children with spelling ages as high as 10 and 11 years.

Conclusions

This study has looked at the way in which taught dyslexic children cope with the phonological aspect of spelling. It focuses on what happens between the early mastery of phonic skills and the development of reliable fluency. This phase is marked by a curious period of instability. The children in this study had learned the short vowels and consonant blends and could spell regular one-syllable words in isolation. Yet in the tests which they were given they made many errors. Moreover, words which were incorrect in the tests tended to be properly spelled on a second occasion (see p. 108). Overall, the newly acquired phonological skills appeared to be insecure.

At first glance the data suggested a general phonological difficulty and a long period of consolidation. However, a more careful analysis revealed an interesting picture. The errors which the children made were not random ones. Only a small range of phonemes were vulnerable and the errors which they produced occurred in a predictable way.

If a phoneme was misrepresented this was not a careless slip or a lapse in letter–sound knowledge. The unstable phonemes tended to be those that are acquired late in the development of speech (th/f, r/w) and those that have a 'partner' which is articulated in a similar way (e.g. c/g, p/t, e/a). When an error occurred, the phoneme was almost invariably written as its perceptually similar 'partner', and there was never any difficulty in the case of phonemes that were clearly contrasted. Thus 'b', for instance, was never written as 'l', 'f' or 's'.

It is incorrect, therefore, to speak of a *general* phonological weakness. Rather, the difficulty seems to centre on (1) the less noticeable phonemes in consonant clusters and (2) a small group of phonemes which happen to have a 'partner' with a similar basis in speech; errors involving voicing are particularly common. The problem for these children appears to be *the fine discrimination of speech sounds*, and this difficulty remains for a long while after the easier phonological distinctions are comfortably secure.

A glance through the data in Appendix I will show the general influence of this limited phonological difficulty. Even when words are misspelled in a wide variety of ways, the errors themselves tend to be restricted to the phonological difficulties outlined above. The range of errors produced by the word 'blend', for example, can all be explained in terms of cluster reduction and the b/p, e/a, b/d and l/r confusions (bland {3}, brend, dlend, pad, band). Even a spelling as seemingly remote as 'pad' is simply a combination of two cluster reductions + e/a and b/p.

It is clear, also, that the difficulties of the dyslexic child are not simply the result of maturational lag; otherwise the controls matched for spelling age would have produced similar phonological errors. It does seem that the dyslexic children's phonological difficulties exert persistent effects on their spelling skills. One possibility is that the dyslexic children's phonological problems derive from difficulties in processing the rapidly changing acoustical information in speech (Tallal, 1980); this would make sense if there are limiting conditions in the magnocellular pathways of the auditory system just as there are in the visual system (Livingstone et al., 1991). However that may be, the results of this study clearly show that even when there has been appropriate teaching the weakness of dyslexic children at perceiving and labelling speech sounds still persists and that it is particularly apparent when these speech sounds are embedded in more complex words.

Acknowledgement

The authors are grateful to Des Guiry both for his help with the testing and for his many useful suggestions. They would also like to thank Dr John Everatt for his comments on an earlier draft of the chapter.

References

Baron, J., Treiman, R., Wilf, J.W. and Kellman, P. (1980). Spelling and reading by rules. In U. Frith (ed.), *Cognitive Processes in Spelling*. London: Academic Press.

Catts, H.W. (1989). Phonological processing deficits and reading disabilities. In A.G.Kamhi and H.W.Catts (eds), *Reading Disabilities: A Developmental Language Perspective*. Boston: Little Brown & Co.

Critchley, M. (1970). *The Dyslexic Child*. London: Heinemann Medical Books

Frith, U. (1980). Unexpected spelling problems. In U. Frith (ed.), *Cognitive Processes in Spelling*. London: Academic Press.

Hallgren, B. (1950). Specific dyslexia (congenital word blindness). A clinical and genetic study. *Acta Psychiatrica et Neurologica Supplementum* 65, i–xi, 1–287.

Hinshelwood, J. (1917). *Congenital Word-Blindness*. London: H.K. Lewis.

Jorm, A.F. (1981). Children with reading and spelling retardation: functioning of whole word and correspondence rule mechanisms. *Journal of Child Psychology and Psychiatry*, 22, 171–178.

Liberman, I.Y., Shankweiler, D., Fischer, F.W. and Carter, B. (1974). Explicit sylla-ble and phoneme segmentation in the young child. *Journal of Experimental Child Psychology*, **18**, 201–212.

Livingstone, M.S., Rosen, G.D., Drislane, F.W. and Galaburda, A.M. (1991). Physiological and anatomical evidence for a magnocellular defect in develop-mental dyslexia. *Proceedings of the National Academy of Science of the USA*, **88**, 7943–7947.

Marcel T. (1980). Phonological awareness and phonological representation: investi-gation of a specific spelling problem. In U.Frith (Ed.), *Cognitive Processes in Spelling*. London: Academic Press.

Miles, T.R. (1982). *The Bangor Dyslexia Test*. Cambridge: Learning Development Aids.

Miles, T.R. (1993). *Dyslexia: The Pattern of Difficulties*, 2nd edn. London: Whurr.

Naidoo, S. (1972). *Specific Dyslexia*. London: Pitman.

Orton, S.T. (1937, 1989). *Reading, Writing, and Speech Problems in Children and Selected Papers*. Austin, Texas: PRO-ED.

Rack, J.P. (1985). Orthographic and phonetic coding in developmental dyslexia. *British Journal of Psychology*, **76**, 325–340.

Read, C. (1971). Pre-school children's knowledge of English phonology. *Harvard Educational Review*, **41**, 1–34.

Read, C. (1971). *Children's Creative Spelling*. London: Routledge & Kegan Paul.

Read, C. (1986). *Children's Creative Spelling*, 2nd edn. London: Routledge & Kegan Paul.

Roach, P. (1983). *English Phonetics and Phonology*. Cambridge: Cambridge University Press.

Schonell, F.J. and Schonell, F.E. (1952). *Diagnostic and Attainment Testing*. Edinburgh: Oliver & Boyd.

Snowling, M.J. (1980). The development of grapheme-phoneme correspondence in normal and dyslexic readers. *Journal of Experimental Child Psychology*, **29**, 294–305.

Snowling, M.J., Goulandris, N., Bowlby, M., and Howell, P. (1986). Segmentation and speech perception in relation to reading skill: a developmental analysis. *Journal of Experimental Child Psychology*, **41**, 489–507.

Stanovich, K., Cunningham, A., and Cramer, B. (1984). Assessing phonological awareness in kindergarten children: issues of task comparability. *Journal of Experimental Child Psychology*, **38**, 175–190.

Sweeney, J.E. and Rourke, B.P. (1978). Neuropsychological significance of phoneti-cally accurate and phonetically inaccurate spelling errors in younger and older retarded spellers. *Brain and Language*, **6**, 212–225.

Tallal, P. (1980). Auditory temporal perception, phonics, and reading disabilities in children. *Brain and Language*, **9**, 182–198.

Thomson M.E. (1991a). *Developmental Dyslexia*, 3rd edn. London: Whurr.

Thomson, M.E. (1991b). Teaching the dyslexic child reading and spelling. In J. Stein (ed.), *Vision and Visual Dyslexia*. Basingstoke: Macmillan Press.

Treiman, R. (1993). *Beginning to Spell: A Study of First-grade Children*. New York: Oxford University Press.

Appendix I: A Corpus of Phonological Errors

Notes

1. If a particular misspelling of the same word occurred more than once the number of occurrences is given in brackets.
2. A dash indicates that no errors were made on the word in question.
3. If comparisons are made with Tables 7.1–7.8 it should be remembered that a single word may contain more than one error.

Exploratory study

Non-words: CVC

Non-word	Misspelled as	Non-word	Misspelled as
tun	–	hib	hip, hid (3)
vap	–	cos	–
mog	–	nim	–
deg	dag (2)	lep	lap
san	sen	suf	–

Non-words: CCVC

Non-word	Misspelled as	Non-word	Misspelled as
plid	pled (2)	tron	-
prag	plag, parg	twif	tfil, tref
clon	clo, clong	blan	ban, blam, blang, dlan
crin	crim, grin, clin, cren	brop	blop, brip, drop
drit	dit, grit, drot, dret	glom	glon, clom
frap	thap	grod	crod
spid	spad, sped	stam	sam, sate
scap	sgat, sgap	snat	stat, spat
slub	slud (3), slab (2)	swip	sip, swep

Non-words: CVCC

Non-word	Misspelled as	Non-word	Misspelled as
belk	blck	pold	bold, poed
dimp	–	sant	senat, sankt
felp	falp	polt	pot (2), pult, put
gand	gamd	menk	mank, migl, megk, mink, make
gupt	gupd, gut, gumpt,gump, gup	mact	mack
milf	mif, melph, muf	neft	naft
losp	lost, lope	kest	cast

Non-words: CCVCC

climp	clip, climb, climk, glimp	trilt	strit, trit, trilpt, trlet
crend	ckend, grand, crand, crnd, criend	plisk	splisk, plis
flond	flound	crolf	krofe, grolf (3), crof (2), crouf
skump	skub, scup, sump	crisk	scick
glalt	glout (6), gloot, glat, glant	snelf	snefe, snalf, snlef

Non-words: CCCVC

thrim	thrib, frim	shram	sram, cram, sham (2)
spleg	splg, sleg (2), slag	stron	strog
scrib	srib, sricb, scrip	squin	scin, skrin, swin, scrin
sprad	–		

Words: CVC

TAP	–	LOG	–
HEN	han	PIG	peg
BUS	–	HOT	–
FAN	–	NUT	unt
PEG	pag	LID	rid, led

Words: CCVC

PLOT	pot	TRIP	trig, trep (2)
PLAN	pan	TWIN	tin, trin, trwn, twen
CLAP	crap	BLOT	bot (2), brot, dlot
DRAG	drg, dag	CROP	grop
BRAN	bron	GLUM	glad, glam
FLIP	flig, flep (2), fick	GLAD	gad, gland
SPIN	sin	STAB	stap (4), stad (3)
SCUM	scam, sgum, scom	SMACK	–
SNUG	snag, snud, slug, snog, suge		
SLAM	–	SWIG	sweg

Words: CVCC

SILK	sike, sick	FOLD	fowd
DUMP	dum, domp	LENT	lant
HELD	hld, hell	TANK	tac, take, tack (2)
HELP	hlep, hep, halp	MEND	–
FACT	fat, fatck, fack (2)	SOFT	sofd, sefed
WASP	–	SELF	sef (2)
MIST	mest	RISK	rick, rist, resk

Words: CCVCC

TRUST	–	BLINK	blick, dlick, blic
CRAMP	crap	FLASK	flarck (2)
CRUST	cust	BLEND	blund, bland
FLINT	fint, flent	BRAND	brad
CREPT	crapt (3), repted	TRUNK	truc, tunk, truck (2), tronk
CLAMP	clap (2), clanp	GLINT	gint, glit
SPEND	spind	CRISP	crist, crip, crips
BLUNT	dlont	SKULK	sgulg, skolk, stock, skuc, suclk, skunk, sclak, sonk, scoap
TRAMP	–	CREST	crast
STUMP	stup, sump, stomp	TWIST	twet

Words: CCCVC

THROB	throd, thob (2), thrub, frob, frod	SHRED	srand, shead, shed (2), shrad
SPLIT	spit, stlet	SCRAM	scrum, scam, cram (2), stcram
STRIP	sprip, stip, strib, ship	SQUID	scid, swid, scrid, stcwd
SPRIG	spig, srig, sbrig, stbig		

Study 1

Word	Misspelled as	Word	Misspelled as

Words: CVC

HEN	han	JAM	jan
WIN	wen (2)	MOTH	mof (3), morth, mot, math, moff, monf, mofe, mougth
RAG	–	YAP	lap, yep, jap, rap
BUZZ	bazz (2), buse, buss (2), bes, bzz, bus	MOSS	mase
THIN	fin (3), fen, then	HOT	–
ROD	yod, road	LIVE	wev
YET	jet, let, yeat	ZIP	zep (3), sip, ssep
HOP	–	NUT	net, nat
WET	wat, weat	JAZZ	jas, jass (2), yaz, jasf, geas
WAG	wang	JOG	–

Note It is possible that the confusions between 'j' and 'y' in the above list – 'jap' for YAP, 'jet' for YET, and 'yaz' for JAZZ – along with 'yust' for JUST in the CVCC list below, are not phonological errors but are the result of an uncertainty over letter production. All four errors were made by the same boy. They have not been included in the analysis.

Words: CCVC

CLOTH	clouth, cofe, clof (6), cloath, coth (2), cloof, clofe	GRAB	crab, crad, gad
BLOT	bot, blop, brat	FLUFF	fulff, flafe, fluth (4), futh, flof, frath, floth
SMELL	smal (3), small (4), smale, snel, smle	PRAM	pam (4)
GRIN	gein, gren (2), crim, grim, gen	FLOP	folp, thop, frop
SPIN	spen (4), spim spein	STUFF	stofer, stuth (3), stof, staf (3), tof
SCUM	scame, sgum (2), scam sum, same	BRIM	brem, brin, dem, bame, bem, breim
PRESS	pase, pras (3), pess (2), prass, pise	SNUG	sage, snog (3), snuc, stug, snag (2), snuck, scung
DROP	jrop, dop (2), brop, grop (2)	TWIG	teiger, tweg (4), tig (2), trig (2), swig
GLAD	gad, gade (2), gid	FROTH	throth (2), fofe, flove, frof (7), throf (3), frot, thof (2), froff, froofl, flof, thaf, faoth, fof
STEM	stam (5), sdam, sem, stom, steem	PLOT	polt, slot, port

Words: CVCC

LOFT	loth, lotht, lofed, looth, loaft	RENT	rate, rant (3)
JUNK	juck (3), juc, gace, guk, guck, juk (2)	THANK	thac (2), fack (2), thag, thak, frack, thunk
JUST	yust, jus, jusd, jast (2), jat	FACT	fated, fat (3), fak, fack, fate
HUMP	hap, hup (3), hamp (2), hunpm	YELP	yell, yep (2), lap, lep, hlap, yall, lelp, ylep
RUST	rest, rast (2), raust	SOLVE	sove (6), sulf, sov, sovel, sulve, sof (2), save, sole, solw, swof, sofe
MEND	med, made, mand (3), ment, mabe	BULB	boldm, buld (3), bolb (7), blub, bold (2), dad, bobe, blad, bowb, boab (2), bub
WIDTH	with (6), whith (5), wite (2), wifu, whiht, withe (2), wither wight (2), wids, weth (2), whih, wive	WIND	wide
VALVE	vave, vav (2), vaule, volve,vovle (2), vove, vive, vaver, fave, vov, vaf, velve, vouth, vavell, vowel, volv	HINT	hnit, hent (2), het, hit (2), hete
RISK	resk (4), wrik, resc (2), resg, rest, rick	FILTH	thelth, feelth, fith (3), fillf (2), thilf, filf (4), filfe, felf (2), felve, fheth, flef, feve, hith, fifh, fif, thilth, fefe
KEPT	kelpted, gopted, capt (3), kapt, cetp	LEFT	laft, lefd, late, lenth

Note The words VALVE, WIDTH and FILTH were classified as CVCC because the study was concerned with the ability to represent phonemes, not the ability to represent letters.

Words: CCVCC

PRINT	prant, prit (2), prent, pint (2), pete	SLEPT	slap, shaped, sletp, sleet, slet, slapt, sliped
DRUNK	druc, druck (2), drank (2), drac, druk (2), dunk, drug, duck	CRAMP	crump, quap, crap (3), camp (2), cremp, crapem, cram
TWELVE	tewel, twele, twew, twelf (2), twave, tave, twive, twleve, twlv	CRISP	crip (4), chirp, chisp, crap, cisp
BLEND	bland (3), brend, dlend, pad, band	TRUNK	truc, truck (2), tunck, trug, truk (3), trank, trak
CLAMP	glamp, clam, clap (4), lamp, camp, caped, clump, cramp	TWIST	list, twest, test, wist, twish, twet
CREPT	crepe, crapt (2), craped, crit, ceted, capt, crad, crapet, creet	GLINT	gerlit, glant, gimed, gint (4), clint, gent, get, glent (3), genet, clent, glet
BRAND	band, daded, bland, bab, brend	CRUST	crusd, crasted, crast, crshe, cruts
SKULK	scolk (2), skluk, scluc, sulk, scul, scock (2), sanck, scapk, srlek, scoce, scok, stoak, scolck (2), skul, scooc	TRAMP	tram, trap (3), tamp, twemp
CREST	crasd, cest, cast, crsd, crast (3)	PLUMP	plup (3), plamp (2), plap (2), pap, pulp, pulmp, plumb, blump, pup, pumlp
SWIFT	switht, sifed, swif, shed, swit, sweft, swifed, swith, swieft	SCAMP	scam, samp (4), scap (2), sgamp, ckap, sape

Words: CCCVC and CCCVCC

STRIP	srip (6), siper, slip, srep, streep	SCRUB	crumb, srub, (2), scrab (2), sreb, crub, scumb, scub (2), shad, srube, srgud
SPLINT	slent, spit, spint, splent, split, slint (4), sert, sent	SCRAP	crap (2), scape, srap (4), srape (2), cr--p, srap, srep
THROB	frob (4), thob (3), thobe, trode, fop, fab, trob (5),throd, thorb, thap, throp, thob	STRICT	stict, stit (2), strit, srik, strick (2), scrict, strik, srict, scrited, stikt, shat, srite, stet, stricitic
SQUINT	squit, swin, swint (2), scrint, swit, scint (2), srat	THRUST	frust (5), thunst, thust, (2), fast, throst, trust (2), frst, thoust, thrat, thast
SQUID	sied, scid, scrid, swid, sqid, s--, skid, sead, swed (2), qwid, squd	SCRAM	skan, quam, scam (2), sram (5), scame, s--, cram (2), sham, sgam

Appendix II: List of Words Used in Study 2

top	spin	jam	left	clamp	twig	stem	loft	tramp	bit
scrap	bed	snug	crept	twist	fat	plump	mend	cut	throb
grin	hump	crest	log	split	tent	risk	scrub	plank	twist

Chapter 8
Behavioural Development and Reading Disabilities

BARBARA MAUGHAN

Introduction

Many studies suggest that children with reading and other learning disabilities may be more than usually vulnerable to emotional and behavioural problems. Links have been reported with a wide range of difficulties: depression (Livingston, 1990); anxiety (Cornwell and Bawden, 1992); low self-esteem (Huntington and Bender, 1993); dysfunctional attributions (Bryan and Bryan, 1990); poor achievement motivation (Oka and Paris, 1987); inattentiveness and overactivity; and with disruptive behaviour problems, aggression and delinquency (Hinshaw, 1992).

These findings raise important questions, both practical and theoretical. What are the aetiological implications of poor readers' increased vulnerability to behaviour difficulties? Are there developmental changes in the picture with time, so that different patterns of behaviour problems are likely in younger and older reading-disabled groups? Do co-occurring behaviour problems affect children's academic progress, further compounding their cognitive difficulties? And what are the long-term implications for social adjustment and psychological well-being in adulthood?

This chapter focuses on just two of these issues: the probable aetiology of reading–behaviour problem overlaps, and changes in the developmental picture over time. Before turning to these questions, however, it is important to pause briefly and attempt to place the overall pattern of findings in some perspective. As noted, the literature suggests *some* increased vulnerability to behavioural difficulties among reading-disabled groups. In practice, estimating the extent of that vulnerability is by no means straightforward. Many current findings come from studies of clinic samples, or of children enroled in special treatment programmes, where rates of co-occurring or co-morbid problems are almost always likely to be high (Caron and Rutter, 1991). Much of the available evidence on links between reading difficulties and anxiety and depression, for example, is of this kind. Although these may indeed be areas of vulnerability for some reading-disabled adolescents, we need more evidence from school or community-based samples to know how far the clinic findings can be generalised.

Even in more widely researched areas, estimates of the extent of overlaps between reading and behaviour problems vary widely (Cantwell and Baker, 1991; Hinshaw, 1992). Methodological variations – in sampling strategies, measurement instruments and definitional criteria – are all likely to play a part here. Semrud-Clikeman et al. (1992), for example, showed that a relatively liberal definition of reading disability identified over twice the rate of overlap with attention deficit disorder – 38% by comparison with only 15% – estimated when more stringent criteria were applied. Although formal tests of this kind have not been used in other studies, it seems highly likely that they too would be sensitive to definitional variations.

In general, the most reliable pointers to the extent to which poor readers are at risk come from data on non-referred, epidemiologically defined samples. Studies of this kind suggest that, in the early school years, low achieving readers may be vulnerable to emotional as well as conduct problems (Richman, Stevenson and Graham, 1982; Jorm et al., 1986), but that underachievement in reading is more strongly linked with disruptive behaviours. Early reports pointed to particular associations with conduct problems: in the Isle of Wight epidemiological studies of 10 year olds, for example, a quarter of specifically retarded readers (reading two or more standard deviations below expectations based on age and IQ) showed antisocial behaviour, and a third of those with conduct problems were also reading retarded (Rutter, Tizard and Whitmore, 1970). This overlap was much higher than would be expected by chance. Much subsequent work on the possible aetiology of reading–behaviour problem linkages has taken these Isle of Wight findings as a starting point.

Understanding the Overlap in Early Childhood

Rutter, Tizard and Whitmore (1970) set out three plausible hypotheses which might account for the overlap they observed in the Isle of Wight study. The first two were unidirectional, and assumed that one set of difficulties was primary, and acted – more or less directly – as a risk factor for the other. Early behaviour problems might interfere with a child's learning, or early reading problems lead, perhaps through lowered self-esteem or frustration, to the expression of behavioural disorder. The third model suggested a more intrinsic connection, with both difficulties sharing common roots in organic, temperamental or environmental adversities. Low social class (Offord and Poushinsky, 1981), maternal depression and anxiety (Richman, Stevenson and Graham, 1982), adverse temperamental features in the child, cognitive deficits (August and Garfinkel, 1990), speech and language problems (Silva, 1987), and neurodevelopmental immaturity (Beitchman, 1985) have been among the most frequently canvassed possibilities here.

A variety of different strategies can be used to test these contrasting possibilities. One, building on cross-sectional and retrospective data, is to compare the correlates of 'pure' and overlapping cases. If the overlap group has correlates in common with one disorder but not the other, this is *prima facie* evidence of the primacy of that disorder. Using this approach, Rutter, Tizard and Whitmore (1970) found that antisocial retarded readers differed from children with only antisocial problems, but were similar to reading-disabled children without behaviour problems, on a number of individual and family correlates. This argued for disruptive behaviours arising as a secondary consequence of reading difficulties. Varlaam (1974) reached similar conclusions in a large-scale inner London study. Sturge (1982), however, found a more equivocal picture, with antisocial retarded readers falling somewhere between pure antisocial and pure reading-retarded groups. Sturge's sample, drawn from a quite disadvantaged inner city population, showed high rates of both reading and behaviour problems (Berger, Yule and Rutter, 1975), and also high levels of family adversity. This suggested a further basis for possible overlaps: reading and behaviour problems might each have distinct patterns of risk factors, but those risks might themselves be correlated in some samples.

A second approach involves the use of genetic strategies, assessing how far common genetic influences may be responsible for observed co-morbidities between reading and behavioural disorders. Very few studies using these new techniques have been reported in the literature as yet, and these have yielded somewhat inconsistent findings. Gilger, Pennington and DeFries (1991), for example, concluded that reading disability and attention–deficit hyperactivity disorder (ADHD) were primarily genetically independent, whereas Stevenson et al. (1993), using spelling problems rather than reading as their marker, found that when co-morbidity between spelling disability and hyperactivity did occur (at a rate of just over 4% in this epidemiologically defined twin sample), it was largely the result of common genetic influences. Methodological differences may account for these different conclusions; we must await further studies using these potentially informative techniques to resolve the role of genetic effects.

A third approach, especially appealing in testing how far difficulties in one domain may predispose to problems in another, is to trace children's progress prospectively over time. A number of studies have now taken this strategy, beginning at the start of schooling (McMichael, 1979; Jorm et al., 1986; Pianta and Caldwell, 1990) or in the pre-school period (Richman, Stevenson and Graham, 1982; McGee et al., 1988). These have highlighted two important issues.

First, many children who go on to develop reading problems show elevated rates of behaviour difficulties from the very start of schooling, before they have been exposed to a formal curriculum. This argues against reactions to school failure as the only source of behaviour problems, and suggests instead that either children may begin reacting to language-related precursors to reading difficulties in very early childhood, or shared or correlated risk factors are important.

Second, the early childhood studies have also provided some support for the proposal that reading difficulties do affect behavioural development in the early years of schooling. Pianta and Caldwell (1990), for example, documented increasing correlations between externalising behaviours and learning problems from nursey school to first grade, and data from the New Zealand Dunedin longitudinal study (McGee et al., 1988) extended this picture up to age 11. Increases in externalising behaviours, most notably in the areas of inattentiveness and overactivity, occurred for both generally backward and specifically retarded reading boys, soon after school entry for the first group and rather later, from age 7 years, for the second. Poor reading girls also showed increases in behaviour problems over the same period. In addition, McGee, Williams and Feehan (1992) have recently shown that, although ADHD normally has an onset in the pre-school period, one sub-group of boys in their study did show an onset only after school entry. These boys' problems appeared to be relatively specific to the school setting, and were identified by teachers, and later by the boys themselves, but not by parents. Perhaps most important, in marked contrast to the wide-ranging cognitive deficits shown by pre-school onset cases, their only discernible deficit was a poorer level of reading from age 7 years onwards. For some disabled readers, early difficulties at school may clearly play a role in the development of behaviour problems.

Developmental Change

Longitudinal studies have also suggested some developmental change
in the nature of the behaviour problems characteristic of poor readers
of different ages. Both the London and Isle of Wight studies (Rutter,
Tizard and Whitmore, 1970; Sturge, 1982) found high rates of poor
concentration, restlessness and overactivity among poor readers in
middle childhood. Hinshaw (1992), reviewing a range of evidence,
argued that hyperactivity and inattentiveness may be the more usual
early concomitants of underachievement, and that more directly con-
duct-related problems, when they occur, may arise at a later point.
Supporting these suggestions, Frick et al. (1991) used multivariate
statistical techniques to unravel the associations between IQ-dis-
crepant reading difficulties, conduct disorder and ADHD in a clinic
sample of boys. Reading disabilities showed direct links only with
ADHD, whereas associations with conduct problems were essentially
contingent on these, arising from the co-morbidity of conduct disorder and ADHD. In a similar way, the Dunedin study found no achievement deficits in children classified as aggressive-only at age 7 years
(McGee et al., 1988), and Taylor et al. (1991) found no elevated rates
of reading difficulties in a 'pure' conduct-disordered group at age 8
years. Where poor readers do show conduct problems in middle
childhood, they may arise as much from associated inattentiveness as
from reading difficulties per se.

Links between reading problems and attention–deficit hyperactivity disorder have been identified in both clinic and epidemiological
samples (Cantwell and Satterfield, 1978; Lambert and Sandoval,
1980; Holborow and Berry, 1986; McGee and Share, 1988), although
estimates of the extent of the overlap vary widely. Here, comparisons
of the cognitive deficits shown by children in each group provide a
further approach to testing aetiological questions. In general, studies
taking this approach have identified a consistent pattern of verbal
deficits associated with reading disability, but more equivocal results
for ADHD children. In part, this seems to reflect methodological
problems (McGee and Share, 1988). Pennington, Groisser and Welsh,
(1993), however, reported a double dissociation between reading disabilities and ADHD on carefully selected tasks chosen to reflect probable core deficits in each area. Reading-disabled boys showed
significant impairment on phonological processing tasks but not on
measures of executive function, whereas ADHD-only boys showed the
reverse pattern. More important, the overlap group, meeting diagnostic criteria for both reading and attentional problems, only showed
deficits in phonological processing.

As Pennington, Groisser and Welsh (1993) argue, these findings support a phenocopy hypothesis of ADHD in the overlap group, where boys with primary reading disabilities developed the behavioural symptoms of ADHD secondary to their reading problems, but showed no evidence of the cognitive deficits associated with the full ADHD syndrome. These authors highlighted a series of family environment measures (more mother-only households, more family members with other mental health problems, and so forth) that differentiated reading-disabled only and co-morbid groups. They went on to put forward a speculative model of the development of this pattern of conjoint difficulties, where mild early language problems interact with environmental stressors to give rise to beginning ADHD symptoms in the pre-school period, and these are then exacerbated as the child faces more specific learning difficulties on school entry.

Experiences at school might act to reinforce early family problems of this kind in a variety of ways. There is strong evidence that schooling influences children's behavioural development in general (Reynolds, 1992), and more detailed studies have highlighted a series of classroom-based factors that may be especially important for poor readers (see Hoffman, 1991; Weinstein, 1991, for reviews). Paradoxically, it seems that the social organisation of low ability teaching groups may often make them particularly difficult contexts in which to learn. Imai et al. (1992), for example, have recently reported a detailed and elegant study of factors affecting children's attention in reading lessons. Reading groups differed markedly in overall levels of attention, with the striking finding that nominal reading group ability level (simply rated on a 1–3 scale, from high to low) was a stronger predictor of children's attentiveness than individual measures of reading comprehension and fluency. These authors suggested that higher ability groups develop 'subcultures' supportive of attention, whereas in low ability groups the norms of behaviour in many ways act to reinforce inattentiveness. Although these processes will clearly not be universal, it may not be uncommon for the child entering school, vulnerable to both attentional and reading problems, to find his or her difficulties compounded by classroom experiences of this kind.

Experiences of failure and frustration at school, and their implications for self-esteem, have frequently been posited as further mediating links in the development of problem behaviours. From middle childhood onwards, academic self-esteem is clearly sensitive to underachievement at school, and perhaps especially to difficulties in reading (Chapman, Lambourne and Silva, 1990). Although very young children's self-assessments seem relatively unrelated to external referents (Harter, 1983), differentiated self-concepts, influenced both by teacher evaluations and by social comparisons with peers, are evident from about age 8 years. The role of peer comparisons may be especially important here. Renick and Harter (1989), for example, found that learning-disabled children rated their cognitive competence significantly higher when comparing themselves with other children with learning disabilities than with their non-disabled classmates. In addition, their views of their competence decreased markedly by comparison with normal peers between grades 3–4 and 7–8, but showed no such developmental changes when compared with other students with learning disabilities. Very similar processes may well occur among poor readers, most of whom will remain in normal classrooms with predominantly competent-reading peers.

These and other findings thus suggest a series of quite complex developmental linkages in early and middle childhood, possibly differing for different subgroups of children. By no means all poor readers will be vulnerable to behaviour difficulties at this stage. For those who are, shared or correlated risks factors may be important in some instances, and environmental stressors in others. Attentional problems seem the most likely concomitant of reading failure in early childhood; for some children, more directly oppositional and anti-social behaviours may also develop at a rather later stage.

Adolescence

The social adjustment and psychological well-being of disabled readers in adolescence and adulthood have received much less systematic attention to date. Here, although cross-sectional studies are revealing, longitudinal data are important in addressing two issues of particular importance: first, how far reading problems make it likely that childhood behaviour difficulties will persist and, second, whether they increase vulnerabilities to new disorders, arising for the first time in adolescence or adulthood.

On the first point, follow-ups of the Isle of Wight, inner London and Dunedin samples all found that reading problems played little, if any, role in the persistence of psychiatric disorder after middle childhood; children with reading difficulties were no more and no less likely to show continuing problems than their peers (Rutter et al., 1976; Maughan, Gray and Rutter, 1985; McGee et al., 1992). On the second issue – links with new adolescent disorders – findings are more mixed. The Isle of Wight studies suggested, in strong contrast with the picture in childhood, that adolescent disorders showed few links with educational difficulties of any kind. The Dunedin study (McGee et al., 1992), however, showed a small but significant effect of reading problems on new disorders at age 15 years, but only in boys. Kellam et al. (1983) linked early learning difficulties with depression in the teens, and studies of clinical populations have suggested that learning-disabled adolescents may experience higher levels of trait anxiety than their peers (see Huntington and Bender, 1993).

In adolescence, delinquency becomes an important additional indicator of behaviour problems, and the possibility of associations between reading disabilities and delinquency has aroused major concerns (Cornwell and Bawden, 1992). Evidence from the delinquency field has consistently demonstrated strong links between school failure and juvenile offending. Reviews of this extensive literature (Hirschi and Hindelag, 1977; Rutter and Giller, 1983; Hawkins and Lishner, 1987; Brier, 1989) suggest a range of possible causal mechanisms, many paralleling those put forward to account for reading–behaviour problem links in childhood. Elevated rates of offending among low achievers might reflect shared or correlated risk factors, problems in the verbal mediation of behaviour, continuities from earlier behaviour difficulties, or experiences of failure at school that at these older ages alienate young people from mainstream societal values, reduce bonds to the conventional social order, and encourage them to seek status and satisfaction elsewhere.

Although a number of studies have identified links between poor reading achievement and delinquency, in practice much of the existing delinquency literature has focused on general underachievement at school rather than reading difficulties per se. Wadsworth (1979) found that links between early reading scores and delinquency up to age 21 could largely be accounted for by social class and birth order effects. Maguin, Loeber and LeMahieu (1993) also questioned any direct connections between reading and delinquency. Studying a large US sample from quite young ages, they found no change in the strength of the association with age, and a strong impact of correlated attentional problems; once attentional difficulties had been included in the analyses, reading performance made no direct contribution to the prediction of delinquency.

In a follow-up of the inner London boys studied by Sturge (1982), Maughan, Gray and Rutter, (1985) found a trend towards higher rates of juvenile offending in both conduct-disordered and non-conduct problem poor readers, suggesting some increased risk of offending for boys with 'uncomplicated' reading difficulties. A further follow-up of the inner London sample in adulthood, however, revealed a different picture. In their twenties, childhood poor readers were no more likely to have been involved in officially recorded offending than their peers. Any increased susceptibility to delinquency in the teens seemed more strongly associated with non-attendance at school – a clear problem area for poor readers – than with persistent tendencies to antisocial behaviour per se. As outlined below, the few other follow-up studies which have examined offending in adulthood have reached broadly similar conclusions.

Adulthood

Follow-ups assessing social and psychological characteristics in adulthood are relatively limited. Most current data still come from clinic samples, or from studies of groups defined somewhat more broadly than in terms of childhood reading problems per se.

Small-scale early clinic studies (Balow and Blomquist, 1965; Carter, 1967) suggested that childhood poor readers showed elevated rates of problems on questionnaire assessments of personality and social adjustment in adulthood. More impressionistically, Balow and Blomquist (1965) also noted that many '... had a negative and slightly defeatist attitude to life. They do not appear to feel that they are "masters of their own destiny" but give one the clinical impression that they feel awash in a sea of forces fashioned by others' (p. 48).

This theme has been picked up more recently in a large-scale US study of high school underachievers (McCall, Evahn and Kratzer, 1992). Underachievers (with problems in a range of academic areas, not solely confined to reading difficulties) showed less planning and persistence in their working and personal lives, and lowered aspirations by comparison with their peers. The authors interpreted this as reflecting a possible characterological trait of underachievers, further exacerbated by experiences of failure at school.

Low achievement motivation has also been reported in a number of school-age studies of poor readers. As Oka and Paris (1987) point out in reviewing this evidence, findings of this kind are open to two rather different interpretations. On the one hand, low achievement motivation will clearly be dysfunctional in many contexts, and may well act to compound poor readers' cognitive difficulties. From a rather different perspective, however, it might be seen in a more positive light, as a coping strategy designed to maintain self-esteem. If the likelihood of failure is high, selecting task demands that are within one's competence may well hold benefits, reducing the risk of threats to self-esteem. Evidence from other adult follow-ups suggests that childhood poor readers may well adopt strategies of this kind in choosing courses of further study or career options. Finucci, Gottfredson and Childs (1985), for example, found that socially privileged alumni from a specialist boarding school for dyslexic children were over-represented in business rather than arts or science courses during their college years, and tended to enter less 'literacy-intensive' careers in adulthood. Although these choices placed some inevitable ceilings on their occupational attainments, they may also have served more positive functions in maintaining psychological well-being.

Further pointers that this may be an area of vulnerability in adulthood come from the early adult follow-ups of subjects in two of the British birth cohort studies (ALBSU, 1987; Bynner and Ekynsmith, 1994). Both studies included self-reports of continuing basic skills problems in adulthood, and self-completion questionnaires tapping low mood. The second study also included literacy and numeracy tests. Once again, the 'basic skills' groups were defined more widely than in terms of reading difficulties per se, and focused specifically on subjects with continuing problems in early adulthood. The findings were important, however, in showing consistently lower mood in the 'basic skills' groups, most obviously for women, and, when both tested literacy skills and self-reports were available, for subjects who perceived themselves to have continuing problems. Vulnerability to low mood seemed associated with *perceptions* of difficulties as much as with tested literacy skills.

To date, the most wide-ranging data on adjustment in adulthood come from two studies of childhood clinic attenders (Bruck, 1985; Spreen, 1987), and from our own inner London follow-up. In Bruck's (1985) study, data on childhood and adult adjustment were gained from interviews with each subject, and separately with his or her parents. Poor overall adjustment was subdivided into: 'withdrawn' (subjects who were depressed, highly sensitive, somewhat withdrawn, or worriers); 'acting-out' (subjects who showed immature and volatile reactions to stress or conflict); 'conduct disordered' (subjects who were repeatedly aggressive, and had committed a number of antisocial acts); and 'situational disorders' (subjects who had unrealistic perceptions of, or an inability to deal with, specific problem areas). In addition, specific records were made of reports of delinquent acts and drug and alcohol use.

The sample was selected to exclude children with primary behavioural or emotional problems. Even so, high levels of childhood problems were reported, with 85% of the learning-disabled subjects rated as showing poor overall adjustment in childhood. Thirty-seven per cent received comparable ratings in late adolescence and adulthood; over half of those showing problems in childhood were thus regarded as well adjusted at follow-up. Problem rates were, however, higher than in a peer control group. This difference was largely accounted for by the higher rate of problems among learning-disabled women;

rates for men were not significantly different from controls. The main specific difference from controls was in the 'acting-out' domain, but the largest single problem category in the learning-disabled group, accounting for almost half of those with adolescent or early adult problems, was withdrawal. There were no differences in rates of psychological problems between learning-disabled subjects in their teens and early twenties, and none of the adjustment measures showed associations with severity of initial learning disability. Finally, there were no group differences in the relatively low rates of delinquency recorded, nor in rates of heavy drug or alcohol use. Although problem rates were higher in the learning-disabled than the control group, few if any suggested evidence of major psychopathology. Only 5% of learning-disabled subjects had recent histories of counselling or psychiatric help. Spreen (1987) also collected retrospective accounts of childhood behaviour, along with standardised assessments and self-reports in early adulthood. Here, as in Bruck's (1985) study, relatively high rates of childhood problems were reported. Questionnaire personality and adjustment measures showed depressed scores in the 'teens and mid-twenties, though few fell in a range suggestive of psychopathology. Rates of difficulty were most clearly elevated for subjects with associated neurological impairment.

Learning-disabled subjects were more likely than controls to have been seen by psychologists or psychiatrists in their teens, but rates of psychiatric consultation were much lower in the twenties, and showed no group differences. Self-reports of offending were no higher in the learning-disabled than the comparison group, and there were no differences in reported use of street drugs (at high levels in both groups) or in alcohol use.

These studies suggest a number of important trends. First, although accounts of childhood behaviour were based on retrospective reports in both cases, rates of adjustment problems seemed considerably lower in adulthood than during the school years. Second, although previously reading-disabled subjects showed some increased vulnerability to adult problems, these rarely reflected clinically significant levels of psychopathology. Third, there were suggestions from Bruck's (1985) findings in particular that rates of adult difficulties might be slightly higher among women.

Both of these studies involved clinically referred groups, where, as noted earlier, rates of conjoint behaviour problems might be expected to be somewhat elevated. The inner London study focused on non-referred samples, albeit from socially disadvantaged backgrounds. There, on wide-ranging assessments of social functioning in the early twenties – encompassing performance at work, in marriage, friendships and other social relationships, negotiations requiring assertiveness and in day-to-day coping (Hill et al., 1989) – poor readers showed few if any tendencies to higher levels of difficulty than their competent-reading peers. A global measure of self-esteem showed no overall differences between the groups, although, as in the birth cohort studies, young adults who saw themselves as still impaired in reading did tend to poorer self-views. General patterns of attribution for success and failure were similar between poor and competent readers, though poor readers did show a pattern of negative, self-blaming attributions about their reading difficulties as such (Hagell, 1992). As outlined earlier, rates of offending were no higher among men with a history of reading difficulties, nor were other self-reported indicators of aggression or alcohol use. There was some increased vulnerability to psychiatric problems – primarily anxiety and depression – among women with specific reading retardation, and a small group of men showed quite severe avoidant personality problems. In general, however, psychiatric problems in adulthood were not significantly elevated. Somewhat unexpectedly, however, women with histories of reading problems had faced a much increased likelihood of broken marriages and co-habitations by their late twenties. Tracing possible pathways to these problems, it seemed that poor school-leaving qualifications and limited labour market opportunities may have combined to restrict opportunities in other domains, and predispose poor reading women to move into marriages and co-habitations earlier than their peers. As has been reported in many studies, early partnerships were less supportive than those embarked on rather later, and more prone to other difficulties. As women with childhood reading problems were more likely to enter relationships early, they faced proportionately more problems of this kind. By their late twenties, over 60%, by contrast with only 20% in the comparison group, had experienced marital breakdown.

Conclusions

This brief overview gives some flavour of the extent of our current knowledge – and the gaps in our understanding – of the behavioural and emotional difficulties that may affect reading-disabled young people. The picture is perhaps clearest in early and middle childhood, when inattentiveness and overactivity seem particularly characteristic of some children with reading problems, and conduct difficulties may compound these at a later stage. Aetiologically, these problems are likely to be heterogeneous: shared or correlated risk factors may be important in a proportion of cases, but there is also evidence that reading disabilities can exacerbate behaviour problems, possibly before and almost certainly after the start of schooling.

Moving to adolescence and early adulthood, findings are more scattered and not always consistent. Data from representative samples in the teens suggest that reading difficulties are unlikely to affect the persistence of existing behaviour problems, but it is less clear how far they may be associated with the development of new adolescent difficulties. To date, follow-up studies have found little evidence of severe psychopathology in adulthood, but have suggested increased vulnerability to more minor, but nevertheless distressing, problems, especially in terms of anxiety and low mood. Women may be somewhat more vulnerable here than men. Where adult problems do arise, it is unclear how far they should be attributed to awareness of on-going literacy problems, to the sequelae of childhood experiences of failure, or possibly to more indirect processes, mediated through current life circumstances. All of these issues warrant further study.

References

ALBSU (Adult Literacy and Basic Skills Unit) (1987). *Literacy, Numeracy and Adults: Evidence from the National Child Development Study*. London: ALBSU.

August, G.J. and Garfinkel, B.D. (1990). Comorbidity of ADHD and reading disability among clinic-referred children. *Journal of Abnormal Child Psychology*, **18**, 29–45.

Balow, B. and Blomquist, M. (1965). Young adults ten to fifteen years after reading disability. *Elementary School Journal*, **66**, 44–48.

Beitchman, J.H. (1985). Speech and language impairment and psychiatric risk: toward a model of neurodevelopmental immaturity. *Psychiatric Clinics of North America*, **8**, 721–735.

Berger, M., Yule, W. and Rutter, M. (1975). Attainment and adjustment in two geographical areas II: the prevalence of specific reading retardation. *British Journal of Psychiatry*, **126**, 510–519.

Brier, N. (1989). The relationship between learning disability and delinquency: a review and reappraisal. *Journal of Learning Disabilities*, **22**, 546–553.

Bruck, M. (1985). The adult functioning of children with specific learning disability: A follow-up study. In I. Siegel (ed.), *Advances in Applied Developmental Psychology*, pp. 91–129. Norwood, NJ: Ablex.

Bryan, J.H. and Bryan, T. (1990). Social factors in learning disabilities: attitudes and interactions. In G. Th. Pavlidis (ed.), *Perspectives on Dyslexia*, Vol. 2, pp. 247–281. London: Wiley.

Bynner, J. and Ekynsmith, C. (1994). *Young Adults' Literacy and Numeracy Problems: Some evidence from the 1970 British Cohort Study*. London: ALBSU.

Cantwell, D.P. and Baker, L. (1991). Association between attention deficit-hyperactivity disorder and learning disorders. *Journal of Learning Disabilities*, **24**, 88–95.

Cantwell, D.P. and Satterfield, J. H. (1978). Prevalence of academic underachievement in hyperactive children. *Journal of Pediatric Psychology*, **3**, 168–171.

Caron, C. and Rutter, M. (1991). Comorbidity in child psychopathology: concepts, issues and research strategies. *Journal of Child Psychology and Psychiatry*, **32**, 1063–1080.

Carter, R.P. (1967). The adult social adjustment of retarded and non-retarded readers. *Journal of Reading*, **11**, 224–228.

Cornwell, A. and Bawden, H.N. (1992). Reading disabilities and aggression: a critical review. *Journal of Learning Disabilities*, **25**, 281–288.

Finucci, J.M., Gottfredson, L.S. and Childs, B. (1985). A follow-up study of dyslexic boys. *Annals of Dyslexia*, **35**, 117–136.

Frick, P.J., Kampaus, R.W., Lahey, B.B., Loeber, R., Christ, M.A.G., Hart, E.L. and Tannenbaum, L.E. (1991). Academic underachievement and the disruptive behavior disorders. *Journal of Consulting and Clinical Psychology*, **59**, 289–294.

Gilger, J.W., Pennington, B.F. and DeFries, J.C. (1991). A twin study of the etiology of comorbidity: attentional deficit disorder and dyslexia. *Journal of the American Academy of Child and Adolescent Psychiatry*, **30**, 309–318.

Hagell, A. (1992). *The social psychology of illiteracy: An attributional perspective*. Unpublished PhD Thesis, University of London.

Harter, S. (1983). Developmental perspectives on the self-system In E.M. Hetherington (ed.), *Socialization, Personality and Social Development*, Vol IV. *Mussen's Handbook of Child Psychology*, 4th edn, pp. 275–385. New York: Wiley.

Hawkins, J.D. and Lishner, D.M. (1987). Schooling and delinquency. In Johnson E.H. (ed.), *Handbook on Crime and Delinquency Prevention*. New York: Greenwood Press.

Hill, J., Harrington, R., Fudge, H., Rutter, M. and Pickles, A. (1989). Adult Personality Functioning Assessment (APFA): An investigator-based standardized interview. *British Journal of Psychiatry*, **155**, 24–35.

Hinshaw, S.P. (1992). Externalizing behavior problems and academic underachievement in childhood and adolescence: causal relationships and underlying mechanisms. *Psychological Bulletin*, **111**, 127–155.

Hirschi, T. and Hindelag, M.J. (1977). Intelligence and delinquency: a revisionist review. *American Sociological Review*, **42**, 571–587.

Hoffman, J.V. (1991). Teacher and school effects in learning to read. In R. Barr, M.L. Kamil, P.B. Mosenthal and P.D. Pearson (Eds), *Handbook of Reading Research*, Vol. II, pp. 911–950. New York: Longman.

Holborow, P.L. and Berry, P.S. (1986). Hyperactivity and learning disabilities. *Journal of Learning Disabilities*, **19**, 426–431.

Huntington, D.D. and Bender, W.D. (1993). Adolescents with learning disabilities at risk? Emotional well-being, depression, suicide. *Journal of Learning Disabilities*, **26**, 159–166.

Imai, M., Anderson, R.C., Wilkinson, I.A.G. and Yi, H. (1992). Properties of attention during reading lessons. *Journal of Educational Psychology*, **84**, 160–173.

Jorm, A.F., Share, D.L., Matthews, R. and Maclean, R. (1986). Behaviour problems in specific reading retarded and general reading backward children: a longitudinal study. *Journal of Child Psychology and Psychiatry*, **27** 33–43.

Kellam, S.G., Brown, C.H., Rubin, B.R. and Ensminger, M.E. (1983). Paths leading to teenage psychiatric symptoms and substance use: developmental epidemiological studies in Woodlawn. In S.B. Guze, F.J. Earls, and J.E. Barratt (eds), *Childhood Psychopathology and Development*, pp. 17–51. New York: Raven Press.

Lambert, N.M. and Sandoval, J. (1980). The prevalence of learning disabilities in a sample of children considered hyperactive. *Journal of Abnormal Child Psychology*, **8**, 33–50.

Livingston, R. (1990). Psychiatric comorbidity with reading disability: a clinical study. *Advances in Learning Disabilities: A Research Annual*, Vol. 6, pp. 143–155. Greenwich: JAI Press.

McCall, R.B., Evahn, C. and Kratzer, L. (1992). *High School Underachievers: What Do they Achieve as Adults?* Newbury Park: Sage.

McGee, R. and Share, D. (1988). Attention deficit–hyperactivity and academic failure: which comes first and which should be treated? *Journal of the American Academy of Child and Adolescent Psychiatry*, **27**, 318–325.

McGee, R., Williams, S. and Feehan, M. (1992). Attention deficit disorder and age of onset of problem behaviours. *Journal of Abnormal Child Psychology*, **20**, 487–502.

McGee, R., Share, D., Moffitt, T.E., Williams, S. and Silva, P.A. (1988). Reading disability, behaviour problems and juvenile delinquency. In D.H. Saklofske and S.B.G. Eysenck (eds), *Individual Differences in Children and Adolescents: International Perspectives*, pp. 158–172. London: Hodder and Stoughton.

McGee, R., Feehan, M., Williams, S. and Anderson, J. (1992). DSM-III disorders from age 11 to age 15 years. *Journal of the American Academy of Child and Adolescent Psychiatry*, **31**, 50–59.

McMichael, P. (1979). The hen or the egg? Which came first – antisocial emotional disorder or reading disability? *British Journal of Educational Psychology*, **49**, 226–235.

Maguin, E., Loeber, R. and LeMahieu, P.G. (1993). Does the relationship between poor reading and delinquency hold for males of different ages and different ethnic groups? *Journal of Emotional and Behavioral Disorders*, **1**, 88–100.

Maughan, B., Gray, G. and Rutter, M. (1985). Reading retardation and antisocial behaviour: A follow-up into employment. *Journal of Child Psychology and Psychiatry*, **26**, 741–758.

Offord, D.R. and Poushinsky, M.F. (1981). School performance IQ and female delinquency. *International Journal of Social Psychiatry*, **21**, 267–283.

Oka, E.R. and Paris, S.G. (1987). Patterns of motivation and reading skills in underachieving children. In S.J. Ceci (Ed.), *Handbook of Cognitive, Social, and Neuropsychological Aspects of Learning Disabilities*, Vol. II, pp. 115–145. Hillsdale, NJ: Lawrence Erlbaum Associates.

Pennington, B.F., Groisser, D. and Welsh, M.C. (1993). Contrasting cognitive deficits in attention deficit hyperactivity disorder versus reading disability. *Developmental Psychology*, **29**, 511–523.

Pianta, R.C. and Caldwell, C.B. (1990). Stability of externalizing symptoms from kindergarten to first grade and factors related to instability. *Development and Psychopathology*, **2**, 247–258.

Renick, M.J. and Harter, S. (1989). Impact of social comparisons on the developing self-perceptions of learning disabled students. *Journal of Educational Psychology*, **81**, 631–638.

Richman, N., Stevenson, J. and Graham, P.J. (1982). *Pre-school to School: A Behavioural Study*. London: Academic Press.

Reynolds, D. (1992). Research on school effectiveness and school improvement: an updated review of the British literature. In D. Reynolds and P. Cuttance (eds) *School Effectiveness: Research, Policy and Practice*, pp. 1–24. London: Cassell.

Rutter, M. and Giller, H. (1983). *Juvenile Delinquency: Trends and Perspectives*. London: Penguin.

Rutter, M., Tizard, J. and Whitmore, K. (eds) (1970). *Education, Health and Behaviour*. London: Longman and Green.

Rutter, M., Tizard, J., Yule, W., Graham, P. and Whitmore, K. (1976). Isle of Wight studies 1964–1974. *Psychological Medicine*, 6, 313–332.

Semrud-Clikeman, M., Biederman, J., Sprich-Buckminster, S., Krifcher Lehman, B., Faraone, S.V. and Norman, D. (1992). Comorbidity between ADDH and learning disability: a review and report in a clinically referred sample. *Journal of the American Academy of Child and Adolescent Psychiatry*, 31, 439–448.

Silva, P.A. (1987). Epidemiology, longitudinal course, and some associated factors: An update. In W. and M. Rutter Yule (Eds), *Language Development and Disorders*, pp. 1–15. Oxford: MacKeith.

Spreen, O. (1987). *Learning Disabled Children Growing Up: A Follow-up into Adulthood*. Lisse, Netherlands: Swets & Zeitlinger.

Stevenson, J., Pennington, B.F., Gilger, J.W., DeFries, J.C. and Gillis, J.J. (1993). Hyperactivity and spelling disability: testing for shared genetic aetiology. *Journal of Child Psychology and Psychiatry*, 34, 1137–1152.

Sturge, C. (1982). Reading retardation and antisocial behaviour. *Journal of Child Psychology and Psychiatry*, 23, 21–31.

Taylor, E., Sandberg, S., Thorley, G. and Giles, S. (1991). *The Epidemiology of Childhood Hyperactivity*. Oxford: Oxford University Press.

Varlaam, A. (1974). Educational attainment and behaviour at school. *Greater London Intelligence Quarterly*, 29, 29–39.

Wadsworth, M. (1979). *Roots of Delinquency: Infancy, Adolescence and Crime*. Oxford: Martin Robertson.

Weinstein, C.S. (1991). The classroom as a social context for learning. *Annual Review of Psychology*, 42, 493–525.

Part III
The Remediation of
Reading Difficulties

Chapter 9
Phonological Processing Skills and Reading Remediation

WILLAM E. TUNMER

How do children learn to read? Two general views have emerged in the literature. According to the first view, the ability to read evolves naturally and spontaneously out of children's pre-reading experiences in much the same way that their oral language develops (Goodman and Goodman, 1979; Goodman and Altwerger, 1981; Harste, Burke and Woodward, 1982). As children are exposed to print in their environment, they acquire print-meaning associations for environmental labels and signs which, in turn, provide the basis for learning about the graphic system. Initially children are unable to read the words in labels and signs. They can only point to the location where it says 'milk' or 'stop'. However, after repeated exposure to these labels and signs, children eventually learn to recognise the words from the graphic cues alone.

This view of early reading is associated with an overall model of reading acquisition proposed by Goodman (1967) and Smith (1978). According to this model, skilled reading is primarily an activity of using the syntactic and semantic redundancies of language to generate hypotheses about the text yet to be encountered. Efficient readers are thought to pay little attention to the bulk of the words of text because the flow of language follows a predictable pattern. Instead, they use as few cues as possible to make a prediction and test their guess against their hypotheses about meaning. The major conclusion derived from these claims was that, unlike fluent readers, poor and beginning readers are less able to make use of contextual redundancy in ongoing sentence processing. Reading instruction should therefore place little emphasis on using visual information to identify individual words and more on using context to guess words.

According to the first view, then, all that is needed is for children to learn a few sight words and focus on the meaning of text; the rest will take care of itself. In short, children 'learn to read by reading'. As it is assumed that children are naturally predisposed to learn written language, reading failure is thought to result from methods of instruction that conflict with the natural course of events. Goodman (1986), a leading proponent of the 'whole language' approach to literacy learning and instruction, argues that teachers make learning to read difficult 'by breaking whole (natural) language into bite-size abstract little pieces' (p.7). Training in such skills as phonemic segmentation provide little or no benefit to beginning readers because language is not kept 'whole'. Word study activities should emphasise the process of 'making meaning', not the mechanics of reading words in isolation or translating written words into sounds. Focusing on the latter prevents beginning readers from making important generalisations through context clues. If children are immersed in a print-rich environment in which the focus is on the meaning of print, they will readily acquire reading skills, according to this view.

In opposition to this view is the claim that learning to read is not natural (see Liberman and Liberman, 1992, for a review of research and theoretical arguments). Gough and Hillinger (1980) proposed a two-stage model of beginning reading. During the first stage, children quickly learn to recognise dozens of words through the natural strategy of selective association, the pairing of a partial stimulus cue to a response. As Gough and Juel (1991) point out:

> Any cue which will distinguish the word will suffice. It might be a character, or a matching pair of characters, or even the font in which the characters appear; if the child knows the names of some letters, it might be the name of one of them (cf. Ehri and Wilce, 1985). Or it might be a property of the whole word; it might be its colour, or its length, or even the resemblance of the whole to some familiar object. Whatever the child might notice, the child will associate the word with that cue, and with that cue only. The child will select that cue, and so his association will be selective.
>
> (p.49)

Beginning readers who continue to learn in this way, however, will face two serious problems (Gough, Juel and Griffith, 1992). First, although the hypothesis of selective association predicts that the beginning reader will easily acquire a few visually distinct sight words, it also predicts that the child's natural strategy of associating a familiar spoken word with some feature or attribute of the word's printed form will eventually break down. Each new word will become increasingly harder to acquire because of the difficulty of finding a unique cue to distinguish it from those that have already been learned. Beginning readers will make an ever increasing number of errors, and become confused and frustrated, unless they discover or are led to discover an alternative strategy for establishing the relationship between the written and spoken forms of the language.

Second, the strategy of selective association based on distinctive visual cues is not generative, i.e. it provides no way of recognising unfamiliar words. This is an important consideration because most of the words that the beginning reader encounters in print are novel. Beginning reading materials typically employ upwards of 1500 words, each of which must be encountered a first time. Moreover, when a new word does appear in print it does not suddenly begin appearing with great frequency. Approximately 35–40% of the words used in beginning reading materials appear only once (Jorm and Share, 1983). Thus beginning readers are continually encountering words that they have not seen before and may not set eyes on again for some time. Sentence context will be of little help because research has demonstrated that the average predictability of content words in running text is about 0.10, as compared to about 0.40 for function words (e.g. *on, the, to*), which are typically short, high-frequency sight words that the child can already recognise (Gough, 1983). In other words, unless a child is reading a very low level text with repeated sentence structures, a high degree of predictability and a large amount of picture support, he or she will have a one in ten chance of guessing the correct word.

Gough and colleagues argue that normal progress in learning to read can occur only if the child makes the transition to the next stage of acquisition, the *cipher* stage. Entering this stage requires that the child becomes conceptually aware of the interrelatedness of the visual patterns and sounds shared by different words. Gough and Juel (1991) refer to this awareness as *cryptanalytical intent*. The child 'must grasp that there is a system of correspondences to be mastered' (p.51). Unlike the first stage, where the child naturally (and subconsciously) associates a spoken word with some particularly salient visual cue in the corresponding written word, the cipher stage is not natural. Rather, it is characterised by fully analytical processing which requires an explicit and conscious awareness of the relationship that exists between alphabetic shapes and phonological segments. According to this view, then, reading skill is not picked up simply through exposure to print but almost always requires extensive adult intervention to promote the development of analytic processing. A basic discontinuity in the acquisition of word recognition skill is therefore proposed.

Research has supported Gough and Hillinger's (1980) two-stage conceptualisation of beginning reading. A study by Masonheimer, Drum and Ehri (1984) indicated that, in contrast to the views of

Goodman and others, environmental print experiences alone do not enable children to advance to the cipher stage of beginning reading, i.e. later stages of beginning reading are not *continuous extensions* of the kind of spontaneous word learning that results from exposure to environmental print. Byrne (1991, 1992) reported the results of a series of experiments demonstrating that pre-readers are largely ignorant of phonological segments, adopting instead a non-analytical strategy in which new words are learned by associating some distinguishing feature of the printed word with its spoken counterpart as a whole. Pre-school children with no knowledge of reading or the sounds of individual letters could be taught to discriminate FAT from BAT but this did not enable them to discriminate FUN from BUN at a level above chance. Byrne concluded that the failure of pre-readers to develop analytical links between print and speech results from the extension of the more natural non-analytical strategy, a strategy which can, however, be altered by explicit instruction in phonemic segmentation and letter–phoneme relations (Byrne and Fielding-Barnsley, 1989). More recently, Gough (1993) reported the results of two experiments providing further evidence of a visual cue reading stage in beginning reading.

Reading Disabilities and Reading Remediation

To advance to the cipher stage of beginning reading, the child must come to realise that there are systematic correspondences between elements of written and spoken language. Cipher knowledge, or phonological recoding skill, may be defined as the ability to translate letters and letter patterns into phonological forms. The process of converting a graphemic representation of a word into its corresponding phonological representation may involve sequentially converting graphemic units into phonemes (a process that may be subject to position-specific constraints and 'marker' letters), analogising to known words that are stored in lexical memory (a process that may involve the subsyllabic units of onset and rime, which are easier to segment than phonemic units), or, most probably, some combination of these two processes (Bruck and Treiman, 1992; Ehri and Robbins, 1992; see Chapter 2).

Research indicates that beginning readers who continue to rely on the strategy of selective association because of phonological processing difficulties will encounter severe problems in learning to read (Snowling, 1987; Rack, Snowling and Olson, 1992). These children will not be able to derive maximum benefit from reading instruction and will be prevented from taking advantage of the reciprocally facilitating relationships between reading achievement and other aspects of development (such as growth in vocabulary, syntactic knowledge and phonological processing skills), which facilitate further growth in reading (Stanovich, 1986). Beginning readers who have phonological processing deficits may be able to overcome their initial weaknesses in the phonological domain and gradually develop along normal lines. They eventually learn to read, but do so more slowly. However, without specific intervention, a more probable possibility is that most of these children will not await phonological development but will rely increasingly on compensatory visual strategies guided by contextual cues (Snowling, 1987; Tunmer and Hoover, 1994).

The reason that the ability to use phonological information is so critical is that sublexical analyses involving phonological information result in positive learning trials (i.e. correct word identifications), which in turn lead to the amalgamation of orthographic and phonological representations in semantic memory (Ehri, 1992). These amalgamated representations provide the basis for rapid and efficient access to the mental lexicon, which in turn frees up cognitive resources for allocation to higher order cognitive functions, such as comprehension monitoring and determining the meanings of unknown words. Children who continue to use compensatory visual strategies at the expense of phonological information will experience progressive deterioration in the rate of reading development as they grow older (Bruck, 1992; Byrne, Freebody and Gates, 1992). As there is little interaction between orthographic and phonological codes in the word processing of poor readers who rely on compensatory strategies, the development of awareness of individual phonemes and knowledge of correspondences between graphemes and phonemes is not promoted. Consequently, the word recognition skills of these children remain relatively weak because they do not develop links between orthographic and phonological representations in semantic memory (see Chapter 1, and Adams and Bruck, 1993, for a discussion of connectionist models of reading).

Remedial reading programmes designed to facilitate the development of phonological processing skills in reading-disabled children may differ on several instructional dimensions. Four dimensions that appear to be particularly important are 'skill and drill' versus metacognitive approaches to instruction in phonological processing skills, systematic versus incidental instruction in alphabetic coding, the degree of reliance on writing as a means of teaching phonological recoding skills, and the use of phonic generalisations versus phonograms (the common elements in word families) in beginning code instruction.

Metacognitive approaches to instruction in phonological recoding skills place particular emphasis on making disabled readers conceptually aware of the interrelatedness of the visual patterns and sounds shared by different words. For example, children may be taught the strategy of reading unfamiliar words by detecting and pronouncing known words and word parts in unfamiliar words (Gaskins et al., 1988; Goswami and Bryant, 1990). This may include making disabled readers aware that some unfamiliar words contain spelling patterns (i.e. *homographic* spelling patterns) that are associated with more than one pronunciation (e.g. *o–w–n* as in DOWN and BLOWN), and that they may need to generate alternative pronunciations until one matches a word in their listening vocabulary. Gaskins et al. refer to this as a 'set for diversity' (p.38). Instruction that places emphasis on metacognitive aspects of learning may also be useful in facilitating the development of phonological awareness in children (Cunningham, 1990). Deficient phonological awareness is widely regarded as a major cause of reading disability (Stanovich, 1986). To discover corespondences between graphemes and phonemes (and vice versa), children must be able to segment spoken words into their constituent phonemic elements (Tunmer and Rohl, 1991). In general, metacognitive approaches to instruction are in sharp contrast to skill-and-drill approaches in which phonic generalisations and phonemic segmentation skills are taught in an isolated, piecemeal fashion with little or no emphasis placed on developing within beginning readers an understanding of how and when to apply such knowledge. In support of a metacognitive approach to remedial reading instruction, Hatcher, Hulme and Ellis (1994; see Chapter 10) found that intervention training in phonemic segmentation skills was more effective when it was integrated with the teaching of reading.

A second important dimension concerns the question of whether remedial instruction in the alphabetic code should arise incidentally in the context of reading connected text, or whether such instruction should be more explicit and systematic. Advocates of the whole language approach to reading instruction argue that word analysis skills should only be taught in context and only as back-up support to confirm language predictions. Strickland and Cullinan (1990), for example, claim that 'phonics is best learned in the context of reading and writing' (p. 429), and that 'the evidence supports a whole language and integrated language arts approach with some direct instruction, in context, on spelling-to-sound correspondences' (p. 433) (see also Clay, 1985, 1991). Research indicates, however, that compared to normally achieving children, at-risk beginning readers are less able to discover grapheme–phoneme correspondences as a by-product of more general reading, suggesting that these children require more explicit instruction in alphabetic coding (Calfee and Drum, 1986). Although a naturalistic, informal, whole language approach to reading instruction (in which word analysis activities arise *incidentally* from the child's responses during text reading) may be suitable for many children, learning-disabled children appear to require a more highly structured, systematic, strategies-based approach with particular emphasis on the development of phonological processing skills. As Adams and Bruck (1993) argue, 'Wherever children who cannot discover the alphabetic principle independently are denied explicit instruction on the regularities and conventions of the letter strings, reading-disability may well be the eventual consequence' (p. 131).

Another instructional dimension concerns the extent to which the development of phonological recoding skills can occur through writing activities. Whole language advocates argue that instruction in the use of letter–sound correspondences to identify unfamiliar words is largely unnecessary because children can acquire knowledge of the alphabetic code through their experiences of attempting to spell words (Clay, 1991). Research has shown, however, that children initially use different strategies in reading and spelling (Goswami and Bryant, 1990). In early spelling the strategies are phonologically based. Analyses of children's early ('invented') spellings indicate that from the very beginning children attempt to figure out the sounds in words and then represent the sounds with alphabetic letters (e.g. 'hkn' for CHICKEN, 'klr' for COLOUR) (Read, 1986; Treiman, 1993). Treiman (1993) found little evidence in these early spellings for the use of visual knowledge of spelling patterns gained through reading. In contrast, the strategies used by children in early reading are visually based. As noted earlier, children learn to recognise their first words by relying on partial visual cues. Research further indicates that direct instruction in phonological recoding skills supports reading growth better than spelling instruction combined with incidental instruction in phonological recoding skills (Foorman et al., 1991). Vellutino (1991) suggests that a possible explanation of this difference is that learning to read depends on the ability to blend letter sounds whereas learning to spell does not. The acquisition of blending skills may require experience of the type received from direct instruction in the use of letter–sound correspondences.

A fourth instructional dimension concerns the issue of exploiting phonograms in remedial reading programmes as opposed to relying solely on individual letter-to-sound correspondences. Phonograms are the common elements in 'word families' (e.g. the letter sequence 'ight' in LIGHT, FIGHT and RIGHT). There appears to be three advantages of focusing initially on phonograms in remedial reading instruction. First, the use of phonograms enables children to take advantage of the intrasyllabic units of onset and rime, where *onset* is the initial consonant or consonant cluster, and *rime* is the vowel and any following consonants (Treiman, 1992). Research indicates that awareness of onsets and rimes precedes the development of full-blown phonemic segmentation ability (Goswami and Bryant, 1990). As onsets and rimes are more accessible to young children and because onsets often comprise single phonemes (e.g. *f–un*), an initial focus on word families may greatly facilitate the process of learning to isolate and recognise individual phonemes, a skill that reading-disabled children normally find difficult to acquire. A second advantage in using phonograms in remedial instruction is that the complexity of vowel generalisations is greatly reduced. Vowel sounds are generally quite stable in the rime phonograms that appear in beginning reading materials (Adams, 1990). Teaching reading-disabled children to recognise stable phonograms may be a very useful first step in making these children more aware of sublexical relationships between written and spoken words. Eventually, however, they will need to acquire more specific grapheme–phoneme correspondences to learn to recognise words that either begin with constant clusters or do not share common rime spelling patterns with other words (e.g. CLIFF, STRICT, HORSE, LIZARD, LAMB, TIGER, LION) (Gough, 1993). A third advantage of initially focusing on teaching phonograms is that it temporarily delays the need for acquiring the ability to blend individual phonemes within rime spelling patterns, the latter being a difficult operation to perform because of the large amount of processing required (Perfetti et al., 1987).

Recent Research

Aspects of the four instructional dimensions that I have discussed were investigated in two recent studies (Iversen and Tunmer, 1993; Greaney and Tunmer, 1994). The first study examined the instructional strategies used in reading recovery, a remedial reading programme that was developed in New Zealand by Marie Clay (1985) to reduce the number of children with reading and writing difficulties. The programme focuses on 6-year-old children who, after 1 year in school, are identified by teachers as not making good progress. The children are assessed with a battery of tests and observational procedures constituting the diagnostic survey (Clay, 1985). The children selected for assistance are provided with 30–40 minutes of individual instruction per day by a specially trained reading recovery teacher. The aim of the instruction, which supplements the children's regular classroom literacy programme, is to help children to reach a level of reading performance that is at or above the class average, in as little time as possible. This process usually takes between 12 and 20 weeks, at which time the child's reading recovery programme is discontinued.

Research indicates that reading recovery is much more effective than remedial instruction in small groups (Pinnell, De Ford and Lyons, 1988). However, similar findings have been reported for other remedial programmes involving one-to-one tutoring but employing altogether different approaches than that used in reading recovery (e.g. Slavin et al., 1991), which suggests that it may be the intensive, one-to-one nature of these programmes that is primarily responsible for their superiority over small group instruction. A major aim of the study, therefore, was to determine whether the specific procedures and instructional strategies of reading recovery are more effective than other remedial approaches when the basic parameters of the programme are held constant. We were particularly interested in determining whether the inclusion of more explicit and systematic instruction in phonological recoding skills would increase the effectiveness of the reading recovery programme. Clay (1985) argues that instruction in alphabetic coding should only arise incidentally in the context of reading connected text and that explicit instruction in the use of letter-to-phoneme correspondences is largely unnecessary because children can acquire knowledge of the alphabetic code through spelling.

Three carefully matched groups of 32 children each were formed: a modified reading recovery group, a standard reading recovery group and a standard intervention group that involved small group instruction. The children were all first graders who had been identified as being at risk for reading failure on the basis of their performance on the diagnostic survey and the Dolch Word Recognition Test. The diagnostic survey comprises a letter identification task, a word recognition task, a concepts about print task, a writing vocabulary task, a dictation task and an assessment of text level. In addition to the diagnostic survey and Dolch Word Recognition Test, the children were also given a phoneme segmentation test, a phoneme deletion test and a pseudoword decoding test.

The children in the standard and modified reading recovery groups received regular reading recovery lessons, but the children in the modified reading recovery group also received explicit training in phonological recoding skills as part of their lesson. The aim of the instruction incorporated into the modified reading recovery programme was to make the children more aware that words with common sounds often share the same spelling patterns. The procedures were similar to those developed by Bryant and Bradley (1985), and included an initial focus on phonograms. The children were asked to manipulate magnetic letters to make, break and build new words that had similar visual and phonological elements. Beginning with the manipulation of initial sounds/letters, the teacher modelled the task and then within each lesson gradually passed control over to the child. This procedure was then repeated daily with different words until the child demonstrated that he or she knew how to manipulate initial sounds/letters/clusters. The teacher then moved to final and then medial sounds/letters/clusters. The instruction focused not only on making children aware that words are visually and phonologically similar but also, in the context of the surrounding lessons, on developing strategies for knowing how and when to apply such knowledge. Whenever possible the teacher required the children to use their newly gained strategic knowledge to help them identify unfamiliar words in text. In short, the emphasis was on developing metacognitive knowledge and strategies for identifying unfamiliar words, not on 'knowing' a particular list of words.

An analysis of the pre-treatment data confirmed that there were no significant differences between the means of the three comparison groups for all pre-treatment measures. The pre-treatment data also revealed that the children in the three intervention groups performed extremely poorly on the three phonological processing measures. An analysis of the same measures at discontinuation showed that the two reading recovery groups performed at very similar levels, and that both groups performed much better on all measures than the standard intervention group.

The most significant finding of the study is presented in Table 9.1. Although the two reading recovery groups performed at very similar levels on all measures at discontinuation, the results shown in Table 9.1 indicate that it took the children receiving the standard reading recovery programme much longer to reach the same point. The difference in the mean number of lessons to discontinuation was highly significant, and indicates that the standard reading recovery programme was 37% less efficient than the modified reading recovery programme. To rule out the possibility that the extra lessons received by the standard reading recovery group children enabled them eventually to overtake the children in the modified reading recovery group, an analysis of measures taken at the end of the year revealed no differences between the two groups.

Table 9.1 Mean number of lessons to discontinuation as a function of type of reading recovery programme

Type of reading recovery programme	*n*	Mean	Standard deviation	*t*[62]
Modified	32	41.75	10.62	5.70*
Standard	32	57.31	11.22	

*$p < 0.001$.

A path analysis of the data was carried out to determine the structure of relationships between measures at discontinuation and measures at the end of the year. The results suggest that phonological awareness is primarily responsible for the development of phonological recoding ability, that phonological recoding ability is in turn primarily responsible for the development of context-free word recognition ability, and that context-free word recognition ability is in turn primarily responsible for the development of the ability to read connected text. The simple predictive correlations between spelling measures and end-of-year reading measures failed to reach significance, suggesting that letter-to-phoneme knowledge, not phoneme-to-letter knowledge as claimed by Clay (1991), is primarily responsible for 'driving' the development of word recognition skills.

In summary, the results of the study indicated the following: that systematic instruction in phonological recoding skill was much more effective than incidental instruction; that the inclusion of direct instruction in phonological recoding skill yielded better results than relying on writing activities as the primary means of developing knowledge of the alphabetic code; and that a metacognitive approach to code instruction that included the use of phonograms could be a very effective intervention strategy for at-risk readers. The results further indicated that the children selected for reading recovery were particularly deficient in phonological processing skills, and that their progress in the programme was strongly related to the development of these skills.

The study by Greaney and Tunmer (1994) focused on older poor readers from 9 to 11 years of age. Using a reading-age match design, they found that younger normal readers performed as well as or better than older poor readers on four measures of onset-rime sensitivity (i.e. rhyme awareness), and performed better on a task that measured children's ability to take advantage of analogical units when reading lists of words that varied in whether the words containing the common unit were presented contiguously or non-contiguously, and in whether the unit constituted the rime portion of the words or was embedded in the rime portion of the words.

A follow-up intervention study was carried out to determine whether poor readers could be taught to use analogies when they encountered unfamiliar words while reading connected text. The poor readers were divided into two carefully matched groups. The treatment group received instruction in the use of orthographic analogies, whereas the comparison group received standard remedial instruction emphasising context cue usage.

The children in both training groups were asked to read one of four prose passages twice, once before and once after the training procedures. As the children read a passage their errors were under-lined by the experimenter on a copy of the passage. The children were informed before the reading that any errors they made would be underlined by the experimenter, but the experimenter provided no prompting or feedback during the reading.

For the children in the analogy training group, the following pro-cedure was then carried out. On the experimenter's copy of the pas-sage (and adjacent to the actual text), the children were asked to spell a frequently occurring word that contained an analogical unit identical to one that appeared in the misread word. If the spelling was incorrect, other examples were selected. If all spelling attempts were incorrect (which was rare), the experimenter wrote down a word for the child that contained the relevant orthographic unit. The child was then asked to locate the common analogical unit, to say the sound and then to copy it in a separate column. For example, a child who could not read the word *gently* was asked to spell the words *went, bent* and *tent*, and then to identify, say and write down the common sound unit *ent*. This procedure was repeated for as many of the reading errors as possible (some of the errors did not contain suitable analogical units from which example spellings could be based). As with the previous study by Iversen and Tunmer (1993), the purpose of the procedure was to develop metacognitive knowledge and strategies for identifying unfamiliar words, not on 'knowing' a particular list of words.

The children in the control group were encouraged to make use of context cues to identify unfamiliar words. The experimenter taught the children a variety of meaning-based strategies and used prompts to encourage them to make use of these strategies.

Following the completion of the training procedure, the children in both groups were asked to read the passage a second time. The children in the analogy group were asked to attend to the spellings and common sound units of the words previously misread, whereas the children in the context cue group were encouraged to make use of context cues to identify the unfamiliar words encountered during the first reading of the text.

The mean number of reading errors made by each training group before and after training are presented in Table 9.2. Although both groups showed significant reductions in the mean number of post-treatment reading errors, the children in the analogy training group made considerably fewer post-treatment errors. This finding suggests that poor readers can be taught to use analogies to identify unfamiliar words, and that analogy training is more effective in increasing the error corrections of poor readers than training in context cue usage (compare Chapter 2).

Table 9.2 Mean number of reading errors as a function of group and time of testing

| | | Time of testing | |
| | | Pre-treatment reader errors | Post-treatment reader errors |
Group	*n*		
Analogical transfer	15	20.20 (6.17)	7.13 (5.60)
Context cue usage	15	21.00 (4.52)	13.20 (3.88)

* Values in parentheses are standard deviations.

Concluding Remarks

In summary, this chapter started with a description of two general views of how children learn to read. According to the first view, reading ability evolves naturally and spontaneously in much the same way that oral language develops. Reading failure is thought to result from methods of instruction that conflict with the natural course of events. In contrast, the second view proposes a two-stage conceptualisation of beginning reading. During the first stage children naturally (and subconsciously) associate a spoken word with some particularly salient visual cue in the corresponding written word. However, movement into the second stage requires explicit and conscious awareness of the relationship that exists between alphabetic shapes and phonological segments. It is claimed that reading problems occur when children continue to rely on partial visual cues because of phonological processing difficulties. Arguments and evidence were presented in support of the second view of beginning reading.

This led to a discussion of phonological recoding skill, which I defined as the ability to translate letters and letter patterns into phonological forms. It was argued that beginning readers must acquire phonological recoding skill to identify unfamiliar words and to gain the practice required for developing speed and automaticity in recognising words in text. It was then noted that remedial reading programmes designed to facilitate the development of phonological recoding skill differ on several instructional dimensions and that four of these dimensions may be particularly important. In the final section two studies were described in which aspects of these four dimensions were investigated. The results of both studies suggest that a metacognitive approach to code instruction which exploits the use of phonograms can be a very effective intervention strategy for children experiencing reading difficulties.

References

Adams, M.J. (1990). *Beginning to Read: Learning and Thinking about Print.* Cambridge, MA: MIT Press.

Adams, M.J. and Bruck, M. (1993). Word recognition: The interface of educational policies and scientific research. *Reading and Writing: An Interdisciplinary Journal* 5, 113–139.

Bruck, M. (1992). Persistence of dyslexics' phonological awareness deficits. *Developmental Psychology*, 28, 874–886.

Bruck, M. and Treiman, R. (1992). Learning to pronounce words: The limitations of analogies. *Reading Research Quarterly*, 27, 375–388.

Bryant, P.E. and Bradley, L. (1985). *Children's Reading Problems.* Oxford: Blackwell.

Byrne, B. (1991). Experimental analysis of the child's discovery of the alphabetic principle. In L. Rieben and C. Perfetti (eds), *Learning to Read: Basic Research and Its Implications*, pp. 75–84. Hillsdale, NJ: Lawrence Erlbaum Associates.

Byrne, B. (1992). Studies in the acquisition procedure for reading: Rationale, hypotheses, and data. In P.B. Gough, L. Ehri and R. Treiman (eds), *Reading acquisition*, pp. 1–34. Hillsdale, NJ: Lawrence Erlbaum Associates.

Byrne, B. and Fielding-Barnsley, R. (1989). Phonemic awareness and letter knowledge in the child's acquisition of the alphabetic principle. *Journal of Educational Psychology*, 81, 313–321.

Byrne, B., Freebody, P. and Gates, A. (1992). Longitudinal data on the relations of word-reading strategies to comprehension, reading time, and phonemic awareness. *Reading Research Quarterly*, 27, 141–151.

Calfee, R.C. and Drum, P.A. (1986). Research on teaching reading. In M.C. Wittrock (ed.), *Handbook of Research on Teaching*, pp. 804–849. New York: Macmillan.

Clay, M. (1985). *The Early Detection of Reading Difficulties.* Auckland: Heinemann.

Clay, M. (1991). *Becoming Literate: The Construction of Inner Control.* Auckland: Heinemann.

Cunningham, A. (1990). Explicit versus implicit instruction in phonemic awareness. *Journal of Experimental Child Psychology*, 50, 429–444.

Ehri, L. (1992). Reconceptualising the development of sight word reading and its relationship to recoding. In P. Gough, L. Ehri and R. Treiman (eds), *Reading Acquisition*, pp. 107–143. Hillsdale, NJ: Lawrence Erlbaum Associates.

Ehri, L.C. and Robbins, C. (1992). Beginners need some decoding skill to read by analogy. *Reading Research Quarterly*, 27, 13–26.

Ehri, L. and Wilce, L. (1985). Movement into reading: Is the first stage of printed word learning visual or phonetic? *Reading Research Quarterly*, 20, 163–179.

Foorman, B.R., Francis, D.J., Novy, D.M. and Liberman, D. (1991). How letter-sound instruction mediates progress in first-grade reading and spelling. *Journal of Educational Psychology*, 83, 456–469.

Gaskins, I.W., Downer, M.A., Anderson, R.., Cunningham, P.M., Gaskins, R.W., Schommer, M. and the Teachers of the Benchmark School (1988). A metacognitive approach to phonics: Using what you know to decode what you don't know. *Remedial and Special Education*, 9, 36–41.

Goodman, K.S. (1967). Reading: A psycholinguistic guessing game. *Journal of the Reading Specialist* 6, 126–135.

Goodman, K.S. (1986). *What's Whole in Whole Language: A Parent–Teacher Guide*. Portsmouth, NH: Heinemann.

Goodman, K.S. and Goodman, Y.M. (1979). Learning to read is natural. In L.B. Resnick and P.A. Weaver (eds), *Theory and Practice of Early Reading*, Vol.1, pp. 137–154. Hillsdale, NJ: Lawrence Erlbaum Associates.

Goodman, Y.M. and Altwerger, B. (1981). Print awareness in preschool children: A working paper. *A Study of the Development of Literacy in Preschool Children*. Occasional Papers No.4, Program in Language and Literacy, University of Arizona.

Goswami, U. and Bryant, P. (1990). *Phonological Skills and Learning to Read*. Sussex: Lawrence Erlbaum Associates.

Gough, P. (1983). Context, form and interaction. In K. Rayner (Ed.), *Eye Movements in Reading: Perceptual and Language Processes*, pp. 203–211. San Diego, CA: Academic Press.

Gough, P. (1993). The beginning of decoding. *Reading and Writing: An Interdisciplinary Journal*, 5, 181–192.

Gough, P. and Hillinger, M. (1980). Learning to read: An unnatural act. *Bulletin of the Orton Society*, 30, 179–196.

Gough, P. and Juel, C. (1991). The first stages of word recognition. In L. Rieben and C. Perfetti (eds), *Learning to Read: Basic Research and Its Implications*, pp. 47–56. Hillsdale, NJ: Lawrence Erlbaum Associates.

Gough, P., Juel, C. and Griffith, P. (1992). Reading, spelling, and the orthographic cipher. In P. Gough, L. Ehri and R. Treiman (eds), *Reading Acquisition*, pp. 35–48. Hillsdale, NJ: Lawrence Erlbaum Associates.

Greaney, K. and Tunmer, W. (1994). *The Development of Onset-Rime Sensitivity and Analogical Transfer in Normal and Poor Readers*, in press.

Harste, J., Burke, C. and Woodward, V. (1982). Children's language and world: Initial encounters with print. In J. Langer and M. Smith-Burke (eds), *Bridging the Gap: Reader meets Author*, pp. 105–131. Newark, DE: International Reading Association.

Hatcher, R., Hulme, C. and Ellis, A. (1994). Ameliorating early reading failure by integrating the teaching of reading and phonological skills: The phonological linkage hypothesis. *Child Development*, 65, 41–57

Iversen, S. and Tunmer, W. (1993). Phonological processing skills and the Reading Recovery program. *Journal of Educational Psychology*, 85, 112–126.

Jorm, A. and Share, D. (1983). Phonological recoding and reading acquisition. *Applied Psycholinguistics*, 4, 103–147.

Liberman, I.Y. and Liberman, A.M. (1992). Whole language vs code emphasis: Underlying assumptions and their implications for reading instruction. In P.B. Gough, L.C. Ehri and R. Treiman (eds), *Reading Acquisition*, pp. 343–366. Hillsdale, NJ: Erlbaum Associates.

Masonheimer, P., Drum, P. and Ehri, L. (1984). Does environmental print identification lead children into word reading? *Journal of Reading Behaviour*, 16, 257–271.

Perfetti, C., Beck, I., Bell, L. and Hughes, C. (1987). Phonemic knowledge and learning to read are reciprocal: A longitudinal study of first grade children. *Merrill-Palmer Quarterly*, 33, 283–319.

Pinnell, G.S., De Ford, D. and Lyons, C. (1988). *Reading Recovery: Early Intervention for At Risk First Graders*. Arlington, VA: Educational Research Service.

Rack, J.P., Snowling, M.J. and Olson, R.K. (1992). The nonword reading deficit in developmental dyslexia: A review. *Reading Research Quarterly*, 27, 28–53.

Read, C. (1986). *Children's Creative Spelling*. London: Routledge & Kegan Paul.

Slavin, R.E., Madden, N.A., Karweit, N.L., Dolan, L.J. and Wasik, B.A. (1991). Research directions: Success for all: Ending reading failure from the beginning. *Language Arts*, 68, 404–409.

Smith, F. (1978). *Understanding Reading*. New York: Holt, Rinehart & Winston.

Snowling, M. (1987). *Dyslexia: A Cognitive Developmental Perspective*. Oxford: Basil Blackwell.

Stanovich, K.E. (1986). Matthew effects in reading: Some consequences of individual differences in the acquisition of literacy. *Reading Research Quarterly*, 21, 360–406.

Strickland, D. and Cullinan, B. (1990). Afterword. In M.J. Adams (ed.), *Beginning to Read: Thinking and Learning about Print*, pp. 425–434. Cambridge, MA: MIT Press.

Treiman, R. (1992). The role of intrasyllabic units in learning to read and spell. In P.G. Gough, L.C. Ehri and R. Treiman (eds), *Reading Acquisition*, pp. 65–106. Hillsdale, NJ: Erlbaum.

Treiman, R. (1993). *Beginning to Spell: A Study of First Grade Children*. New York: Oxford University Press.

Tunmer, W. and Hoover, W. (1994). Components of variance models of language-related factors in reading disability: A conceptual overview. In M. Joshi and C.K. Leong (eds), *Reading Disabilities: Diagnosis and Component Processes*, in press. Dordrecht, The Netherlands: Kluwer Academic Publishers.

Tunmer, W. and Rohl, M. (1991). Phonological awareness and reading acquisition. In D. Sawyer and B. Fox (eds), *Phonological Awareness in Reading: The Evolution of Current Perspectives*, pp. 1–30. New York: Springer-Verlag.

Vellutino, F. (1991). Introduction to three studies on reading acquisition: Convergent findings on theoretical foundations of code-oriented versus whole-language approaches in reading acquisition. *Journal of Educational Psychology*, 83, 437–443.

Chapter 10
An Integrated Approach to Encouraging the Development of Phonological Awareness, Reading and Writing

PETER J. HATCHER

There is an impressive amount of evidence that links children's progress in reading to their underlying phonological skills (see Wagner and Torgesen, 1987; Adams, 1990; Goswami and Bryant, 1990; Hulme and Snowling, 1991, for reviews). However, in spite of the weight of this evidence, no study has succeeded unequivocally in demonstrating a causal relationship between phonological awareness and learning to read. Rather, it seems probable that adequate phonological skills are necessary, but not sufficient, for learning to read effectively (Tunmer and Nesdale, 1985; Juel, Griffith and Gough, 1986; Tunmer, Herriman and Nesdale, 1988; Byrne and Fielding-Barnsley, 1989). In line with this view, a number of studies have shown that, when phonological training is combined with teaching children to read, it is effective in boosting reading (Goldstein, 1976; Haddock, 1976; Wallach and Wallach, 1976; Williams, 1980; Bradley and Bryant, 1983, 1985; Ball and Blachman, 1988, 1991; Bradley, 1988; Cunningham, 1990).

The research linking the teaching of reading with training in phonological skills has important implications for teachers of reading. A problem with these combined phonological and reading training studies, however, has been that they have not taken account of the possibility that their success may have arisen from the reading part of the programme rather than from the effect of combining phonological training with the teaching of reading.

To try and resolve this issue, Hatcher, Hulme and Ellis (1994) carried out a training study aimed at improving the reading skills of 7-year-old poor readers. This chapter will outline the training study and go on to describe the intervention programme that was most effective.

Phonological Training and Learning to Read

Hatcher, Hulme and Ellis (1994) assigned four matched groups of poor readers to one of three experimental teaching conditions. In the first condition, reading with phonology, children received training in phonological skills and help in learning to read. In the second and third conditions they received teaching in reading alone or phonological training alone respectively. A control group received their normal teaching without any additional provision from our study. The details of the four groups are shown in Table 10.1.

Table 10.1 Means (average scores) for age, BAS word reading age, and WISC-R Full-Scale IQ* for the four groups ($n=124$)

Group	Age (years)	Reading age (years)	IQ
'Reading and phonology' ($n=32$)	7;6	5.9	93.6
'Reading alone' ($n=31$)	7;6	5.9	93.1
'Phonology alone' ($n=30$)	7;6	5.9	94.6
Control ($n=31$)	7;7	6.0	93.2

* Wechsler (1994).

During the period of intervention, which lasted 20 weeks, each of the taught groups received 40 30-minute teaching sessions. To measure the progress of the four groups during that period, the children were assessed on a large number of measures before and after the intervention. The measures included tests of reading, spelling and phonological awareness. The children's arithmetic skills were also assessed to be sure that any effects of the three teaching programmes were specific to reading and not of a general nature. Finally, given that an aim was to see whether any effects on reading persisted beyond the period of intervention, the children's attainments in reading and spelling were assessed again some 9 months after the intervention had ceased.

Four different measures of reading were used. An Early Word Recognition Test was devised to assess progress at the very early stage of acquiring a 'sight vocabulary'. This test required the children to read aloud words that commonly appear in the first books children come across in their reading. The British Ability Scales (BAS) Word Reading Test: Test A (Elliot, Murray and Pearson, 1983) was used as a normative measure of 'word reading' and the Neale Analysis of Reading Ability: Form 1 (Neale, 1989) was used as a measure of reading accuracy in context (i.e. when reading passages of text rather than just single words). The Neale also measures reading comprehension through questions asked about each passage. The fourth measure of reading, a non-word reading test, which contained items such as 'um', 'bac', 'blod' and 'unplint', was used to provide a relatively pure measure of phonic decoding skill.

The Schonell and Schonell (1956) Graded Word Spelling Test: List B was used to measure spelling ability and the BAS Basic Number Skills Test: Test A (Elliot, Murray and Pearson, 1983) was used to measure arithmetic skills.

Four measures were used to measure the children's development of phonological skills, or their ability to reflect upon and manipulate the sounds of spoken language. One of the tasks required the children to delete individual speech sounds (referred to as phonemes) from words and say what remained after the deletion (e.g. removing the 's' from 'spin' to make 'pin'). This is quite a difficult skill that is usually acquired after two or more years of learning to read. Another task required the children to split words, in this case non-words, into their individual speech sounds. This type of skill (commonly referred to as 'phoneme segmentation') is, like phoneme blending, normally acquired at about the time of learning to read. A phoneme blending task, which required the children to blend a sequence of sounds into non-words, was also included. The fourth test was a version of Bradley's (1984) sound categorisation test. This required the children to identify the 'odd word out' in sets of words, all but one of which shared a common sound. For example, in the set of words PIN, SIT, WIN, FIN, three words share the rhyme 'in', so, SIT is the odd word out. In addition, the sound categorisation test required children to identify words with a different medial sound (e.g. 'hat' in LOT, COT, POT, HAT), and a different initial sound (e.g. 'rug' in BUN, BUD, RUG, BUS).

The Intervention Programmes

The 93 children in the three experimental groups were taught by a total of 23 teachers who were granted relief from their normal duties to receive 3-day training in how to use the materials and how to carry out the research interventions. During the intervention period, each teacher worked individually with between two and nine children. To reduce the effects of any differences between teachers most of the teachers taught sets of three children (one from each experimental group). Another factor that was taken into account was the time of the day that the children received their intervention. It was purposefully varied, so as to avoid children always being taught at the same time of the day.

The aim of the study was to determine the relative effectiveness of the three teaching programmes in helping children who were experiencing difficulties in the early stages of learning to read. We were therefore interested in the relative progress of the groups in learning to read and spell between the first and second assessments.

Results of the Intervention

The reading, spelling and arithmetic results are shown in Table 10.2. For most of the tests the results are shown as attainment ages. Thus, if we look at the performance of the 'reading plus phonology' group on the accuracy measure of the Neale Analysis of Reading Ability, it can be seen that at the first assessment (t1), before the intervention

Table 10.2 Means (average scores) for the pre- and post-intervention attainment measures of reading, spelling and arithmetic in the four groups

Measure	Group			
	'Reading and phonology' (n=32)	'Reading alone' (n=31)	'Phonology alone' (n=30)	Control (n=31)
Early word identification*				
t1	20.2	20.1	21.0	20.9
t2	32.7	32.3	29.7	29.3
BAS Word Reading†				
t1	5.9	5.9	5.9	6.0
t2	6.7	6.6	6.6	6.6
Neale accuracy†				
t1	5.1	5.0	5.2	5.1
t2	6.1	5.8	5.8	5.7
t3	6.8	6.2	6.3	6.3
Neale comprehension†				
t1	5.3	5.3	5.4	5.4
t2	6.4	6.0	5.9	5.9
t3	7.0	6.5	6.5	6.4
Non-word reading‡				
t1	4.3	3.6	6.0	3.7
t2	15.6	10.8	15.5	11.9
Schonell spelling†				
t1	5.8	5.8	5.9	5.8
t2	6.8	6.5	6.7	6.5
t3	7.2	6.9	7.0	6.9
BAS arithmetic†				
t1	6.6	6.8	6.8	6.7
t2	7.4	7.5	7.4	7.4

*Maximum score = 42; †attainment ages expressed in years; ‡maximum score = 70.
t1 = first assessment; t2 = second assessment; t3 = third assessment.

began, the 7.5-year-old poor readers were performing at a level that would be expected in normal readers aged just over 5 years. By the time of the second assessment, following 20 weeks of intervention, they had gained a whole year in reading age, advancing from 5;1 to 6;1 years.

The statistical analysis that was adopted ensured that any differences between the literacy scores of the groups at the time of the first assessment were statistically accounted for, and contrasted the scores of each of the three experimental groups at the second assessment with those of the control group.

The analyses indicated that the 'reading with phonology' group made significantly more progress than the control group on all of the measures of reading. These included, early word recognition word recognition, text reading accuracy, and comprehension and non-word reading. The reading with phonology group also made significantly more progress in spelling than the control group.

On only one measure did the 'reading alone' group make more progress than the control group. This was 'early word reading', a test in which children were encouraged to pick out words, selected from early reading material, that they recognised. The progress of the children who received 'reading alone' on this test might be accounted for by the ease with which children's first words can be learned through visual, 'logographic' strategies (Frith, 1985; Seymour and Elder, 1986) or 'selective association' (Gough and Juel, 1991). The 'phonology alone' group did not make significantly greater progress than the control group on any of the measures of literacy.

In view of the fact that the 'reading alone' group received 'the same' reading training as the 'reading with phonology' group, apart from the omission of any reference to letter–sound association activities and phonology, it seems unlikely that the positive effect of the combined phonological and reading programme was the result of its reading component alone. It was also not the result of its phonological element alone. The 'phonology alone' group was the only group (Table 10.3) to make significantly more progress in phonological skills than the control group but, as noted above, it did not make comparable improvements in literacy skills.

Changes in arithmetic skills were similar in all four groups, with the three experimental groups failing to make faster progress than the control group. This indicates that the treatment effects found for reading and spelling were specific to those skills, and were not the result of any general factor such as motivation or increases in teachers' expectations.

Further statistical analyses indicated that the 'reading with phonology' group had maintained its advantage over the control group, on

Table 10.3 Means (average scores) for the pre- and post-intervention raw scores on measures of phonological ability for the four groups

| Measure | Group | | | |
	'Reading and phonology' (*n*=32)	'Reading alone' (*n*=31)	'Phonology alone' (*n*=30)	Control (*n*=31)
Sound deletion*				
t1	2.9	2.9	3.8	2.4
t2	9.9	6.2	13.7	7.4
Non-word segmentation†				
t1	9.3	10.3	11.4	8.3
t2	15.8	16.1	18.6	14.9
Sound blending†				
t1	6.9	6.0	7.6	7.1
t2	12.1	10.7	14.4	11.0
Sound categorisation†				
t1	14.3	13.8	14.6	13.3
t2	17.6	16.9	18.3	15.7

*Maximum score = 24; †maximum score = 30.
t1 = first assessment; t2 = second assessment.

the text reading accuracy and comprehension measures, even 9 months after the intervention had finished. As before, neither the 'reading alone' nor the 'phonology alone' group differed significantly from the control group. The results with spelling were more disappointing, with none of the treatment groups differing significantly from the control group at the 9-month reassessment.

The results of this study provide strong support for the importance of linking phonological training with learning to read. They are also in keeping with another study that linked phonological training with Clay's (1985) teaching procedures (Iversen and Tunmer, 1994; Tunmer, 1994; see also Chapter 9) and are consistent with the findings that phonic-based methods of teaching reading are more effective than methods that omit explicit phonic teaching (for reviews see Chall, 1983; Adams, 1990). As the effects obtained by Hatcher, Hulme and Ellis (1994) are likely to generalise to younger children and may also be helpful for children with specific reading difficulties, the purpose of this chapter is to convey the nature of the 'reading with phonology' programme so that important aspects of it can be implemented by teachers.

The 'Reading with Phonology' Programme

The 'reading with phonology' training package was modelled on Marie Clay's (1985) early intervention procedures, but included additional phonological activities. Some of these were to be completed on their own; others were to be explicitly linked with reading and writing.

In line with the research design, teachers presented children in the 'reading with phonology' group with 40 30-minute teaching sessions over the 20 weeks of teaching. The first four sessions were taken up with the assessment of their reading and writing, through a series of diagnostic tests and reading text. Based on the data obtained, teachers were able to identify children's reading strengths, and areas of reading confusion and weakness. They were also able to identify teaching goals that were likely to maximise the children's reading progress.

Each of sessions 5–40 followed a similar format and consisted of three main sections, each containing a number of different activities. The first and last sections involved reading text and the middle section involved writing and work on words, letters and sounds.

Section 1: reading text at the easy level and recording children's reading behaviour

Re-reading an 'easy' book

Each session began with children reading a book (or books) which could be read with at least 95% accuracy (one error or less in 20 words). The purpose of this was to provide them with the opportunity to rehearse known words in as many different contexts as possible, and to read with fluency and phrasing. The teachers praised children for aspects of their reading that were being consolidated. For example, if a child corrected an error for the first time, the teacher would make a positive comment about that point.

Reading the book introduced at the end of the previous session

Having read an easy book, children then read the book that had been introduced during the third part of the previous session. While the children were reading, the teachers used a coding system to record the children's responses to between 100 and 200 running words. Clay (1985) refers to this as taking a 'running record' of children's reading. If a book was found to have been read with 90–94% accuracy (commonly called the instructional level of reading), teachers introduced another book from the same level at the end of the session. Where children had read books fluently and with greater than 94% accuracy on two or more consecutive sessions, teachers introduced a book at a higher level at the end of the session.

The books used were selected mainly from the series 'Story Chest' (Arnold Wheaton, Leeds), 'Oxford Reading Tree' (Oxford University

Press, Oxford), 'Shorty' books (Ginn, Aylesbury, Bucks), and 'Monster' books (Longman, Harlow, Essex), and approximately three to four books were provided at each of 20 levels of text difficulty. Often, more books were required at each level, particularly at the initial shared-reading levels. For this reason, teachers were provided with a list of about 1200 books categorised according to the twenty levels of the New Zealand 'Ready to Read' series (New Zealand Department of Education, 1985, 1987).

In addition to helping determine a book's 'reading level', the running record provided data about children's reading behaviour. This enabled teachers to determine whether children had exhibited appropriate directional movement, i.e. whether they had read from left to right and from the top to the bottom of the page? It also enabled them to consider the 'errors' the children had made. Of particular interest, in this regard, was whether children realised they had made errors and whether they attempted to correct them. The teacher looked for evidence of children using the meaning of the text, the structure of the sentences, the visual appearance of words and letter–sound relationships to 'guess' at unknown words. They also looked for evidence that children were using these strategies in combination. Of equal importance was evidence which enabled teachers to praise children for implementing skills they were acquiring, or consolidating.

Having completed the running record, teachers selected one or two teaching points, which they believed would be maximally effective, and worked on them with the children. At a very early stage of learning to read, children might have spent time acquiring a sense of print directionality, or the ability to 'finger-point' to words while they were being read. Children who were more advanced in their reading were encouraged to search for semantic, syntactic, visual and letter–sound clues, to cross-check clues when reading unknown words in text and to correct their own errors. The essence of this level of work was to encourage the children to question whether what they were reading made sense, whether it sounded right and, of particular importance to this study, whether their attempts at unknown words corresponded to the letter–sound sequence of the printed words.

Section 2: letter identification, phonological training, writing and phonological linkage activities

Letter identification

Where necessary, the middle part of every session began with children learning the names and sounds of letters. This was accomplished through a multi-sensory approach (feeling, writing and naming) and through the construction of individual alphabet books containing pictures and words associated with each letter.

Phonological training

The isolated phonological training involved exercises from the phonological training package used by the 'phonology alone' group. This consisted of a graded sequence of tasks derived from the work of researchers such as Lewkowicz (1980), Lundberg, Frost and Petersen (1988), Rosner (1975), Stanovich, Cunningham and Cramer (1984), and Yopp (1988).

The first set of tasks from the phonological training programme helped children to recognise and manipulate rhyme. One of the tasks simply required them to identify which of three words rhymed with a stimulus word. For example, given the stimulus word 'house', the word 'mouse' would be the correct response from 'monkey', 'dog' and 'mouse'.

The next set of tasks was concerned with the perception of words as units within sentences. In line with Elkonin's (1973) technique, one of the tasks (word segmentation) required children to push plastic counters into a line of squares marked on a card while simultaneously saying each word of a sentence. For example, given four counters and the sentence 'That is my bike', children would have been expected to push the counters into the squares while simultaneously saying each of the four words.

Once children were able to complete rhyme and word tasks with 80% accuracy, they were encouraged to listen for, and to manipulate, syllables in words. Tasks within this section included children clapping in time with rhythmic rhymes (e.g. 'One, two, three, four, five, Once I caught a fish alive'), blending syllables to form common words (e.g. tel–e–vi–sion to television), syllable segmentation using plastic counters, and syllable deletion (e.g. deleting the word farm from farmhouse to leave the word house).

The introduction to individual speech sounds (phonemes) was undertaken by getting children to vary the speed with which they said words such as FISH, SNEEZING and SUPERMAN. With the aid of pictures, they were then encouraged to listen for specific sounds at the beginning (e.g. 'ssss' in SNAKE, and 'ffff' in FAN), at the end and in the middle of words. Following success with this type of activity, children were asked to discriminate between words on the basis of their initial, end and medial sounds. For example, when presented with a set of three pictures for MOON, MAN and DOG, they were asked to touch the two pictures with the same sound at the beginning. A related but more difficult task was indicating which of four words ended with a different sound. For example, 'shoot' would be the correct response given the words KNIFE, SHOOT, SCARF and LEAF. After this they progressed to blending sounds into words. At first, they were simply shown two pictures and asked to identify which of the two they thought teachers were trying to say. For example, they would have been expected to choose the picture of a 'boy' rather than the picture of the 'sea' when teachers articulated the sounds 'b', 'oy'.

Writing a story

Another key activity within this section was children writing a short story. The story consisted of one or two sentences and was written on the bottom page of an unlined exercise-book which had been turned through 90°. The top page was used as a practice pad. One of the aims of the writing activity was to help children add to the list of words that they could write fluently.

Teachers generally used the multisensory approaches described by Clay (1985) and Bryant and Bradley (1985) to help children acquire an initial sight vocabulary. Clay's procedure of 'trace and say, imagine and say, look and say, and write and say' draws children's attention to the overall appearance of words. Bryant and Bradley's approach of 'look and say, write and say the letter names, and look and say' draws children's attention to words being formed of sequences of distinct letters. In either case, children would have been encouraged to write the words in as many different settings as possible (e.g. using sand, chalk, paint, wet windows, plastic letters, large crayons and felt pens, etc.), as well as in their story and the word would have been added to a list of words that was accessible to both the teachers and children.

Once children had acquired a reasonable 'sight vocabulary' and were proficient at the types of phonological activities referred to above, they were introduced to phoneme segmentation through phonological linkage activities such as Bradley's (Bryant and Bradley, 1985) plastic letter technique. Bradley's technique involves choosing a word from one of a set of words known to a child (e.g. 'hen' from HEN, MEN and PEN) and encouraging the child to form the word with plastic letters. The child is then encouraged to make further words from the same set until such time as he or she realises that it is only necessary to change the first letter of the word.

Running parallel with the use of plastic letters, children were encouraged to complete 'phoneme segmentation' exercises using counters and the card with the line of squares on it. In this exercise, children were asked to push counters into the squares while simultaneously articulating each sound of the word. For example, for the word LOCK, children would have been given three counters and expected to say 'l–o–ck' slowly, while simultaneously pushing the three counters into the squares.

Once children were proficient at perceiving sounds within words and were able to identify letters by name or by sound, they were introduced to the notion of using sounds to write words. Naturally, this fitted in well with the writing of a story activity. Using simple phonemically regular words that children wished to write in their stories, teachers drew boxes for each sound segment of a word on the top page of the children's writing a story book. They articulated the words slowly and encouraged children to either push counters into the boxes (see Elkonin, 1973), or to listen for a sound, think (and possibly practise) how it would be written, and consider which box it should be written in. Initially, children might only have been able to write the first or last sound. The correct sequencing of letters was attended to after children were able to write each of the letters in the right box without too much trouble.

Cut-up-story

Once children had completed their written story, they were encouraged to re-read it. If necessary, they were asked to point to each word while doing so. If one-to-one reading and finger pointing was difficult, teachers wrote the stories on card and cut the cards into language units (e.g. phrases or words) for the children to re-assemble. The children would then either check their responses by placing the segments on top of or below the teacher's model, or simply read the words aloud. The cut-up-story activity remained a part of each session until firm one-to-one finger pointing had been established.

Section 3: introduction to a new book

Being introduced to a new book

The last segment of each 'reading with phonology' session involved children reading a new book. When introducing a new book (capable of being read by children at the instructional level, i.e. with 90–94% accuracy), teachers assisted the children in discussing the plot and drew their attention to any unusual language within the book.

Attempting to read the new book

With support being given when difficulties were met, the children were then encouraged to read the stories on their own. Teachers would almost certainly have derived a teaching point from their reading. Finally, teachers and children read the books together to encourage fluency of reading.

Reading progression within the 'reading with phonology' programme therefore followed Clay's (1985) cycle: consolidation of children's reading strengths with material that could be read with more than 94% accuracy; working to overcome confusions and learning new skills with text that could be read with 90–94% accuracy; and identifying the set of skills to be taught at the next level through a running record of children's responses to text at that level. It also included additional phonological and phonological linkage activities which were linked to the children's writing and reading.

Implications of the Results

The results of this study indicate that a combined phonological–literacy skills training approach is effective in boosting the reading skills of reading-delayed 7 year olds. Spending an equivalent amount of time on either reading or phonology, on their own, was less effective. The results are impressive, particularly because the children in the 'reading with phonology' group spent less time reading than the 'reading alone' group.

Sceptics might argue that there are two reasons why the results of the 'reading with phonology' group should be interpreted with caution. It might be argued that the programme was modelled on Clay's (1985) approach and that the group performed well because of that. In contrast, the 'reading alone' group performed less well because it did not receive all aspects of Clay's programme. This argument would appear to be refuted by a study carried out by Iversen and Tunmer (1994) (see also Chapter 9) in the State of Rhode Island. Iversen and Tunmer (1994) compared an unchanged reading recovery programme with a programme in which children also received systematic phonological training. The modified programme was 37% more effective than the reading recovery programme alone.

Another argument that might be levelled against the findings of Hatcher, Hulme and Ellis (1994) is that explicit linkage activities are not essential. All that is needed is to provide children with both reading and phonological training; children will then make the connection for themselves. The results of Byrne and Fielding-Barnsley's

(1989) study would suggest that this is not the case. Byrne and Fielding-Barnsley found that in order for children to understand that particular phonemes in words are matched by particular letters it is necessary for three components to be in place. These are that children can isolate phonemes within words, appreciate that sounds can be common between words, and that specific sounds can be represented by particular letters. The first two components are not enough. The children in their study needed to be explicitly taught to make the connection between letters and sounds within words.

Having shown the advantage of explicitly linking phonological training with reading, the question of generality arises. The subjects in this study were poor readers corresponding, roughly, to the bottom 25% in reading skills. These 7 year olds were struggling with the earliest stages of learning to read. It seems probable, however, that the effects of a combined reading and phonological training programme would generalise to a wider range of children.

Given Iversen and Tunmer's (1994) findings with reading-delayed 6-year-old children, there is little reason to believe that the effects would not generalise to 6 year olds with reading difficulties. There is also evidence that children of high IQ with specific reading difficulties commonly experience phonological difficulties (see review by Hulme and Snowling, 1991). I would suggest that it is likely that such children would show an equivalent pattern of benefit from an integrated approach to teaching reading and phonological skills. However, it is also possible that some children with severe phonological problems might be immune to the effects of phonological training. Examples of such cases are discussed in several papers (Snowling and Hulme, 1989; Hulme and Snowling, 1992; Stackhouse and Snowling, 1992). Nevertheless, given the results of this study it would seem worth while to explore the use of a combined phonological and reading programme with dyslexic children.

One slightly disappointing aspect of the results was that the reading accuracy and comprehension scores of the 'reading with phonology' group, although still significantly ahead of the control group 9 months after the period of intervention, were tending to diminish. This is an important point, because a similar lack of long-term effect with reading recovery in New Zealand has also been identified (Glynn et al., 1989). Tunmer (in Chapter 9) argues that the reading recovery programme pays too little attention to phonological awareness and to letter–sound relationships, and without that element its effectiveness fades. Although the 'reading with phonology' programme specifically included activities of this nature, it is possible that some of the children in the study of Hatcher, Hulme and Ellis (1994) needed more than the 40 30-minute teaching sessions they received. It is also possible they may have continued to benefit from the programme had it been integrated with the provision made by their schools. Clay (1985, 1987) argues that her teaching procedures need to form part of a total system of provision involving the children, their parents, their teachers, and the educational system at school and regional levels. These are important issues for future studies to address.

Another important issue is the degree to which the 'reading with phonology' teaching procedures need to be carried out on an individual basis. Clearly some of the procedures used in the present research need to be conducted on an individual basis (e.g. children reading and having their errors corrected by teachers). However, some of the key elements of the programme, such as relating letters to sounds, making explicit links between the sounds of words and their spelling patterns, and certain phonological training exercises, could be modified for use in small groups.

Finally, the findings from this study, and others that have been considered here, suggest the following ideas for good teaching practice with reading-delayed children:

1. The teaching of reading and writing are integrated.
2. Text is provided at an appropriate level (90–94% reading accuracy).
3. Awareness of words' component sounds is explicitly taught.
4. Letter names and sounds are both taught.
5. An explicit link is made between sounds and letters within words.
6. Children are taught how to cross-check visual, letter–sound, syntactic and semantic clues.

Reading-delayed children need all the help they can get, in every sense!

References

Adams, M.J. (1990). *Beginning to Read: Learning and Thinking about print*. Cambridge, MA: MIT Press.

Ball, E. W. and Blachman, B.A. (1988). Phoneme segmentation training: Effect on reading readiness. *Annals of Dyslexia*, 38, 208–225.

Ball, E. W. and Blachman, B.A. (1991). Does phoneme awareness training in kindergarten make a difference in early word recognition and developmental spelling? *Reading Research Quarterly*, 26, 49–66.

Bradley, L. (1984). *Assessing reading difficulties: A diagnostic and remedial approach* 2nd edn. London: Macmillan Education.

Bradley, L. (1987). *Categorising sounds, early intervention and learning to read: A follow-up study*. Paper presented at the British Psychological Society conference, London, December 1987.

Bradley, L. (1988). Making connections in learning to read and spell. *Applied Cognitive Psychology*, **2**, 3–18.

Bradley, L. and Bryant, P.E. (1983). Categorising sounds and learning to read: a causal connexion. *Nature*, **301**, 419–421.

Bradley, L. and Bryant, P.E. (1985). *Rhyme and Reason in Reading and Spelling.* International Academy for Research in Learning Disabilities Monograph Series, No. 1. Ann Arbor: University of Michigan Press.

Bryant, P.E. and Bradley, L. (1985). *Children's Reading Difficulties.* Oxford: Blackwell.

Bruce, D. J. (1964). The analysis of word sounds by young children. *British Journal of Educational Psychology*, **34**, 158–170.

Byrne, B. and Fielding-Barnsley, R. (1989). Phonemic awareness and letter knowledge in the child's acquisition of the alphabetic principle. *Journal of Educational Psychology*, **81**, 313–321.

Carver, C. (1970). *Word Recognition Test.* London: Hodder and Stoughton.

Chall, J.S. (1983). *Learning to Read: The Great Debate*, 2nd edn. New York: McGraw-Hill.

Clay, M. (1985). *The Early Detection of Reading Difficulties*, 3rd edn. Tadworth, Surrey: Heinemann.

Clay, M. (1987). Implementing reading recovery: systematic adaptions to an educational innovation. *New Zealand Journal of Educational Studies*, **22**, 35–58.

Cunningham, A. E. (1990) Explicit versus implicit instruction in phonemic awareness. *Journal of Experimental Child Psychology*, **50**, 429–444.

Elkonin, D.B. (1973). USSR. In J. Downing (ed.), *Comparative Reading: Cross-national Studies of Behaviour and Processes in Reading and Writing.* London: Collier-Macmillan.

Elliott, C.D., Murray, D. J. and Pearson, L. S. (1983). *British Ability Scales.* Windsor: NFER-Nelson.

Frith, U. (1985). Beneath the surface of developmental dyslexia. In: K.E. Patterson, J.C. Marshall and M. Coltheart (eds), *Surface Dyslexia: Neuropsychological and Cognitive Studies of Phonological Reading.* London: Lawrence Erlbaum Associates.

Glynn, T., Crooks, T., Bethune, N., Ballard, K. and Smith, J. (1989). *Reading Recovery in Context.* Wellington: Department of Education.

Goldstein, D.M. (1976). Cognitive–linguistic functioning and learning to read in preschoolers. *Journal of Educational Psychology*, **68**, 680–688.

Goswami, U. and Bryant, P. (1990). *Phonological Skills and Learning to Read.* London: Lawrence Erlbaum Associates.

Gough, P.B. and Juel, C. (1991). The first stages of word recognition. In L. Rieben and C. Perfetti (eds), *Learning to Read: Basic Research and Its Implications.* Hillsdale, NJ: Lawrence Erlbaum Associates.

Haddock, M. (1976). Effects of an auditory and an auditory–visual method of blending instruction on the ability of preschoolers to decode synthetic words. *Journal of Educational Psychology*, **68**, 825–831.

Hatcher, P.J., Hulme, C. and Ellis, A.W. (1994). Ameliorating early reading failure by integrating the teaching of reading and phonological skills: The phonological linkage hypothesis. *Child Development*, **65**, 41–57.

Hulme, C. and Snowling, M. (1991). Phonological deficits in dyslexia: A 'sound' reappraisal of the verbal deficit hypothesis? In N. Singh and I. Beale (eds), *Progress in Learning Disabilities*, pp. 260–283. New York: Springer-Verlag.

Hulme, C. and Snowling, M. (1992). Deficits in output phonology: A cause of reading failure? *Cognitive Neuropsychology*, 9, 47–72.

Iversen, S. and Tunmer, W.E. (1994) Phonological processing and the reading recovery program. *Journal of Educational Psychology*, in press.

Juel, C., Griffith, P.L. and Gough, P.B. (1986). Acquisition of literacy: A longitudinal study of children in first and second grade. *Journal of Educational Psychology*, 78, 243–255.

Lewkowicz, N. K. (1980). Phonemic awareness training: What to teach and how to teach it. *Journal of Educational Psychology*, 72, 686–700.

Lundberg, I., Frost, J. and Petersen, O. (1988). Effects of an extensive program for stimulating phonological awareness in pre-school children. *Reading Research Quarterly*, 23, 263–284.

Neale, M. D. (1989). *Neale Analysis of Reading Ability – Revised British Edition*. Windsor: NFER-Nelson.

New Zealand Department of Education (1985). *Reading in Junior Classes: With Guidelines to the Revised Ready to Read Series*. Wellington: Department of Education.

New Zealand Department of Education (1987). *Classified Guide of Complementary Reading Materials – Books for Junior Classes: A Classified Guide for Teachers*. Wellington: Department of Education.

Raven, J. C. (1965). *The Coloured Progressive Matrices Test*. London: Lewis.

Rosner, J. (1975). *Helping Children Overcome Learning Difficulties: A Step-by-step Guide for Parents and Teachers*. New York: Walker and Company.

Schonell, F.J. and Schonell, F. E. (1956). *Diagnostic and Attainment Testing: Including a Manual of Tests, Their Nature, Use, Recording and Interpretation*. London: Oliver & Boyd.

Seymour, P.H.K. and Elder, L. (1986). Beginning reading without phonology. *Cognitive Neuropsychology*, 3, 1–36.

Snowling, M. and Hulme, C. (1989). A longitudinal case study of developmental phonological dyslexia. *Cognitive Neuropsychology*, 6, 379–401.

Snowling, M. and Hulme, C. (1991). Speech processing and learning to spell. In R. Ellis and R. Bowler (eds), *Language and the Creation of Literacy*, pp. 33–39. Baltimore: Orton Dyslexia Society.

Stackhouse, J. and Snowling, M. (1992). Barriers to literacy development in two cases of developmental verbal dyspraxia. *Cognitive Neuropsychology*, 273–299.

Stanovich, K.E., Cunningham, A.E. and Cramer, B.B. (1984). Assessing phonological skills in kindergarten children: Issues of task comparability. *Journal of Experimental Child Psychology*, 38, 175–190.

Tunmer, W.E. (1994) Phonological processing and reading recovery: A reply to Clay. *New Zealand Journal of Educational Studies*, in press.

Tunmer, W.E. and Nesdale, A.R. (1985). Phonemic segmentation skill and beginning reading. *Journal of Educational Psychology*, 77, 417–427.

Tunmer, W.E., Herriman, M.L. and Nesdale, A.R. (1988). Metalinguistic awareness abilities and beginning reading. *Reading Research Quarterly*, 23, 134–158.

Wagner, R.K. and Torgesen, J.K. (1987). The nature of phonological processing and its causal role in the acquisition of reading skills. *Psychological Bulletin*, 101, 192–212.

Wallach, M.A. and Wallach, L. (1976). *Teaching All Children to Read*. Chicago: University of Chicago Press.

Wechsler, D. (1974). *Wechsler Intelligence Scale for Children – Revised*. New York: The Psychological Corporation.

Williams, J.P. (1980). Teaching decoding with an emphasis on phoneme analysis and phoneme blending. *Journal of Educational Psychology*, **72**, 1–15.

Yopp, H. K. (1988). The validity and reliability of phonemic awareness tests. *Reading Research Quarterly*, **23**, 159–177.

Chapter 11
Reading Difficulties can be Predicted and Prevented: A Scandinavian Perspective on Phonological Awareness and Reading

INGVAR LUNDBERG

Introduction

Almost 20 years ago we carried out a small study (later reported in Lundberg, 1982) in which reading-disabled students in grade 2 were compared with normal, age- and gender-matched readers on two different types of phonological processing tasks. One task only required the automatic and non-reflective, implicit processing of phonological segments of words. By contrast, the other task required explicit, conscious awareness and deliberate control of the phonemic segments of words, a shift of attention from semantic content to linguistic form.

The implicit task was taken from a sub-test of the Illinois Test of Psycholinguistic Abilities (ITPA – Kirk, McCarthy and Kirk, 1968). The students were presented with a partially fragmented spoken word where one sound was deleted (e.g. air_lane instead of airplane) and the task was to identify the intended target word, i.e. a simple listening task. The explicit task was also a phoneme-deletion task, but here the experimenter explicitly named the target word and asked what would be left if a sound was deleted (e.g. what is left if the first sound is deleted from the word chair – correct answer: air). To solve this kind of task the child needs to be able consciously to segment a word and manipulate phonemic units.

The difficulty of the explicit task was well illustrated by a severely reading-disabled child who had problems already at the practice–trial stage. He reacted violently when he was told that the sound /dile/ had been deleted from the word 'crocodile'. Instead of trying to analyse the word, he answered with resentment: 'You have cut off his tail.' Apparently, he was unable to shift his attention from content to linguistic form. Maybe, this is also why he failed in learning to read. In any case, the requirement of this task was more cognitively advanced, less natural and less 'modularised' than the perceptual requirement of the ITPA where a more direct 'closure' mechanism seemed to be in operation. All users of spoken language are, by a long evolution, provided with neurological mechanisms or a processing module which normally functions automatically when coping with the complicated phonological structure of speech (Mattingly and Studdert-Kennedy, 1991). Thus, the study highlighted the distinction between the functioning of the automatic speech module and the explicit, deliberate control of the speech segments.

The two tasks were designed so that their average difficulty level for normal children was about the same (the proportion of correct responses was 0.67 for the ITPA task and 0.64 for the phonemic awareness task). However, although the retarded readers were significantly inferior to the normal readers on both tasks, the difference was far greater for the phonemic awareness task, as can be seen in Figure 11.1.

Both tasks were phonological in nature. Yet, a clear dissociation

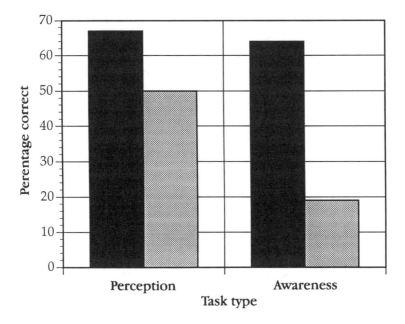

Figure 11.1 Percentage correct responses on two different tasks: one perceptual task (auditory closure in ITPA) and one phonological awareness task (phoneme deletion). Normal (■)and retarded (□) readers in grade 2 are compared

was found. Only one of the tasks, the one requiring explicit and conscious control of phonemic segments, had a clear diagnostic value in the identification of reading disability. By now, literally hundreds of other empirical studies have given evidence of the critical role of phonological awareness in learning to read (for reviews, see, for example, Wagner and Torgesen, 1987; Adams, 1990; Goswami and Bryant, 1990; Brady and Shankweiler, 1991; Leong, 1991; Sawyer and Fox, 1991; Bentin, 1992; Stanovich, 1993; Wagner et al., 1993).

According to Bryant and Goswami (1987) 'the discovery of a strong relationship between children's phonological awareness and their progress in learning to read is one of the great successes of modern psychology' (p. 439). This is certainly not a typical British understatement but rather close to a gross exaggeration. The success referred to in the quotation is mainly related to the remarkable stability, robustness and consistency of the findings. The relationship has been replicated over and over again, across languages, ages and tasks used to measure phonological awareness. Less successful, perhaps, have been the attempts to understand and interpret the relationship. As most of the evidence presented so far is correlational in nature, causal inferences cannot be made with any certainty.

One popular interpretation of the relationship is that the emergence of phonological awareness is simply a rather trivial by-product of learning to read in an alphabetic script. Letters of the alphabet are external representations of the sequence of the abstract perceptuo-motor units (phonemes) in which our internal lexical items (words or morphemes) are stored. Letters are then the vehicles that take us beneath the surface of the spoken word to a level where temporary, sometimes irrelevant, sound variations, co-articulations, assimilations and reductions are disregarded, and where the abstract, invariant segments of the word are represented in our consciousness. Phoneme awareness, in this view, is an almost inevitable consequence of becoming literate (Morais, 1991).

However, it could be the other way around. To learn how to read and spell one must discover that units of print (letters) map on to units of sounds. Thus, the understanding of the alphabetic principle requires the ability to segment the speech stream into units of phoneme size. In this sense, phoneme segmentation is located at the very heart of reading and spelling development. The establishment of functional orthographic representations for rapid, automatic word recognition is then assumed to depend on explicit segmental phonology where the full and detailed anatomy of words is attended to. In this sense, phonological awareness might be regarded as a prerequisite for the acquisition of literacy (see also Lundberg, 1978).

A third, and most probable, alternative is reciprocal causation. According to this view there are causal connections running in both directions: phonemic awareness facilitates the acquisition of reading and spelling and, at the same time, increasing literacy skill sharpens the phonological insight (e.g. Perfetti et al., 1987). Whereas most researchers now seem to agree that the relationship between phonemic awareness and reading is reciprocal in nature, the question of which affects the other most and earliest is far from settled. Neither is the exact nature of the transition from implicit to explicit control of the segmental structure of spoken words well known.

In the present chapter, I shall attempt to clarify some fundamental issues on the relationship between phonological awareness and reading by reviewing a series of studies carried out by my group in Umeå (Sweden), Bornholm (Denmark) and Stavanger (Norway). A distinct advantage of doing research in this field in Scandinavia is that one can find perfectly healthy and cognitively well-developed children who, by the age of 7 years, only know a few letters and cannot read a single word. This is simply because they have not enjoyed the benefit of reading instruction. In the Scandinavian countries, children do not start school until the end of August in the year they are 7 years old. In many parts of Scandinavia, the level of informal literacy socialisation before school is very modest. There is a general attitude among parents that the teaching of reading should wait until a competent school teacher gives the proper foundation. Although some might find this educational policy questionable from a research perspective, it has some obvious advantages. In comparison to North America and the UK, where most of the current reading research is performed, Scandinavians are well placed to examine phonological skills in children before they have begun to learn to read.

This takes on particular importance when we consider that the cognitive demands of developing phonemic awareness may be rather high. It seems to require a kind of basic ability to shift attention from content to form which is similar to what is required in Piagetian tasks tapping decentration ability. Many 7 year olds are supposed to be able to decentre. By studying older, non-literate children the relationship between phonemic awareness and more general aspects of cognitive development can be explored.

In the research reviewed here, using this Scandinavian advantage, we have attempted to answer a number of questions discussed in the current literature on the relationship between phonological awareness and reading. For example:

Can phonemic awareness be observed among children who are not able to read and who do not even know the letters of the alphabet?

Can phonological awareness be developed by training outside the context of reading instruction?

What are the components of phonological awareness?

Which aspect of phonological awareness is most closely related to success in reading acquisition?

Are there any long lasting effects of early training in phonological awareness?

Can early training in phonological awareness prevent the occurrence of reading disability?

Is lack of phonological awareness also typical of older reading-disabled students?

Is there any neurobiological correlate of poorly developed phonological awareness?

Can Phonemic Awareness be Observed Among Pre-readers?

Phonological awareness refers to awareness and access to the sound structure of one's language (Mattingly, 1972). In general, pre-readers can perform tasks such as rhyming or syllable segmentation. The ability to segment words into phonemes, however, is not expected among pre-readers. If one could demonstrate phonemic awareness among young children who are clearly not able to read and who do not even know the letters of the alphabet, one would certainly have a strong case against the position that reading instruction is necessary for the development of phonemic awareness. Lundberg (1991) presented a re-analysis of earlier data on phonological awareness in nursery school and identified 51 pre-school children out of a sample of 200 (aged 6–7 years) who did not demonstrate any sign of reading ability. Most of these non-readers also had very low scores on tasks assessing phonemic awareness (phoneme segmentation, phoneme synthesis, phoneme position identification and phoneme reversal). However, a small number of the non-readers (three or four children) showed a remarkable level of phonemic awareness, comparable to what was found among the best precocious readers in the pre-school sample. When observing this exceptional facility with the phonemic tasks, it was striking that they, in fact, were completely unable to read the simplest words and that they had never received any formal reading instruction.

In another sample of 387 6-year-old pre-school children, where most of the children at the time of testing must be considered as non-readers, the children solved 75% of the rhyming tasks and about 50%

of the tasks requiring syllable segmentation. However, only 9% of the tasks requiring phoneme manipulation were solved. In spite of a total lack of reading ability and very limited letter knowledge, 8 of the 387 children managed to solve more than 50% of the phonemic tasks.

Most pre-readers, thus, seem to have developed some phonological awareness on a super-phonemic level without having explicitly been taught such skills. However, in most cases they seem to lack phonemic awareness. Only in rare cases do we find non-readers with well-developed phonemic awareness. The fact that such children exist indicates that it is possible, at least in principle, to develop phonemic awareness without the support of letter knowledge and without formal reading instruction in school. Exactly how this is accomplished remains to be understood.

One speculation mentioned by Lundberg and Høien (1991) was that the discovery of the phonemic unit of speech, in the absence of letter experience, may emerge when the child spontaneously produces rhymes in playful settings and happens to encounter a non-word together with a real word, i.e. a confrontation of meaning and phonology. This meeting might facilitate and encourage the discovery of the critical segment of differentiation. Although such spontaneous discoveries do not seem to be made by most pre-school children, it still might be possible to develop phonemic awareness by explicit training. Are there ways outside reading instruction to get children to notice the phonemes, to discover their existence and separability?

Can Phonemic Awareness be Developed by Training without the Use of Letters?

A number of studies have demonstrated that activities designed to develop phonemic awareness per se are far more effective and productive when phonemes are related to letters (Bradley and Bryant, 1983; Hohn and Ehri, 1983; Byrne and Fielding-Barnsley, 1990, 1993; Cunningham, 1990; Ball and Blachman, 1991; see also Chapter 10). The letters seem to serve as external representations of the elusive structure of words; providing concrete symbols to stand for abstract phonemes. The conventional letter names also provide imperfect cues to the sounds of speech which the phonemes represent. But are letters necessary for developing phonemic awareness?

We have found a training programme with no letters and no involvement of text or print to be highly successful. Lundberg, Frost and Petersen (1988) designed a programme which required daily activities in group settings over a full pre-school year of more than 8 months. It included listening games, rhymes and ditties, playing with sentences and words, and discovering the initial sounds of words, and ended with phoneme games. The programme is now available in English by an adaptation made by Adams and Huggins (cited in Adams, 1990).

The effectiveness of the programme was demonstrated by comparing pre- and post-test scores for trained and untrained children on an assessment battery. The training effects were very specific, being modest or even absent on general linguistic skills and on rhymes and syllables, but quite dramatic on phonemic awareness tasks. Thus it could be confidently concluded that phonemic awareness can be developed among pre-readers by training, without introducing letters or written text. More crucial than letters seems to be the *explicit* guidance of children when they are trying to access, attend to and extract the elusive, abstract and implicit segments of speech.

Did the Pre-school Training Facilitate Literacy Acquisition in School?

Two steps have now been taken in the direction of demonstrating that phonemic awareness is not just a by-product of learning to read, but has an independent status and can act as an important causal factor in early literacy development. First, I have reported a few cases of non-readers with well-developed phonemic awareness. Although these were exceptional cases, they nevertheless make it hard to hold the strong view that reading skill and reading instruction are necessary conditions for phonemic awareness to develop. Second, the study by Lundberg, Frost and Petersen (1988) has clearly demonstrated that phonemic awareness can successfully be developed among pre-readers without support from letters and reading instruction.

A third line of evidence provided by our group (Lundberg, Olofsson and Wall, 1980) and later by a large number of other researchers (Bradley and Bryant, 1983; Mann, 1984; Mann and Liberman, 1984; Share et al., 1984; Stanovich, Cunningham and Cramer, 1984; Tunmer and Nesdale, 1985; Ellis and Large, 1987) concerned the remarkably predictive power of pre-school phonological awareness for achievement in reading several years later: what develops later in time (reading) can hardly be the cause of something preceding it. Thus, the longitudinal research has brought us a step closer to an understanding of the causal relationship. However, even a longitudinal study may be open to alternative interpretations. Some factor that lies outside our control or remains unidentified might be the underlying cause of the observed relationship. Although serious attempts were made to include several critical factors in the path model, such as non-verbal intelligence and decentration ability, there is no guarantee that some other unknown factor is not at work which causes the observed relationship between phonological skills and later reading ability.

Having established that it is possible to develop phonemic awareness among non-reading pre-schoolers by explicit training, it should be asked whether such training also facilitates later reading and spelling acquisition in school. Only if we can demonstrate a reliable and long-lasting positive effect on literacy learning are we in a position to regard phonemic awareness as a causal factor and not just a by-product of becoming literate.

The 400 children studied by Lundberg, Frost and Petersen (1988) were followed through the first 4 years in school, and reading and spelling achievement were assessed on several occasions. First the level of phonemic awareness was measured when the children started school and it was noted that the trained children still outperformed the untrained children, although 2 months of vacation had elapsed. Thus, there was good reason to believe that the trained children entered school better prepared to work with the alphabetic system than the untrained children. The early discovery of the phoneme as a basic unit of speech should have given the trained children an initial advantage in learning to read and spell. Yet, in other fields of achievement, such as mathematics and IQ, the experimental group performed slightly worse than the controls.

After the children had been in school some 7 months, their reading ability was assessed by a simple test of word recognition (Lundberg and Hoien, 1991). This assessment was repeated with inter-test intervals of about 7 months over the three first grades in school. Figure 11.2 presents the results. The experimental group outperformed the control group on each occasion, indicating the beneficial effect of the pre-school training in phonological awareness, at least on a test of rapid identification of single words. Although the face validity of the test as an indicator of a more general reading ability might seem questionable to some, earlier studies have shown a high correlation with tests on reading comprehension (e.g. Taube, 1988). To broaden the reading assessment, a sentence reading test was given in the beginning and at the end of grade 3. Each item consisted of a sentence or a brief passage accompanied by seven pictures, one of which unambiguously depicted the meaning of the sentence. This test correlated highly with the word reading test ($r= 0.88$). Not unexpectedly, then, the experimental group also outperformed the control group on this test, which is shown in Figure 11.3.

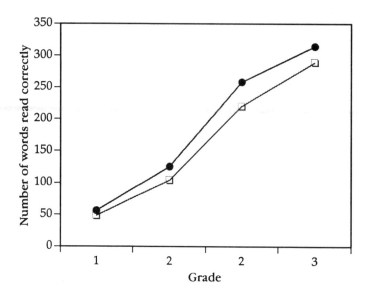

Figure 11.2 The development of word reading over the first three grades in school. Children trained in phonological awareness during the pre-school year (–●–) are compared with untrained control (–☐–) children. Two assessments were made in grade 2

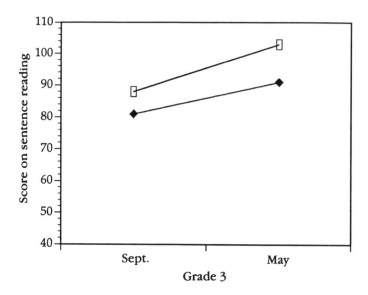

Figure 11.3 Sentence comprehension in grade 3: a comparison between trained (–☐–) and untrained (–◆–) children

The result of a spelling assessment was equally encouraging. Spelling tests were given on six different occasions from grade 1 to grade 4. As different tests were used at the various stages, the scores were transformed to z-scores with the mean of the control group as reference. Figure 11.4 shows that the experimental group spelled significantly more words correctly as compared with the control group and that the superiority was maintained across the four school years, although there was a tendency towards a decreasing gap between the groups.

The total number of comparisons of literacy performance between the two groups now amounts to 12, and on each comparison point the trained children outperformed the untrained controls. This result is even more impressive when considering the fact that the control group actually had a slight initial advantage in general cognitive ability.

On the basis of the follow-up results we can conclude with more confidence than in Lundberg, Frost and Petersen (1988) that preschool training of phonological awareness has a long-term positive effect on reading and spelling development. It can also be concluded that the training programme effectively prevents the occurrence of reading difficulties.

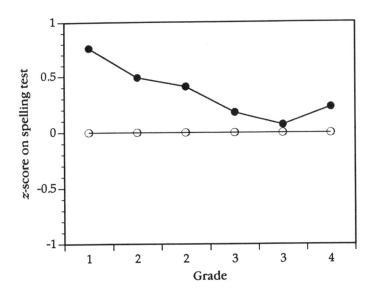

Figure 11.4 The development of spelling over four grades: comparisons between-trained (-●-) and untrained (-⊖-) children. Because of variation in difficulty betweenthe tests, the performance scores were transformed to z-scores with the control group as comparison norm

Can Pre-school Training of Phonological Awareness Prevent Reading Failure in School ?

The preventive power of the pre-school programme was evaluated by identifying children at risk and comparing trained and untrained children when they came to school. On the basis of the very first assessment pre-school before the training period (pre-test), 25 extreme children from each group were selected according to the following criteria:

1. Less than 3 points out of 24 on the phonological awareness tests (including rhyme, words and syllables as well as phonemes).
2. Ability to recognise no more than three letters.
3. No sign of reading ability.

A careful matching between the low-achieving experimental and control children ensured an almost perfect equivalent performance on all pre-tests. The gender composition was also the same in the two groups (16 boys and 9 girls). With current knowledge of the relationship between pre-school phonological skills, letter knowledge and pre-reading skill, on the one hand, and later reading achievement in school, on the other, the children in the extreme groups would be labelled as being at serious risk for developing reading difficulties.

The development of reading and spelling skills in school for the two groups with extremely low pre-test performance was compared to the development of the total sample of non-trained control children. The control group can be regarded as composed of typical children in the ordinary school system and can thus serve as a useful norm for comparisons. The 50 at-risk children were distributed over a large number of different classrooms.

Figure 11.5 presents the development of word-reading skills over four test occasions during the three first grades in school.

The slowest development was observed for the untrained group, and the gap tended to widen over the years, which gives support to the negative Matthew effect suggested by Stanovich (1986). In contrast, the performance of the trained group closely matched the performance of the control group, indicating that the pre-school training of phonological awareness prevented at-risk children from developing reading difficulties.

At the sentence reading test in grade 3, the picture was essentially the same, as can be seen in Figure 11.6. The trained group of children with extremely low performance on the pre-tests showed a normal

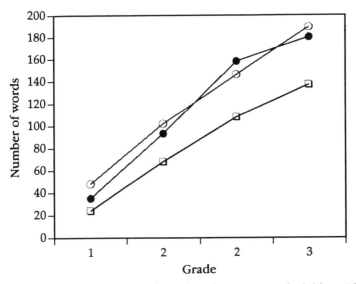

Figure 11.5 The development of word reading among risk children. The experimental children were trained in phonological awareness during the pre-school year. Comparisons are made with the total, untrained control group as reference norm. (-□-) Low achieving control group; (-●-) low achieving experimental children; (-○-) total control group.

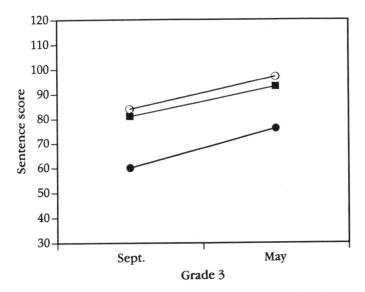

Figure 11.6 Sentence comprehension in grade 3 among risk children. The low achieving experimental (-○-) group had pre-school training of phonological awareness, whereas the low achieving control (-●-) group did not enjoy the benefit of such training. The total control (-■-) group was used as reference norm for the comparisons

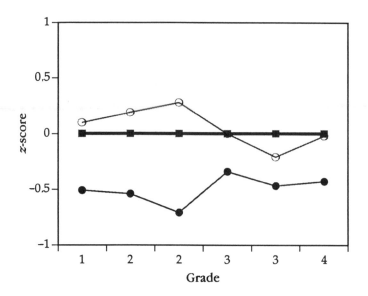

Figure 11.7 The development of spelling among risk children. Trained and untrained risk children are compared. The performance scores are transformed to z-scores with the total control group as reference norm. (–●–) Low achieving control group; (–○–) low achieving experimental children; (–■–) total control group

level of reading ability in school 3 years after the pre-school training, whereas the untrained children performed at a much lower level.

Finally, the results on the sequence of six spelling tests further confirmed the preventive power of the pre-school programme. Here, the performance of the trained group hovered around the level of the control group, whereas the untrained children fell far below this level on all occasions (Figure 11.7).

Taken together, the results for word reading, sentence comprehension and spelling suggest that it is possible to prevent the development of reading and spelling difficulties in school by a carefully designed pre-school programme which brings the children to a level of phonological awareness that is sufficiently high to meet the demands of coping with the alphabetic system. The at-risk children who do not enjoy the benefit of such training seem to face serious obstacles in acquiring literacy skills. Several studies in Scandinavia have also demonstrated the remedial and facilitating power of phonological awareness training in school as part of regular teaching or as an important element in special education (e.g. Tornéus, 1984; Lie, 1991).

Are Phonological Problems Characteristic Deficits among Older Dyslexic Children?

There is now a general consensus among researchers that non-automatic, slow, inaccurate, effortful and dysfluent word recognition is the core symptom of dyslexia (see, for example, Pennington, 1986; Stanovich, 1986). However, relatively little empirical evidence has been presented concerning the role of poorly developed phonological skill or low level of phonemic awareness as an underlying factor, especially among older students.

Snowling (1980, 1981) and Snowling and Hulme (1989) presented convincing evidence on the role of phonological deficits in dyslexia. Pennington et al. (1987) showed that dyslexic individuals almost approached normal levels of orthographic processing in adulthood, whereas their phonological skills continued to be markedly deficient. Manis, Custodio and Szeszulski (1993) showed, in a developmental study, that dyslexic individuals failed to catch up with normal readers in phonological skills. According to Stanovich's (1988) phonological–core-variable difference model of reading problems, dyslexic individuals are readers whose cognitive impairment is specific and typically localised to phonological processing.

Lundberg and Hoien (1990) studied a carefully selected group of 19 15-year-old dyslexic students, 19 age-matched normal readers and 19 reading-level matched young students (about 9 years old). The performance of these groups on a large number of reading and reading related tasks were examined. Here, the focus is only on the phonological tasks.

Many dyslexic children show marked difficulty in reading non-words (Rack, Snowling and Olson, 1992). Although some non-words might be read by using an analogy strategy where the similarity with known words is used, it can be argued that in many cases non-words have to be read by applying grapheme–phoneme correspondences. The typical difficulty with non-words among dyslexic children is then interpreted as an indication of their poor phonological skill, in particular the low level of phonemic awareness.

We have found, in accordance with most studies reviewed by Rack, Snowling and Olson (1992) that the dyslexic children read non-words much slower and with far more errors than did the reading level-matched young students. The fact that the two groups read real words equally well indicates that dyslexic children may use an alternative strategy to identify words, perhaps relying more on orthographic patterns.

The results were similar on the more direct phonological awareness tasks, phonological synthesis and syllable reversal, where the dyslexic children scored far below the comparison students. In fact, the overlap between the dyslexic group and the other two groups was almost non-existent. In a number of tasks which were not related to reading the difference between the dyslexic and comparison groups was small and insignificant. Thus, it seems that the problem for these older dyslexic children is specific to the phonological system.

Is there a Neurological Correlate of the Poor Phonological Skills among Dyslexic Children?

Can the persistent phonological problems found among dyslexic children be explained in neurobiological terms? A step in the direction of finding a neurological correlate of phonological problems was taken in a study by Larsen et al. (1990). The 19 dyslexic children and the age-matched controls referred to above were examined using MRI. Brain scans showed that the planum temporale, an area involved in language processes, tended to be of equal size in the two hemispheres among the dyslexic subjects, whereas an asymmetrical pattern was more common among the normal readers. Seven of the dyslexic subjects showed serious phonological problems. All of them had symmetry of the planum temporale. This is an unusually clear identification of a brain–anatomical substrate of a psychologically defined symptom. It certainly needs replication.

There is no reason to believe that the deviant brain morphology is the result of limited reading experiences or failure in learning to read. It is rather something which has already developed in fetal life (Geschwind and Galaburda, 1987). The cause of this early deviation in brain structure is not known. Recent advances in developmental neurobiology, in molecular genetics and in methods for recording brain processes with high spatiotemporal resolution will certainly open up new ways for understanding the biological bases of dyslexia.

Another example of the biological validity of the phonological deficit is given by Olson (1991). In studies of identical and fraternal twins, he has been able to demonstrate the strong heritability of phonological dysfunction in word recognition, whereas orthographic processing seems to be more related to experiential factors (like teaching or exposure to print).

Components of Phonological Awareness

Phonological processes certainly involve more than phonological awareness. Elbro (1994) has discussed auditory–phonological discrimination and identification, as discussed in the introductory section of this chapter in the context of the ITPA task. Furthermore, Elbro mentioned phonological coding in working memory, articulatory efficacy, naming or phonological code retrieval, segmental phonological representation and distinctness of phonological representations. In all cases there is evidence of an association with dyslexia.

Wagner et al. (1993) have conducted some sophisticated studies of the factorial structure of phonological abilities. Their focus was on testing the differentiability of phonological awareness, phonological memory and naming skills. In contrast, the focus of one of our recent studies (Høien, Lundberg and Stanovich, 1994) was on the factoral structure underlying different types of tasks *within* the domain of phonological awareness.

This study used a sample that was considerably larger than that employed in any extant study of a similar type ($n=1509$), which allowed for a sensitive test of whether phonological awareness skills at various levels (rhyme, syllable, phoneme) should be considered separate constructs or are instead aspects of a unitary underlying construct. In the latter case the various tasks might simply be differentially sensitive or differentially age-appropriate indicators of the same construct.

Lundberg (1978) and later Stanovich (1992) argued that phonological awareness might be viewed as a continuum or hierarchy ranging from 'shallow' to 'deep' sensitivity, where the deeper levels require more explicit analysis of smaller sized phonological units. The task of deciding which words are rhyming, for example, seems to require a small amount of conscious awareness of phonemic segments. The attention is more directed to global similarity between words. One should, then, not be surprised to find rhyming ability among non-reading children. Syllables are also accessible units of the speech signal, more isolable, more salient and less abstract than phoneme units. To attend to syllables, the child does not have to ignore the natural unity of the articulatory act, as is the case with attending to phonemes. A minimum of explicit guidance, then, should be required for the child to manipulate syllables (Mann, 1986).

The study by Høien, Lundberg and Stanovich (1994) supported the view that there are different components of phonological awareness corresponding to the different levels of language analysis required by the task. More than 1500 children in pre-school and in grade 1 were tested with a battery of tasks including rhyme recognition, syllable counting, initial-phoneme identification, phoneme deletion, phoneme synthesis and phoneme counting. Three basic factors were extracted in a principal component analysis: a phoneme factor, a syllable factor and a rhyme factor. It was also demonstrated that the three components of phonological awareness were separate predictors of early word reading ability, with the syllable factor as the weakest predictor. Not unexpectedly, the phonemic factor proved to be the most potent predictor of early reading acquisition. A considerable amount of variance (30%) was explained by this factor even when individual differences in rhyme and syllable awareness were partialled out. Among the phoneme tasks, the phoneme identification tasks were the most powerful predictors of reading, explaining 14% unique variance even after all other tasks had been entered into the regression equation. This is consistent with findings reported by Byrne and Fielding-Barnsley (1993).

Further microanalyses of the structure of phonological abilities will clarify and confirm the picture outlined in this chapter concerning which aspects of phonological processing are critical to understanding reading acquisition and reading difficulties.

Concluding Comments

Collectively, the research presented here gives evidence for the causal role of phonological awareness in learning to read. Phonological awareness can be developed by training outside the context of formal reading instruction. Such training seems to facilitate the acquisition of reading and spelling in school. Even more important, children at serious risk for developing reading difficulties benefit from the early training to the extent that they reach a normal level of performance in reading and spelling. Thus, the research presented leads to rather optimistic educational conclusions. It also gives strong support to the hypothesis that phonological deficits are core symptoms in dyslexia without denying that there might be other factors involved (Breitmeyer, 1989; Lovegrove and Slaghuis, 1989; Stein, 1989). The heterogeneous nature of phonological awareness, as well as its neurobiological basis, has also been clarified.

Although the focus of this chapter has been restricted to the impact of phonological awareness in the research presented here, I also recognise the importance of other aspects of emergent literacy among pre-school children. Pretend writing, invented spelling, letter recognition, story reading, environmental print exposure and other natural experiences with print are all possible components in a broad pre-school programme for early stimulation of literacy development without formal reading instruction. The practical implications of the results presented here should be considered within such a broad perspective on emergent literacy and the prevention of reading failure.

References

Adams, M.J. (1990). *Beginning to Read: Thinking and Learning about Print*. Cambridge, MA: MIT Press.

Ball, E.W. and Blachman, B.A. (1991). Does phoneme awareness training in kindergarten make a difference in early word recognition and developmental spelling? *Reading Research Quarterly*, **26**, 49–65.

Bentin, S. (1992). Phonological awareness, reading, and reading acquisition: A survey and appraisal of current knowledge. In R. Frost and L. Katz (eds), *Orthography, Phonology, Morphology, and Meaning*, pp. 193–210. Amsterdam: North-Holland.

Bradley, L. and Bryant, P. (1983). Categorizing sounds and learning to read: A causal connection. *Nature*, **301**, 419–421.

Brady, S. A. and Shankweiler, D.P. (eds) (1991). *Phonological Processes in Literacy*. Hillsdale, NJ: Lawrence Erlbaum Associates.

Breitmeyer, B.G. (1989). A visually based deficit in specific reading disability. *Irish Journal of Psychology*, **10**, 534–541.

Bryant, P. and Goswami, U. (1987). Beyond grapheme–phoneme correspondences. *Cahiers de Psychologie Cognitive*, 7, 439–443.

Byrne, B. and Fielding-Barnsley, R. (1990). Acquiring the alphabetic principle: A case for teaching recognition of phoneme identity. *Journal of Educational Psychology*, **82**, 805–812.

Byrne, B. and Fielding-Barnsley, R. (1993). Evaluation of a programme to teach phonemic awareness to young children: A one year follow-up. *Journal of Educational Psychology*, **85**, 104–111.

Cunningham, A.E. (1990). Explicit versus implicit instruction in phonemic awareness. *Journal of Experimental Child Psychology*, **50**, 429–444.

Ellis, N.E. and Large, B. (1987). The development of reading: As you seek, so shall you find. *British Journal of Psychology*, **78**, 1–28.

Geschwind, N. and Galaburda, A.M. (1987). *Asymmetry of the Human Brain in Cerebral Lateralization*. Cambridge, MA: MIT Press.

Goswami, U. and Bryant, P. (1990). *Phonological Skills and Learning to Read*. East Sussex: Lawrence Erlbaum Associates.

Hohn, W.E. and Ehri, L.C. (1983). Do alphabet letters help prereaders acquire phonemic segmentation skill? *Journal of Educational Psychology*, **75**, 752–762.

Høien, T., Lundberg, I. and Stanovich, K.E. (1994). Components of phonological awareness. *Reading and Writing: An Interdisciplinary Journal*, in press.

Kirk, S.A., McCarthy, J.J. and Kirk, W.D. (1968). *Examiner´s Manual: Illinois Test of Psycholinguistic Abilities*. Urbana, IL: University of Illinois Press.

Larsen, J.P., Høien, T., Lundberg, I. and Ødegaard, H. (1990). MRI-evaluation of the size and symmetry of the planum temporale in adolescents with developmental dyslexia. *Brain and Language*, **39**, 289–301.

Leong, C.K. (1991). From phonemic awareness to phonological processing to language access in children developing reading proficiency. In D.J. Sawyer and B.J. Fox (eds), *Phonological Awareness in Reading: The Evolution of Current Perspectives*, pp. 217–254. New York: Springer-Verlag.

Lie, A. (1991). Effects of a training programme for stimulating skills in word analysis in first-grade children. *Reading Research Quarterly*, **26**, 234–250.

Lovegrove, W. and Slaghuis, W. (1989). How reliably are visual differences found in dyslexics? *Irish Journal of Psychology*, **10**, 542–550.

Lundberg, I. (1978). Linguistic awareness as related to reading. In A. Sinclair, R.J. Jarvella and W.J.M. Levelt (eds), *The Child's Conception of Language*. New York: Springer-Verlag.

Lundberg, I. (1982). Linguistic awareness as related to dyslexia. In Y. Zotterman (ed.), *Dyslexia: Neuronal, Cognitive and Linguistic Aspects*, pp. 141–153. Oxford: Pergamon Press.

Lundberg, I. (1991). Phonemic awareness can be developed without reading instruction. In S.A. Brady and D. P. Shankweiler (eds), *Phonological Processes in Literacy. A Tribute to Isabelle Y. Liberman*, pp. 47–53. Hillsdale, NJ: Lawrence Erlbaum Associates.

Lundberg, I. and Høien, T. (1990). Patterns of information processing skills and word recognition strategies in developmental dyslexia. *Scandinavian Journal of Educational Research*, 34, 231–240.

Lundberg, I. and Høien, T. (1991). Initial enabling knowledge and skills in reading acquisition: Print awareness and phonological segmentation. In D.J. Sawyer and B.J. Fox (eds), *Phonological Awareness in Reading: The Evolution of Current Perspectives*, pp. 73–95. New York: Springer-Verlag.

Lundberg, I., Frost, J. and Petersen, O.-P. (1988). Effects of an extensive programme for stimulating phonological awareness in pre-school children. *Reading Research Quarterly*, 33, 263–284.

Lundberg, I., Olofsson, A. and Wall, S. (1980). Reading and spelling skills in the first school years predicted from phonemic awareness skills in kindergarten. *Scandinavian Journal of Psychology*, 21, 159–173.

Manis, F.R., Custodio, R. and Szeszulski, P.A. (1993). Development of phonological and orthographic skill: A 2-year longitudinal study of dyslexic children. *Journal of Experimental Child Psychology*, 56, 64–86.

Mann, V.A. (1984). Longitudinal prediction and prevention of reading difficulty. *Annals of Dyslexia*, 34, 117–137.

Mann, V.A. (1986). Phonological awareness: The role of reading experience. *Cognition*, 24, 65–92.

Mann, V.A. and Liberman, I.Y. (1984). Phonological awareness and verbal short term memory. *Journal of Learning Disabilities*, 17, 592–598.

Mattingly, I. G. (1972). Reading, the linguistic process, and linguistic awareness. In J.F. Kavanagh and I.G. Mattingly (eds), *Language by Ear and by Eye: The Relationships between Speech and Reading*, pp. 133–147. Cambridge, MA: MIT Press.

Mattingly, I.G. and Studdert-Kennedy, M. (eds) (1991). *Modularity and the Motor Theory of Speech Perception*. Hillsdale, NJ: Lawrence Erlbaum Associates.

Morais, J. (1991). Phonological awareness: A bridge between language and literacy. In D.J. Sawyer and B.J. Fox (eds), *Phonological Awareness in Reading. The Evolution of Current Perspectives*, pp. 31–71. New York: Springer-Verlag.

Olson, R.K. (1991). The family connection in dyslexia. In I. Lundberg and T. Høien (eds), *Literacy in a World of Change*. Stavanger, Norway: Center for Reading Research/UNESCO.

Pennington, B.F. (1986). Issues in the diagnosis and phenotype analysis of dyslexia: Implications for family studies. In S. Smith (ed.), *Genetics and Learning Disabilities*, pp. 69–95. San Diego, CA: College-Hill Press.

Pennington, B.F., Lefly, D.L., van Orden, G.C., Bookman, M.O. and Smith, S.D. (1987). Is phonology bypassed in normal or dyslexic development? *Annals of Dyslexia*, 37, 62–89.

Perfetti, C.A., Beck, I., Bell, L. and Hughes, C. (1987). Phonemic knowledge and learning to read are reciprocal: A longitudinal study of first grade children? *Merrill-Palmer Quarterly*, **33**, 283–319.

Rack, J.P., Snowling, M.J. and Olson, R.K. (1992). The nonword reading deficit in developmental dyslexia: A review. *Reading Research Quarterly*, **27**, 29–53.

Sawyer, D.J. and Fox, B.J. (eds) (1991). *Phonological Awareness in Reading. The Evolution of Current Perspectives*. New York: Springer-Verlag.

Share, D.L., Jorm, A.F., Maclean, R. and Matthews,R. (1984). Sources of individual differences in reading acquisition. *Journal of Educational Psychology*, **76**, 1309–1324.

Snowling, M. J. (1980). The development of grapheme–phoneme correspondence in normal and dyslexic readers. *Journal of Experimental Child Psychology*, **29**, 294–305.

Snowling, M.J. (1981). Phonemic deficits in developmental dyslexia. *Psychological Research*, **43**, 219–234.

Snowling, M.J. and Hulme, C. (1989). A longitudinal case study of developmental phonological dyslexia. *Cognitive Neuropsychology*, **6**, 379–603.

Stanovich, K.E. (1986). Matthew effects in reading: Some consequences of individual differences in the acquisition of literacy. *Reading Research Quarterly*, **21**, 360–407.

Stanovich, K.E. (1988). Explaining the differences between the dyslexic and the garden-variety poor reader: The phonological-core-variable-difference model. *Journal of Learning Disabilities*, **21**, 590–612.

Stanovich, K.E. (1992). Speculations on the causes and consequences of individual differences in early reading acquisition. In P. Gough, L. Ehri and R. Treiman (eds), *Reading acquisition*, pp. 307–342. Hillsdale, NJ: Lawrence Erlbaum Associates.

Stanovich, K.E., Cunningham, A.E. and Cramer, B.B. (1984). Assessing phonological awareness in kindergarten children. *Journal of Experimental Child Psychology*, **38**, 175–190.

Stein, J. (1989). Visuospatial perception and reading problems. *Irish Journal of Psychology*, **10**, 521–533.

Taube, K. (1988). *Self Concept and Reading Disability*. Umeå, Sweden: Umeå University.

Tornéus, M. (1984). Phonological awareness and reading: A chicken and egg problem? *Journal of Educational Psychology*, **76**, 1346–1358.

Tunmer, W. E. and Nesdale, A.R. (1985). Phonemic segmentation skill and beginning reading. *Journal of Educational Psychology*, **77**, 417–427.

Wagner, R.K. and Torgesen, J.K. (1987). The nature of phonological processing and its causal role in the acquisition of reading skills. *Psychological Bulletin*, **101**, 192–212.

Wagner, R.K., Torgesen, J.K., Laughon, P., Simmons, K. and Rashotte, C.A. (1993). Development of young readers' phonological processing abilities. *Journal of Educational Psychology*, **85**, 83–103.

Chapter 12
The Nature and Treatment of Reading Comprehension Difficulties in Children

SUSAN E. STOTHARD

Reading can be considered to comprise two component skills: word recognition and comprehension. To read effectively a child must be able to identify the individual words of a text and integrate the meaning of these words and sentences to comprehend what is being read. It follows that reading difficulties can arise from either decoding problems, comprehension problems or a combination of the two (see Gough and Tunmer, 1986).

The vast majority of research investigating reading difficulties in children has focused on children with decoding difficulties, often referred to as developmental dyslexic children. This research shows that phonological impairments play a key role in the development of these children's reading difficulties (see, for example, Hulme and Snowling, 1992, for a review, and Chapters 6 and 9–11, for details of some of this research). In comparison, relatively little research has investigated reading comprehension difficulties in children. Approximately 10% of children experience specific difficulties with reading comprehension (Yuill and Oakhill, 1991; Stothard and Hulme, unpublished data). These children, who will be referred to as poor comprehenders, are able to decode accurately, yet have little or no understanding of what has been read. These children often go unnoticed in the classroom because seemingly they can 'read' (i.e. decode) well. However, their comprehension difficulties constitute a problem that has important educational consequences and pose problems for theories of how children learn to read.

Most studies investigating reading comprehension problems in children have examined generally poor readers. Such children have deficits on a variety of tasks including inefficient decoding skills (Perfetti, 1985), global language comprehension problems (Smiley et al., 1977) and poor metacognitive skills (Paris and Myers, 1981).

However, these studies confound decoding and comprehension difficulty and therefore cannot address the causes of specific comprehension problems. The appropriate way to explore this issue is by
selecting children whose comprehension is impaired but whose
decoding skills are normal. This approach has been adopted by
Oakhill and her colleagues (e.g. Oakhill, Yuill and Parkin, 1986) and
Stothard and Hulme (1992). In a series of studies these researchers
have attempted to identify the causes of reading comprehension
problems in children. Before considering the results of these studies,
a number of theories that have been proposed to explain reading
comprehension problems will be reviewed.

Comprehension Problems as a Consequence of Inefficient Decoding

It has been suggested that reading comprehension problems might
be attributable to inefficient decoding processes. The main version of
this theory is Perfetti's decoding bottleneck or verbal efficiency
hypothesis (e.g. Perfetti and Lesgold, 1979; Perfetti, 1985). Similar
theories have also been proposed by LaBerge and Samuels (1974)
and Crain and Shankweiler (1990). The general form of the verbal
efficiency theory is as follows:

> ... individual differences in reading comprehension are produced by indi-
> vidual differences in the efficient operation of local processes. The local
> processes are those by which temporary representations of a text are estab-
> lished.
> (Perfetti, 1985, p.100)

Local processes include schema activation, propositional encoding
and lexical access, inefficient operation of the latter being a particularly strong candidate for comprehension failure. The verbal efficiency theory depends critically upon two general assumptions: that the
component processes of reading are interactive, and that these
processes compete for resources in a limited capacity working memory system. Thus, inefficient lexical access disrupts comprehension in
the following manner. In comparison to efficient readers, who can
decode words quickly and automatically, slow readers will need to
allocate more resources to decoding processes. As processes compete, less capacity will be available for working memory to carry out
such processes as propositional encoding, and therefore comprehension will be impaired. A second feature of this theory is that, because
the contents of working memory decay rapidly, if word recognition is
slow then fewer of its products will be available in memory when

needed and once again comprehension will suffer. An important point to note is that, even when word recognition is not inaccurate, if it is slow and effortful it will consume the resources usually devoted to comprehension and as such text comprehension will be impaired.

Several sources of evidence attest to the plausibility of this theory. In general, reading comprehension and reading speed correlate highly. For example, Hess and Radtke (1981) reported a correlation of –0.47 between reading time and comprehension skill in third to eighth grade children, indicating that the slower readers tended to be poor comprehenders. Using regression analyses they went on to show that reading time was a significant predictor of comprehension skill. Siegel and Ryan (1989) have also shown that slow readers often have poor comprehension skills. They reported that, from a sample of children with adequate word recognition skills but a slow reading speed, 25% could be classified as having a concomitant comprehension deficit.

Evidence frequently cited in support of the theory that children with comprehension difficulties are slow decoders comes from research by Perfetti and his colleagues (Perfetti and Hogaboam, 1975a; Perfetti, Finger and Hogaboam, 1978). For example, Perfetti and Hogaboam (1975a) showed that third and fifth grade less-skilled comprehenders were significantly slower at naming single words and non-words than age-matched skilled comprehenders. There is, however, a major methodological flaw with these studies: both omitted to assess the decoding accuracy skills of the children. As nothing is known about the reading ages of the children, the results are uninterpretable. It is impossible to determine whether the observed differences in comprehension skill are related to the differences in response latencies (as the authors claim), or whether the differences in response latencies are related to differences in decoding accuracy. These findings, therefore, remain ambiguous.

Studies controlling for decoding accuracy skills have failed to report the hypothesised decoding speed differences between good and poor comprehenders. Oakhill (1981, unpublished study presented in Yuill and Oakhill, 1991) found that groups of 7- to 8-year-old good and poor comprehenders, matched for decoding accuracy, did not differ in either accuracy or the time taken to sort pairs of words into groups of rhyming and non-rhyming items. As half of the rhymes were visually dissimilar (e.g. side-cried), phonological recoding was obligatory to make the rhyming judgement. Oakhill therefore found no evidence that poor comprehenders are slow decoders.

Arguably the strongest evidence against the verbal efficiency hypothesis comes from training studies. If slow word recognition is the deficit causing comprehension failure, then overcoming this deficit should improve comprehension. Thus, training poor comprehenders to decode more rapidly should enhance their comprehension skills. However, if comprehension remains poor then it would appear that the relationship is not causal and an alternative explanation of comprehension difficulties must be sought. A number of studies (e.g. Perfetti and Hogaboam, 1975b; Fleisher, Jenkins and Pany, 1979; Yuill and Oakhill, 1988a) have failed to find evidence that increasing decoding speed leads to improved comprehension.

Yuill and Oakhill (1988a) gave groups of good and poor comprehenders, matched for decoding accuracy, practice at reading words as 'quickly and accurately as possible'. Training was successful insofar as children who received rapid decoding practice were able to read single word lists more quickly than matched groups given inference training that taught specific comprehension skills. However, it did not result in the selective improvement of the less skilled group's comprehension skills. Good and poor comprehenders showed a similar rate of improvement. Furthermore, at both pre- and post-tests the two groups did not differ in decoding speed. In fact, there was a tendency, albeit non-significant, for the good comprehenders to read more slowly on both occasions. Yuill and Oakhill conclude that slow decoding is not the cause of these poor comprehenders' comprehension difficulties.

This study, however, has a number of shortcomings which need to be considered before this conclusion can be accepted. Yuill and Oakhill report that following rapid decoding practice, poor comprehenders read the trained word lists more quickly. However, it is not clear whether the effects of this training generalised. Reading times for the comprehension passages are not presented. As the comprehension passages did not appear to be composed of the trained words, it seems doubtful that training would have decreased reading times for these passages. It is therefore unclear whether the poor comprehenders read the comprehension passages more quickly than they would have done before training.

Fleisher, Jenkins and Pany (1979) also trained poor comprehenders to decode more quickly. Comprehension was then assessed for a passage composed from the trained words. Although training significantly increased the decoding speed of single words it did not improve comprehension, suggesting that fast decoding is not sufficient for good comprehension. However, it should be noted that following training, although good and poor comprehenders did not differ in decoding times for the single, isolated word lists, they did differ in reading times for the comprehension passage. The poor comprehenders were significantly slower in reading the words in context. This suggests that poor comprehenders are less able to take advantage of the syntactic and semantic information inherent in context. As the groups still differed in decoding speed for the test passage, it is difficult to determine the precise relationship between comprehension and decoding speed. Furthermore, the poor comprehenders studied in this experiment were also poor decoders. This complicates the interpretation of these results even further and limits the conclusions that may be drawn.

To summarise, a number of researchers have proposed that reading comprehension problems are attributable to inefficient decoding skills. There can be little doubt that, if a child cannot decode adequately, he or she will have difficulty comprehending what is read. However, it does not seem that inefficiencies in decoding are sufficient to explain the problems of many children who have reading comprehension difficulties. An alternative explanation for most of these cases of specific comprehension difficulties is required.

Perfetti's verbal efficiency theory also proposes that comprehension failure might arise from inefficient semantic access. Readers who recover the meanings of words quickly are likely to understand text more easily than readers for whom semantic access is less automatic. Perfetti, Hogaboam and Bell (unpublished experiment, cited by Perfetti and Lesgold, 1979) reported that less skilled comprehenders were slower than skilled comprehenders in completing a semantic categorisation task which involved deciding whether a visually presented word or picture was a member of a given category, e.g. 'animals'. As the two groups did not differ in picture–word matching tasks (e.g. deciding whether a picture of a dog matched the word 'dog' and vice versa), it was concluded that the less-skilled comprehenders were less efficient at retrieving higher-level semantic information. However, Golinkoff and Rosinski (1976) failed to find evidence to support this view. They used Rosinski, Golinkoff and Kukish's (1975) finding that picture-naming time is increased by presenting the picture with a semantically incongruent word name. For example, the picture of a pig with the word 'cat' printed on it will take longer to name than the picture of a pig with the word 'pig' or the trigram 'pog' superimposed. Two groups of children, differing in comprehension skill, were presented with this picture-naming task. Although the less-skilled comprehenders were found to take longer to name the pictures in general, there was no interaction between comprehension skill and naming condition. Both groups took longer to name pictures in the semantically incongruent and trigram conditions than they did in the congruent condition. The fact that even the poor comprehenders were subject to a semantic interference effect indicates that they do not have difficulty accessing meaning. Unfortunately, both studies failed to control for decoding accuracy skills, making interpretation of their results difficult.

Data which do address this issue in a convincing manner are provided by Oakhill (1981, unpublished study presented in Yuill and Oakhill, 1991), in two experiments which are similar to the studies reported above. In the first experiment Oakhill found that skilled and less-skilled comprehenders, matched for decoding accuracy, did not differ in the time taken to decide whether a visually presented word was a member of a given category. She thus found no evidence that poor comprehenders are slower at accessing the meanings of single words. In a second experiment she replicated Golinkoff and Rosinski's findings, i.e. that poor comprehenders are slower at naming pictures than good comprehenders, but that both groups are subject to a general interference effect. For both groups, picture-naming times were shortest in the semantically congruent condition. Furthermore, neither group differed in the time taken to name pictures accompanied by trigrams or semantically incongruent words. This indicates that the interaction is the result of facilitation when words and pictures matched, rather than semantic interference caused by a mismatch. From this it was concluded that poor comprehenders do not have difficulty accessing the meaning of words. There is no evidence, therefore, that automaticity of semantic access is a factor contributing to the poor comprehenders' difficulties.

It is clear that adequate word recognition skills are necessary but not sufficient for adequate comprehension. The research reviewed here suggests that specific reading comprehension difficulties are not generally attributable to underlying word recognition problems. Furthermore, it would seem that most poor comprehenders do not have difficulty accessing the meaning of words. Explanations of comprehension problems have therefore turned to look at processes operating above the single-word level.

Verbal Memory

A number of studies have investigated whether comprehension difficulties might be attributable to poor verbal memory skills. To read and understand prose the incoming information must be held in memory. This is necessary so that the semantic and syntactic relationships among successive words, phrases and sentences may be computed, and a coherent and meaningful representation of the passage be constructed. Skilled reading thus depends on the temporary storage of old information while new information is being processed. It therefore seems reasonable to suggest that poor verbal memory skills might underlie reading comprehension difficulties.

Within the normal range of ability memory span is related to reading comprehension skill. For example, Hulme (1988) in a study of 8- to 10-year-old children found correlations between memory span and reading comprehension of $r = 0.57$ for the younger group and $r = 0.45$ in the older group. Furthermore, these correlations remained significant even when the effects of age, IQ and language comprehension ability were partialled out ($r = 0.31$ and 0.28). Thus it was shown that short-term memory skills are related to differences in reading comprehension ability in children. Research also suggests that memory span is predictive of later reading comprehension skills. Jorm et al. (1984) assessed the short-term memory skills of 5-year-old children before they had learned to read and found that pre-reading memory span was correlated with reading comprehension ability at age 7 years. This suggests that short-term memory skills may be important in the development of comprehension skills.

These correlations indicate that variations in reading comprehension are related to variations in short-term memory skills in unselected groups of children. However, it does not appear that impaired memory skills are a frequent cause of specific reading comprehension difficulties. A number of studies have shown that children with specific comprehension difficulties have normal short-term memory spans (e.g. Oakhill, Yuill and Parkin, 1986; Stothard and Hulme, 1992).

Oakhill, Yuill and Parkin. (1986) examined memory span as a function of word length and presentation modality. Good and poor comprehenders, matched for word-recognition skills, were required to remember sets of words and pictures, whose names were either one, two or three syllables in length. It was found that the groups obtained equivalent memory spans in both modalities with the usual detrimental effect of word length on recall.

Stothard and Hulme (1992) also measured the short-term memory skills of children with specific comprehension difficulties. Children with comprehension difficulties were found to have equivalent digit spans to the normal controls, matched for chronological age and decoding skills. However, the poor comprehenders had significantly larger memory spans than younger children, matched for reading comprehension ability. Thus, the poor comprehenders' short-term memory skills were normal for their age. These findings indicate that comprehension problems are not the product of any simple deficit in short-term memory capacity.

Further support for this conclusion comes from studies examining poor comprehenders' memory and comprehension of text. Oakhill (1981, unpublished study presented in Yuill and Oakhill, 1991) assessed good and poor comprehenders' sentence memory for text in a free recall task. When a strict verbatim criterion was applied to assess performance, the memories of good and poor comprehenders did not differ. However, using a more relaxed gist criterion produced a reliable difference between the memory scores of the two groups, the good comprehenders showing significantly better recall. This indicates that poor comprehenders show normal verbatim memory, remembering the details of sentences in a word-for-word manner. However, their memory for the overall meaning of text is impaired. In comparison, good comprehenders appear to make a more active attempt to understand. The fact that poor comprehenders are able to remember the exact wording of sentences indicates that their ability to hold information in short-term memory is unlikely to be impaired.

The research indicates that poor comprehenders do not have a general deficit in short-term memory capacity. Their difficulties do not lie in the storage of information, but rather in the processing of that information to derive meaning. This suggests that poor comprehenders may show impaired performance on more complex memory tasks, requiring both storage and processing functions simultaneously. In other words, children with comprehension difficulties might be expected to show deficits on tasks measuring working memory skills.

Yuill, Oakhill and Parkin (1989) administered a working memory task to good and poor comprehenders matched for word-recognition skills. This task involved children reading aloud triplets of numbers and then recalling, in order, the final digit in each triplet (e.g. 835–402 response 5–2). Poor comprehenders were found to obtain significantly lower scores than the good comprehenders. Furthermore, performance on this task correlated (0.51) with reading comprehension ability across both groups (although correlations unfortunately are not reported for the two groups separately). These results were interpreted as evidence for a 'general non-linguistic working memory' limitation in the poor comprehenders. This, however, seems a very odd conclusion given that the task is quite clearly verbal: the children read the digits aloud and then reported the final item from each triplet. In a following study, poor comprehenders were found to have difficulties resolving anomalies they heard in text. Yuill and her colleagues argue that such a weakness may be caused by an underlying working memory impairment.

These results suggest that working memory problems may contribute to children's reading comprehension difficulties. However, they leave a number of points unresolved. First, the absence of a comprehension age control group makes it hard to evaluate the severity of the poor comprehenders' difficulties on the working memory task, and the likelihood that it taps a cause of their comprehension problems. A second problem is that the problems on the working memory task, involving reading digits, have not been shown to be independent of modality of presentation. It is possible, for example, that the problems here reflect, at least in part, difficulties with naming digits to encode them into memory rather than problems in the storage and manipulation of information in memory as suggested. Finally, it seems far more likely from other work (e.g. Daneman, 1987) that the working memory processes that relate to reading will be those related to verbal information processing. Hence, the claim by Yuill, Oakhill and Parkin. (1989) for a deficit in a non-linguistic working memory system underlying reading comprehension problems, when their only task involves reading and remembering digit names, seems highly implausible.

Other evidence suggests that children with reading comprehension difficulties do not have impaired working memory skills (Siegel and Ryan, 1989; Stothard and Hulme, 1992). Stothard and Hulme (1992) assessed the working memory skills of poor comprehenders, age-matched controls and younger comprehension age-matched controls. The children were given a listening span task, based on that developed by Daneman and Carpenter (1980). In this task the children heard a series of short sentences and had to assess the validity of each by responding true or false. They also had to memorise the final word from the end of each sentence and recall these words in the correct serial order (e.g. 'Butter goes on bread' (true), 'Giants are small' (false), response → 'bread, small'). The poor comprehenders and chronological age controls did not differ on this working memory task, and there was a tendency for the poor comprehenders to outperform their comprehension age controls. From these results it seems unlikely that working memory deficits are a common cause of specific reading comprehension difficulties.

Integrative and Inferential Processing Skills

It is well established that comprehension is a constructive, integrative process. When presented with a story, the skilled reader spontaneously draws inferences to link together ideas and to fill in information that is only implicit. This process is necessary so that an integrated representation or mental model of the text can be constructed. This meaning-based representation is then retained, memory for the exact wording of the original sentences quickly being forgotten (Bransford,

Barclay and Franks 1972; Barclay, 1973). Thus, comprehension requires the reader to go beyond that which is explicitly stated to derive an abstract representation of the intended meaning of the passage that has been read.

As integrative processing is characteristic of skilled adult readers, it seems reasonable to suggest that children with reading comprehension problems might experience difficulties here. Research indicates that this is indeed true. For instance, Oakhill (1981, unpublished study presented in Yuill and Oakhill, 1991) showed that good and poor comprehenders, matched for decoding skills, did not differ in verbatim memory for a piece of text. They did, however, differ in gist memory, the poor comprehenders showing significantly poorer recall of the overall meaning of the text. It appears that poor comprehenders remember the details of sentences in a word-for-word manner, rather than retaining their meaning. In comparison, good comprehenders seem to make a more active attempt to understand them. Similarly, in a series of studies, Cromer (e.g. Cromer, 1970; Oakan, Wiener and Cromer, 1971; Steiner, Wiener and Cromer, 1971) has identified a group of poor readers whose comprehension problems can be attributed to their reading in a word-by-word fashion, rather than integrating the input into meaningful units (however, see Calfee, Arnold and Drum, 1976, for a critique of this research). Studies by Clay and Imlach (1971) and Weinstein and Rabinovitch (1971) also support the view that poor readers do not integrate word meanings, and instead process only one word at a time.

Oakhill (1982) examined the relationship between children's reading comprehension and their use of constructive memory representations. Good and poor comprehenders, matched for decoding skills, were presented with a series of short stories which they were asked to listen to and try to remember. They were then given a recognition task and had to decide which of a series of test sentences they had heard before. For each story there were two types of recognition foil: one was semantically congruent with the original story and one semantically incongruent. Oakhill found that the good comprehenders made more errors than the poor comprehenders on the valid inference foils, i.e. sentences that had not actually been presented but were semantically congruent with the original passage. However, they made fewer errors than the poor comprehenders on the invalid inference foils. In other words, the children with comprehension difficulties were less likely to make confusions of a semantic nature. It would seem that poor comprehenders are less likely to form constructive memory representations from sets of related sentences, than are their skilled counterparts. In a subsequent study, Oakhill, Yuill and Parkin (1986) demonstrated that these results were not simply an artefact of the skilled group possessing superior memorisation strategies. A similar pattern of results was obtained even when the recognition test was unexpected.

There are a number of possible reasons why poor comprehenders experience difficulty constructing an integrated representation of a story. Integrative processing requires the reader to draw inferences about the text. In fact, a number of studies emphasise the importance of drawing inferences in order to understand (e.g. Winograd, 1972). During reading, two types of inference are required for detailed understanding. Literal inferences involve linking up explicit ideas both within and between sentences. However, texts do not always make the ideas explicit; rather they must be inferred. The reader needs to draw implicit inferences, incorporating relevant knowledge and experience so that such missing information may be filled in. Studies indicate that adults use general knowledge to fill in implicit textual information (e.g. Bartlett, 1932; Dooling and Lachman, 1971). There is also evidence that children make inferences while reading. Several studies have shown that primary school children often infer relations among sentences and store them in memory automatically (Paris and Carter, 1973; Paris and Mahoney, 1974). Thus, children construct inferential relationships when attempting to understand and remember information. The ability to make implicit inferences during reading could conceivably be a major distinguishing feature between skilled and less skilled comprehenders. If poor comprehenders are unable to draw inferences during reading, then this may impair their understanding.

Oakhill (1984) investigated the relationship between children's reading comprehension skill and their use of inferential and constructive processing. Children read a series of short stories and at the end of each were asked a set of comprehension questions. Comprehension questions were of two types, requiring either literal information, i.e. information that was mentioned explicitly, or implicit information, i.e. information that could only be inferred. The questions were asked twice, first with the text removed, the children being required to respond from memory. The text was then returned and the questions repeated, the children being asked to check the text before answering. When answering from memory, the good comprehenders performed significantly better than the poor comprehenders on both question types. However, when the text was available, the superior performance of the skilled group held only for the inferential questions, both groups making very few errors on the literal questions. It would appear that poor comprehenders can scan a text to retrieve information that is explicitly stated; however, they find it difficult to retrieve information that requires an inference to be drawn. These findings indicate that children with comprehension difficulties are less able to draw inferences and use relevant general knowledge when reading a story. This failure to draw inferences will prevent the child from constructing an integrated representation of the meaning of a text which, in turn, will hinder comprehension.

Skilled reading involves not only making inferences about the meaning of sentences, but also making them about the meaning of particular words in a given context. It has been noted that adult readers use context and world knowledge to restrict the meaning and reference of words. They will give a word a more specific interpretation if it is presented in context, rather than in isolation. For example, given the sentence 'The fish attacked the swimmer', the more specific word SHARK will be a better cue for recall than the less specific word FISH which was actually presented (Anderson et al., 1976). Anderson has called this process instantiation. He and his colleagues argue that instantiation plays a major role in sentence comprehension and memory. It has also been shown that children can select particular meanings for words in context. For example, Anderson et al. (1977) reported that first- and fourth-grade children were able to select the contextually most appropriate form of a word when given a choice of four possible pictorial representations. However, although this study shows that children can draw inferences, a number of studies have shown that they do not spontaneously engage in inferential elaboration (e.g. Brown, 1975; Paris and Lindauer, 1976; Paris, Lindauer and Cox, 1977). As poor comprehenders are less likely to draw inferences to integrate the constituent ideas of a text, it seems possible that they will also find it more difficult to draw inferences about the meanings of individual words given the particular context. This idea seems particularly appealing given the observation that young children often experience such difficulties. A number of studies suggest that this might be true (e.g. Merrill, Sperber and McCauley, 1981; Oakhill, 1983).

Oakhill (1983) examined whether poor comprehenders find it difficult to draw inferences about the meanings of words. Children with good and poor comprehension skills were given a cued recall task. They heard a series of sentences which they were asked to 'think about and try to remember'. They were then presented with a set of 'clue' words and had to recall the sentence each clue reminded them of. Each sentence had a general term in the subject–noun–phrase position and the rest of the sentence was designed to cause a certain instantiation of this general term. On each occasion, the clue word was either the general noun which appeared in the original sentence or a specific noun which fitted the context. For example, given the sentence 'The animal chased the mouse', the child may be presented with ANIMAL or CAT as a cue for recall. In the latter case, the child needs to make the inference that the animal is probably a cat. It was argued that, if poor comprehenders fail to draw inferences during reading, then the instantiated clues should produce poorer recall for this group. This is precisely what was found. Good and poor comprehenders were similarly able to recall the original sentences when given the original nouns as cues. However, the good comprehenders showed significantly better recall when given the particular instantiated word cues. Furthermore, the instantiated cues enhanced recall for the good comprehenders whereas they had no effect on the poor comprehenders' performance. A further test indicated that the poor comprehenders possessed the relevant general knowledge to draw the inference although they failed to use it. It was also noted that the good comprehenders responded as quickly to both cue types; however, poor comprehenders took significantly longer to respond to the instantiated than to general cues. This suggests that the good comprehenders spontaneously drew the inferences at the time of comprehension; however, the poor comprehenders did not make the inferences until the time of retrieval. In conclusion, it would appear that poor comprehenders are less likely to draw inferences and that this may result in an impoverished representation of the overall meaning of the text.

These studies indicate that poor comprehenders are less likely to form an integrated representation of a text during reading (or listening). It was suggested that this might be the result of the poor comprehenders finding it difficult to draw inferences. Further evidence supportive of this view comes from the observation that these children also experience significant difficulty resolving pronouns (Oakhill and Yuill, 1986; Yuill and Oakhill, 1988b). The accurate interpretation of pronouns requires the ability to integrate information and make inferences. For example, in the sentence 'Claire gave Jane a present because it was her birthday' it is necessary to infer that 'her' refers to 'Jane' to determine whose birthday it is. The observation that poor comprehenders find pronouns difficult to interpret provides further evidence of these children's poor inferential processing skills.

To summarise, research suggests that poor comprehenders do not engage in constructive processing when reading or listening to text. They are less likely to form an integrated representation of the text's overall meaning. It is easy to see why poor comprehenders fail to make use of integrative processing. They find it difficult to draw inferences, particularly when these are of an implicit nature and they are poor at resolving pronouns. From this it is tempting to conclude that these difficulties play a causal role in comprehension problems. However, these data are correlational. They demonstrate that comprehension difficulties are associated with poor integrative and inferential processing skills, but it is still unclear whether poor inferential skills are a cause of reading comprehension difficulties. Oakhill has conducted several training studies (Yuill and Joscelyne, 1988; Yuill and Oakhill, 1988a) which provide suggestive evidence that inferential skills are causally related to comprehension ability. This issue will be returned to later when methods of remediation are considered.

Metacognitive Skills

Reading is a multidimensional activity in which readers automatically make inferences and bring prior knowledge to bear. Skilled reading also requires an awareness of these strategies, skilled readers being characterised by their ability to monitor and evaluate their own comprehension (Ryan, 1981; Paris, Lipson and Wixson, 1983). This awareness of the reading process, of the strategies involved and a knowledge of one's own cognitive processes is termed 'metacognition'. Skilled readers employ a wide variety of metacognitive processes during reading: they clarify the purposes of reading, identify important aspects of the message, allocate attention to relevant information, monitor their comprehension of the message, and take corrective steps when necessary to recover from disruptions and distraction (Brown, 1980). It is generally acknowledged that these strategies aid comprehension and failure to employ them might be a cause of reading problems. In fact, since the term 'metacognition' was coined in the mid-1970s, it has assumed a major role in theories of reading comprehension (e.g. Baker and Brown, 1984).

Metacognitive awareness is a late developing skill which only occurs after other reading-related variables such as decoding and comprehension have been acquired. It is a higher-level skill in the sense that it requires the ability to reflect upon how such primary skills as decoding and comprehension are being used. Comprehension is far more dependent upon metacognitive awareness than word recognition and decoding. As reading progresses from the beginning stages, metacognitive skills become increasingly important. The meta-level knowledge required to make inferences, integrate information and monitor one's own comprehension is much greater than that required by the beginning reader to identify words.

The assumption that metacognition is an important component of skilled reading, particularly reading for understanding, together with the observation that awareness is a late developing skill, has led many researchers to credit metacognition with a central role when explaining comprehension problems. There is much evidence to support this position. For instance, compared with older and better readers, younger poorer readers exhibit a lack of metacognitive awareness on a variety of measures (e.g. Myers and Paris, 1978; Winograd, 1984). Myers and Paris (1978) found that young children (8 versus 12 year olds) had a poorer understanding of the cognitive aspects of reading, such as skimming, re-reading and paraphrasing. They also had fewer ideas about how to deal with such difficulties as unknown words or difficult sentences, indicating that they did not know how to respond to comprehension failure. Younger children also appear to have different perceptions of reading, considering decoding, rather than comprehension, to be the main point (e.g. Myers and Paris, 1978).

There is also evidence that variations in metacognitive awareness are related to variations in reading ability. A number of studies have compared good and poor readers, matched for chronological age, and found significant differences between the two groups with respect to metacognitive skills. For example, Paris and Myers (1981) assessed good and poor fourth grade readers' (matched for age and mathematics achievement) metacognition about reading. They found that the poor readers showed less evidence of metacognitive awareness. They exhibited less use of spontaneous study strategies, correcting fewer errors during oral reading either spontaneously or when directed to do so. They also used fewer study strategies and were less aware of the negative effects of poor reading strategies such as watching television while reading. However, as Paris, Wasik and Van der Westhuizen (1988) point out, the fact that the poor readers made less use of study strategies does not necessarily mean they lack metacognition about reading. For instance, they may fail to use strategies because they lack specific knowledge, adequate practice or motivation, rather than because they lack awareness.

Other studies indicate that, like young children, poor readers do not make an active attempt to understand text, focusing on decoding rather than extracting the meaning (e.g. Myers and Paris, 1978). In fact, several researchers (e.g. Torgesen, 1977, 1982) have suggested that learning-disabled children might be better characterised as inactive learners whose problems arise from their failure to employ efficient and organised strategies to complete school tasks. According to this view, these individuals do not fail because they lack the ability to do the tasks, but because they do not employ goal-oriented strategies flexibly and efficiently.

These studies demonstrate that children with general reading problems show limited metacognitive awareness. There is also evidence that children with specific comprehension problems perform poorly on such measures. Yuill and Oakhill (1991) reported that children with specific comprehension problems seem to lack an awareness of the goals of reading. When asked what makes someone a good reader, significantly more poor comprehenders than good comprehenders spontaneously responded that 'not knowing words' was a cause of poor reading. Poor comprehenders appear to resemble younger children in terms of their emphasis on decoding rather than understanding.

Poor comprehenders have also been found to have deficits in other aspects of metacognition. Brown (1980) argues that the ability to identify important aspects of a text's message is a feature of metacognitive awareness. In both narrative and expository texts some aspects of the message are essential, whereas others are less important. Skilled readers tend to remember the important details, such as the basic plot, while forgetting other less important information. A number of studies have demonstrated that good and poor readers differ in sensitivity to importance (e.g. Smiley et al., 1977; Winograd, 1984). For example, Smiley et al. (1977) noted that poor readers' recall of stories is less influenced by the importance of the text content than is that of more skilled readers. Nevertheless, even these poor readers recalled more important than unimportant information. However, Yuill and Oakhill (unpublished study cited in Yuill and Oakhill, 1991) failed to find evidence of differential sensitivity to importance in good and poor comprehenders, both groups were better able to answer comprehension questions that tapped important as compared with less important information. Although, in a subsequent experiment, they did find that the poor comprehenders were significantly poorer than good comprehenders in determining the central point of a story.

Winograd (1984) gave eighth grade good and poor comprehenders a number of tasks designed to measure summarisation skills, ability to identify the important points in a story and reading awareness. Good readers were found to be better judges of importance than the poor readers. Furthermore, compared with the good readers, the poor readers showed a much weaker relationship between the information that they considered important and the information that they actually included in their summarisations. In fact, regression analyses indicated that the ability to identify important elements in a text accounted for a significant proportion of the variance in summarisation scores and two measures of reading comprehension, even after the effects of IQ and decoding ability had been taken into account. It would appear that comprehension difficulties might be related to strategy deficits such as the ability to identify the important parts of a text.

The metacognitive skill that has been studied in the greatest detail, particularly in relation to comprehension problems, is comprehension monitoring. An essential feature of metacognition is the ability to monitor one's own comprehension, assessing whether one's understanding is adequate and being able to take corrective action when a lack of comprehension is detected. The theory that comprehension monitoring is an integral component of skilled comprehension can be seen in many models of comprehension (e.g. Goodman, 1976; Rumelhart, 1980; Woods, 1980). Goodman (1976) argues that the reader must 'monitor his choices so he can recognise his errors and gather more cues when needed' (p. 483). Similarly, Baker and Brown (1984) suggest that 'any attempt to comprehend must involve comprehension monitoring' (p. 355). It is argued that readers who monitor their comprehension by periodically pausing to ask themselves questions, paraphrase important points, and look forward and backward in the text will show greater understanding than readers who simply read the text in a word-for-word manner.

Evidence indicates that children with reading problems are less able to monitor their comprehension processes than adequate readers (see Wagoner, 1983; Baker and Brown, 1984; Garner, 1987, for reviews of this literature). For example, Paris and Myers (1981) gave good and poor fourth grade readers passages to read which contained difficult or anomalous information. The poor readers showed less evidence of monitoring, being less likely to make spontaneous self-corrections during oral reading. Furthermore, even when the children were directly asked to monitor their comprehension by underlining any words or phrases they did not know, the poor readers were still less likely to engage in accurate monitoring. Group differences were particularly noticeable for anomalous phrases, poor readers detecting only 35% of the incomprehensible phrases as compared with 70% for the good readers. The poor readers also showed poorer comprehension of the stories, answering significantly fewer questions correctly and recalling less information. Furthermore, they were less aware of the effectiveness of various strategies for reading and tended to focus on the importance of single-word decoding, rather than understanding. In summary, the poor readers showed less evidence of comprehension monitoring. Garner has reported similar results in a series of studies (e.g. Garner, 1980; Garner and Kraus, 1981–1982; Garner and Taylor, 1982).

There is also evidence that children with specific comprehension problems have difficulties monitoring their comprehension. Yuill, Oakhill and Parkin (1989) tested good and poor comprehenders' ability to resolve apparent inconsistencies in a text. Children heard a series of stories describing an adult's apparently inconsistent emotional response to a child's action. For example, in one story a mother is pleased with her son when he refuses to share his sweets with his little brother. This inconsistency is resolved by the information that his little brother is on a diet. Following each story, the children were asked whether the adults should have behaved as they did, and why. In general, the poor comprehenders were poorer at detecting the anomalies than their skilled counterparts, although this just fell short of significance. However, this difference was only true when the anomalous and resolving information was separated by intervening sentences. Thus, the poor comprehenders exhibited significant difficulty resolving anomalies when there was an additional memory load imposed by the interposition of intervening sentences. The poor comprehenders appear to have difficulty in comprehension repair, being less likely to use resolving information to explain the inconsistencies.

In a further study, Yuill and Oakhill (unpublished study cited by Yuill and Oakhill, 1991) investigated poor comprehenders' tendency to recognise implicitly or explicitly anomalies in text. Implicit recognition was assessed by measuring reading time. If the children read the inconsistent information more slowly, it was reasoned that they must have detected the anomaly. Explicit recognition of the anomaly was assessed by direct questioning, asking the children about the content of the story and asking whether there was anything odd about each story. It was found that good comprehenders were significantly more likely to notice inconsistencies than the poor comprehenders. Furthermore, the poor comprehenders did not slow down their reading when they encountered an inconsistency. It was only the good comprehenders who showed longer reading times for the inconsistent information, the difference being significant for the most obvious inconsistencies only. These results suggest that poor comprehenders fail to monitor their comprehension. It should, however, be noted that there is little evidence to support the theory that longer reading times (for inconsistent information) are associated with superior comprehension. Correlations between reading time and detection are typically rather small (e.g. Baker and Anderson, 1982; Zabrucky and Ratner, 1986). The extent to which Yuill and Oakhill's reading time data indicate a lack of monitoring for poor comprehenders is, therefore, questionable. Nevertheless, the fact that the poor comprehenders failed to notice the inconsistencies indicates that they are less likely to monitor their comprehension.

To summarise, research indicates that poor comprehenders are characterised by their passive approach to reading. During reading they are less likely to employ such strategies as re-reading, pausing and self-questioning. In short, they fail to monitor their comprehension. They fail to detect when understanding breaks down and therefore are unable to apply 'fix-up' strategies to restore comprehension. Furthermore, not only are poor comprehenders less strategic readers, they also appear to have different perceptions of the reading task. Whereas good readers acknowledge that reading involves extracting meaning from the text, poor comprehenders view reading primarily in terms of decoding. As these effects have been observed in children with specific comprehension problems, i.e. poor comprehension but adequate decoding skills (e.g. Garner, 1981; Yuill, Oakhill and Parker, 1989), it appears that these difficulties are related to comprehension deficits rather than being a manifestation of a more general reading problem. These observations seem to suggest a possible causal role for metacognitive deficits in comprehension failure. It should, however, be noted that failure to employ such strategies may be a consequence rather than a cause of comprehension problems. The repeated experience of reading texts which make little sense may result in the adoption of a passive, non-strategic approach to reading.

Specificity of Comprehension Problems

An important question about children with reading comprehension problems concerns the specificity of their difficulties. Are the comprehension difficulties specific to reading, or do these children also show relatively poor language comprehension skills? This is a fairly obvious question, with important theoretical and practical implications.

Most previous research suggests that reading and listening comprehension are highly related skills. There are a number of obvious differences between the two modalities, for example, listening is determined by temporal factors whereas reading is dependent upon spatial characteristics, the normal rate of reading is commonly two to three times that of speech, the reader has more control over input than the listener, and spoken language contains explicit prosodic features such as stress and pauses, which are more or less absent in written language. These differences are, however, limited to the surface characteristics of the language. Beyond the modality of input, listening and reading comprehension appear to be dependent upon more or less identical processes. In fact, most researchers interested in comprehension assume that listening and reading comprehension are interdependent processes (e.g. Carver, 1977; Kintsch and Kozminsky, 1977; Sticht, 1979).

Numerous studies support the view that reading and listening comprehension are closely related processes. First, reading and listening comprehension are highly correlated skills (Palmer et al., 1985; Aaron, Phillips, Kleinschrodt and Gregory, 1987 – unpublished, cited in Aaron, 1989). Palmer et al. (1985) assessed the relationship between reading and listening comprehension skills in a group of college students. They found that listening comprehension correlated ($r = 0.82$) with a composite of three reading comprehension measures. Moreover, reading comprehension could be predicted almost perfectly by the listening comprehension measure, listening comprehension accounting for almost all the reliable variance (92%). From this, it was concluded that 'reading comprehension ability is indistinguishable from listening comprehension ability' (p. 59). It has also been noted that this relationship between reading and listening skills increases during reading acquisition. As the absolute level of reading ability increases, listening comprehension accounts for a progressively larger proportion of the variance in reading ability (Sticht, 1979; Curtis, 1980; Stanovich, Cunningham and Feeman, 1984). There is also evidence that the processes involved in understanding written text are analogous to those employed during listening comprehension. For example, research indicates that comprehension following listening and reading is structurally similar, as measured by the propositions recalled (Kintsch and Kozminsky, 1977) and the important ideas remembered (Smiley et al., 1977). This research provides strong support for the view that reading and listening comprehension are dependent upon similar, if not identical, underlying processes.

There is also evidence for an association between reading and listening comprehension skills in children who have general reading problems. A number of studies have reported that children who are poor readers are similarly poor listeners. For example, Berger (1978) investigated the relationship between reading and listening comprehension in 10-year-old good and poor readers. The poor readers had impaired listening as well as reading comprehension skills, suggesting a generally reduced ability to understand language. Similarly, Smiley et al. (1977) found poor listening comprehension in seventh grade poor readers, and a high correlation between reading and listening comprehension skills ($r = 0.85$). Curtis (1980) found that the comprehension skills of poor fifth grade readers were matched to younger skilled third grade readers for both listening and reading ability. In comparison to skilled readers, the poor readers were no better at listening comprehension than they were at reading comprehension. This finding that poor readers are also poor listeners has been replicated in a number of subsequent studies (e.g. Stein, Cairns and Zurif, 1984; Carlisle, 1989). It would appear, therefore, that poor readers suffer from a general comprehension deficit which is evidenced by their poor reading and listening skills.

Children with specific reading comprehension problems also have impaired listening comprehension skills. Stothard and Hulme (1992) examined the listening comprehension skills of a group of children who had reading comprehension difficulties in the presence of normal decoding skills. The poor comprehenders, chronological age controls and younger comprehension age controls were given two tests of language comprehension: a non-standardised test of listening comprehension and Bishop's (1983) Test for the Reception of Grammar (TROG). On both measures the poor comprehenders exhibited marked difficulties, performing at a significantly lower level than their age-matched controls. However, they obtained equivalent scores to the younger children who were matched for reading comprehension skill. In other words, the poor comprehenders showed equivalent deficits on reading and listening comprehension tasks, indicating a general language comprehension deficit. The children's verbal ability was examined further (Stothard and Hulme, unpublished) by administering a short form of the WISC-R (Wechsler, 1974). The poor comprehenders were found to have a selective deficit in verbal IQ. These children obtained significantly lower verbal IQ scores than the chronological age and comprehension age control groups. It should, however, be noted that the raw scores obtained by the poor comprehenders on the verbal sub-tests did not differ from those of the comprehension age controls. In other words, these children with poor comprehension skills had similar reading comprehension, language comprehension and verbal/semantic skills to a group of younger children whose comprehension was normal for age. Hence, it would seem that the low level of comprehension skill exhibited by the poor comprehenders is actually in line with some of their other verbal skills. In this light, these children's comprehension difficulties might be thought of as a manifestation of a more global deficit in verbal/semantic skills.

Snowling and Frith (1986) have also noted that verbal ability may constrain reading comprehension skill. They studied a group of children with moderate learning difficulties ('hyperlexic' readers) and found that children who varied in verbal ability also varied in the strategies they could bring to bear when reading text. Children of higher verbal ability were better able to take account of context in sentence processing (e.g. to work out the correct pronunciation of a homograph such as TEAR) and were more likely to use knowledge of the world when questioned about texts. Furthermore, these children showed equivalent deficits on a written and spoken version of the TROG, suggesting that they had a general language delay.

Taken together, these findings indicate that children with reading comprehension problems also have generally poor language comprehension skills. Furthermore, it appears that comprehension skills vary with verbal ability such that reading comprehension difficulties constitute one component of a more general language comprehension impairment.

Methods of Improving Reading Comprehension Skills

There are three main approaches to improving reading comprehension skills which have been considered (Oakhill and Garnham, 1988). The first is to modify the reading material: various additions or changes can be made to the text to make it easier to understand and remember. For example, pictures can be integrated with the text or summary statements and titles can be added. A second approach is that students can be trained to employ study aids such as underlining, note taking and summarising during and after reading text. Finally, students can be taught a range of reading strategies to improve comprehension, such as encouraging them to think about the information during reading and how it relates to what they already know.

The first approach is clearly very limited because it will not result in general improvements in comprehension in general terms, but will be specific to the materials at hand. The last two approaches, however, aim actually to teach students new skills to improve comprehension: the former by encouraging the use of external aids, the latter by emphasising the value of internal cognitive strategies. This last approach has proved to be particularly popular, probably because it involves teaching children strategies which can be used with any texts, allowing for the transfer of learning.

Considering the first approach, a number of studies have examined the usefulness of providing comprehension aids such as titles, subtitles, questions, summaries, pictures and diagrams in the text. As this approach does not improve comprehension per se, the present discussion of this literature will be brief (see Tierney and Cunningham,

1984, for a more detailed review). A number of studies have shown that adding pictures and titles to a text can enhance comprehension (e.g. Arnold and Brooks, 1976; Harris et al., 1980). For example, Arnold and Brooks (1976) gave second and fifth grade children verbal descriptions of unusual situations, e.g. three children flying through the air on a giant swan. Each description was preceded by a title that either listed the characters in the text or integrated them. It was found that integrated titles enabled the children to make significantly more correct inferences than the non-integrated titles. Arnold and Brooks also found a similar effect when the texts were accompanied by pictures; those that integrated the elements resulted in more correct inferences and better recall of the texts than those that presented the elements in a non-integrated way.

It has also been shown that children with specific comprehension problems can benefit from the use of supplementary integrative pictures and titles. Yuill and Joscelyne (1988) investigated the effects of verbal and pictorial advance organisers. They reasoned that, if the less-skilled group's comprehension deficits are partly the result of a failure to use prior knowledge, or to integrate information in text, then text organisers which integrate the information should be more beneficial for these children than for skilled comprehenders. If, however, their comprehension problems are the result of a lack of past experience or prior knowledge, then such advance organisers should not have any facilitative effects. Children were presented with stories to read in which some of the information was not stated explicitly, although it could be readily inferred by skilled adult readers. The stories were accompanied by either titles or pictures. There were two types of title. Integrative titles made the main consequence of the story explicit, whereas non-integrative titles simply described the main protagonists. Similarly, in the picture condition, the story was accompanied by either one large picture which summarised the whole story, or a series of smaller pictures which illustrated separate events. It was found that integrative pictures and titles improved the comprehension of the poor comprehenders but not the good comprehenders, the effect being most dramatic for the titles. However, it is possible that a ceiling effect was responsible for the lack of effects in the good comprehender group. Yuill and Joscelyne suggest that one possible explanation of the improvement observed among the poor comprehenders might be that these children are unable to integrate information from different parts of a text. Therefore, pictures and titles which indicated how the different pieces of information fitted together aided their comprehension. However, it should be noted that, even with the provision of integrative pictures and titles, the poor comprehenders still did not comprehend the texts as well as their skilled peers. Clearly, a more effective means of improving comprehension is required.

Arguably, the most effective approach to improving comprehension involves teaching children cognitive skills that are known to be employed during skilled comprehension. For example, skilled comprehenders readily make inferences and integrate textual information during reading. Poor comprehenders, however, display impaired inferential and integrative processing skills. Not only do they make less effective use of such cognitive strategies during reading, they also seem to be less aware of their existence and usefulness. However, poor comprehenders can make inferences and use their background knowledge to interpret text (Oakhill, 1982, 1983). It is, therefore, possible that poor comprehenders will show improved comprehension if they are informed of the value and importance of making inferences more regularly. This theory has formed the basis for a number of studies which have attempted to teach children inferential comprehension skills (e.g. Hansen and Pearson, 1983; Yuill and Joscelyne, 1988; Yuill and Oakhill, 1988a).

Yuill and Joscelyne (1988) examined the effect of training children to make inferences from specific words in texts. Good and poor comprehenders, matched for decoding skills, were given stories to read in which the locations and main consequences were not stated explicitly and had to be inferred. The experimental group were trained to search for and use clue words. For instance, they might be trained to use the clue words steamy, soap and towel to draw the inference that the story was set in a bathroom. These children were also provided with summary statements which raised two issues that were central to the story, for example, where the story took place (the setting) and what the main event was (the consequence). Children in the experimental and control groups read the same stories; however, only the experimental children received the summary statements and were trained to search for clue words. Training was found to be successful insofar as poor comprehenders who received training performed significantly better on subsequent comprehension questions about the story than controls. Training, however, had little effect on the performance of good comprehenders. Therefore, following training, poor comprehenders showed improvements in comprehension which raised them to the level of their more skilled peers. Although training did not enhance the comprehension scores of the good comprehenders, it is possible that this was the result of ceiling effects. The skilled group showed a high level of performance regardless of condition, answering 83% and 88% of the comprehension questions correctly in the control and trained conditions, respectively.

In a further study, Yuill and Oakhill (1988a) combined the former inference instruction technique with training children to ask questions about texts. The effectiveness of training was compared for two groups of 7- to 8-year-old children: good and poor comprehenders, matched for decoding skills. Training comprised two major components: lexical inference and question generation. Lexical inference instruction taught the children to look for clue words, as in the previous study. The other main component of training was question generation, children being encouraged to formulate questions about the text during reading. This procedure was designed to increase the children's awareness of their own comprehension and to help them formulate questions to guide comprehension. Trained children were compared with two control groups who spent a similar amount of time either completing standard comprehension exercises or being trained to decode words more rapidly. Effectiveness of instruction was assessed by measuring the children's improvement on a parallel version of the standardised reading test used for initial subject selection. Over the 2 months of study, all groups made gains in comprehension, improvements tending to be greater for the less-skilled group. Further analyses indicated that the poor comprehenders showed a differential effect of instruction, inference training being significantly more effective than rapid decoding practice. In fact, inference training produced a marked gain in comprehension skills for this group, comprehension age improving over 17 months in a 2-month period (compared with 6 months following rapid decoding practice and 14 months following comprehension exercises). This rapid increase in comprehension skills brought the poor comprehenders, on average, to within 6 months of the good comprehenders and well in advance of their chronological age. Hence, the less skilled group benefited more from inference training than the skilled group. Subsequent analyses indicated that these improvements in comprehension skills were not simply a reflection of improved reading accuracy. The good comprehenders did not show a differential effect of instruction.

The effects of training produced in this study are striking. Instruction that increases comprehension skills by over 17 months in a 2-month period is very impressive. However, the fact that poor comprehenders who received the comprehension exercises also showed marked gains in comprehension suggests that inference training alone is not the key to instruction. In fact, inference training was not significantly better than standard comprehension exercises. It should also be noted that children who were already skilled comprehenders (comprehension age being some 16 months in advance of chronological age) made an average gain of 10 months in comprehension skills after receiving rapid decoding practice. Although this effect was not significant, it is still rather large. This latter finding questions the extent to which the improvements represent 'true' gains in comprehension skill, and raises the possibility that they are a reflection of practice effects on the reading test measure. A further problem with this study is the small size of the control groups (six or seven per group). Given these problems, the conclusions must be accepted with caution.

Other training studies have attempted to teach children a variety of cognitive strategies, such as integrative processing skills (e.g. White, Pascarella and Pflaum, 1981), question generation (e.g. Cohen, 1983) and mental imagery (e.g. Levin, 1973). In general, such studies indicate that children show improvements in both strategy usage and comprehension. It appears that children can be trained to engage in more constructive processing, which, in turn, enhances reading comprehension. However, research indicates that, without specific instruction, poor comprehenders are not generally aware of their comprehension problems. For instance, they fail to notice anomalies in text. Poor comprehenders have a lack of awareness; their metacognitive skills are inferior to those of their more skilled peers. This observation has formed the basis for a large number of training studies which have attempted to improve reading comprehension by raising children's level of metacognitive awareness.

The clearest examples of this metacognitive approach to comprehension instruction comes from the work of two groups of researchers: Brown and Palincsar (e.g. Brown and Palincsar, 1982; Brown, Palincsar and Armbruster, 1984; Palincsar and Brown, 1984), and Paris and colleagues (e.g. Paris, Cross and Lipson, 1984; Paris and Jacobs, 1984; Paris and Oka, 1986; Cross and Paris, 1988). Palincsar and Brown (1984) attempted to improve the comprehension skills of seventh grade poor comprehenders whose decoding skills were adequate. During intervention four main cognitive activities – summarising, questioning, clarifying and predicting – were taught through the use of reciprocal teaching whereby the students acted as both tutors and tutees. The children assumed the role of teachers to generate questions, construct summaries of texts, make predictions and ask for clarification. These cognitive skills were taught in the context of reading and in response to a text comprehension problem. In addition, the authors also attempted to enhance the children's understanding of the activities and their sense of competence and control by, for example, teacher praise. Intervention lasted for approximately 20 days. Treatment effects were assessed directly at the end of the project and again 8 weeks later.

Palincsar and Brown found that the reciprocal teaching programme was successful and produced significant gains in comprehension. Following training, the children were significantly better at answering text-comprehension questions and were more able to summarise relevant information and detect errors in text. Furthermore, the effects of teaching generalised, improvements being seen in social studies and science classes. The trained children were better able to answer comprehension questions from texts about geography and life sciences. It should be noted that these improvements were observed both in relation to pre-intervention performance and the performance of a group of control children who received no intervention. Perhaps of most importance is the finding that the children made reliable gains as assessed by their performance on a standardised test. Approximately 3 months after the termination of intervention, the children were re-administered the reading test. The children made no improvement on the vocabulary measure (mean improvement of 1 month). However, they did make substantial gains on the comprehension measure, the six students making an average gain of 15 months.

The results obtained by Palincsar and Brown are, at first sight, impressive and suggest that reciprocal teaching is an effective means of producing substantial and reliable improvements in comprehension. However, these authors unfortunately fail to report data regarding the children's metacognitive strategies either before or after intervention. It is, therefore, unclear whether the observed improvements in comprehension are attributable to the children's enhanced metacognitive skills, or reflect other factors such as motivation. It is also unfortunate that no taught control group was included to assess the specificity of the gains observed.

Paris and colleagues (Paris, Cross and Lipson, 1984; Paris and Jacobs, 1984) also taught children about reading strategies and how to use them. Children received an experimental curriculum, termed 'informed strategies for learning' (ISL), which was designed to increase their awareness and use of effective reading strategies. ISL involved several forms of teaching such as directing the children's attention to the material to be learned, increasing their level of involvement and providing frequent practice and feedback. Cognitive strategies were taught by the use of metaphors such as 'Be a reading detective' to explain the importance of analysing text features before starting to read. Using such metaphors, a variety of strategies were taught: comprehension monitoring, summarising and finding the main idea. Training was given to 8- and 10-year-old children for a period of 4 months, each child receiving a 30-minute group lesson twice a week. Children in control classes also received lessons, but the topics were not related to reading.

ISL proved to be successful, producing marked improvements in both metacognitive awareness and comprehension skills. Compared with controls, children in the experimental classes showed significantly greater gains from pre-test to post-test in strategic reading, as assessed by their ability to detect errors in text and to fill in words in a cloze procedure. Furthermore, children who learned the most about strategies also showed greater gains on these measures of strategic comprehension. It was therefore argued that the effects of intervention appear to be mediated by improvements in metacognitive knowledge about reading strategies.

Although instruction produced significant improvements in metacognition, error detection and cloze performance, it did not produce significant improvements in standardised reading test scores. The two groups did not differ in their ability to answer questions about previously read stories. Similarly, good and poor strategy learners did not differ on the standardised comprehension tests. To explain these conflicting results, Paris, Cross and Lipson (1984) suggest that standardised reading tests do not actually provide robust measures of comprehension skills. They propose that many standardised reading tests should be more accurately described as achievement tests that are determined by general intelligence and background experiences, rather than measures of specific cognitive skills used to aid comprehension. Paris and colleagues suggest that had the children been specifically trained to answer questions on short paragraphs, then they may well have shown significant gains on such standardised measures. This remains to be shown.

Although comprehension involves a number of cognitive skills, it is also clear that understanding is dependent upon the possession of relevant background knowledge; textual information needs to be integrated with relevant prior knowledge if it is to be understood thoroughly. A number of studies have shown that the possession of relevant background knowledge results in superior comprehension (e.g. Marr and Gormley, 1982). In fact, it has been suggested that insufficient background knowledge might play a major role in reading comprehension failure (Beck and McKeown, 1986).

An important form of background knowledge necessary for comprehension is vocabulary knowledge. Correlations between comprehension and vocabulary scores are high and well established (e.g. Stanovich, Nathan and Zolman, 1988). Indeed, as Sternberg and

Powell (1983) note, vocabulary is generally regarded as an excellent measure of verbal comprehension.

A number of training studies have examined the efficacy of teaching vocabulary as a means of improving comprehension. These studies are based on the assumption that comprehension depends, at least in part, on efficient access to word meanings. However, as Pearson and Gallagher (1983) note, although such studies find that pre-teaching vocabulary improves the students' knowledge of word meanings, a number of studies failed to produce a marked effect on comprehension (e.g. Tuinman and Brady, 1974; Pany and Jenkins, 1978; Sylvester, 1981). There are, however, exceptions to this finding (e.g. Beck, Perfetti and McKeown, 1982; Kameenui, Carnine and Freschi, 1982; Stahl, 1983; McKeown et al., 1985). As Beck, Perfetti and McKeown (1982) point out, the fact that virtually all studies succeeded in enhancing vocabulary knowledge, but only a few demonstrated corresponding gains in comprehension shows that something more than knowing the meaning of words is required for skilled comprehension. They suggest that there is an important distinction between knowing the meaning of a word well enough to pass a multiple-choice vocabulary test, and knowing it well enough for use during text comprehension. This suggests that, for instruction to be effective, children need to be taught the meaning of words thoroughly, so they can gain access to their meaning rapidly and automatically.

Beck, Perfetti and McKeown (1982) conducted an experiment to assess whether teaching vocabulary would improve comprehension. Over a period of 5 months, fourth grade children were taught 104 words. Word meanings were taught by a variety of instructional activities and tasks such as defining, sentence generation, classification, oral and written production and word-speeded games. The children were also given tasks that referred to the semantic or affective relationships between target words and previously acquired vocabulary. The effects of instruction were assessed by a variety of tasks tapping word, sentence and discourse level comprehension.

Instruction was successful insofar as children who received vocabulary training showed significantly greater improvement on the experimental vocabulary tests than a group of controls who received language arts instruction following a standard textbook curriculum. Although the groups did not differ in vocabulary knowledge at pretest, at post-test the instructed children knew significantly more of the trained words. They also knew significantly more control words which were not actually taught. Training also produced significant improvements on a standardised vocabulary test. Moreover, vocabulary instruction resulted in significant gains in comprehension:

between pre-test and post-test the instructed children increased from the 37th to the 45th percentile on the reading comprehension measure. The respective performance of controls was at the 36th and 34th percentiles. The instructed group also showed superior performance on a range of other measures. They were significantly quicker on semantic decision and sentence-verification tasks involving taught words. They also showed superior recall for a story containing taught words than the controls, although the groups did not differ on recall of the story containing untaught control words.

This study indicates that vocabulary instruction can produce significant increases in semantic knowledge and result in gains in reading comprehension. As the trained children showed similar gains on the vocabulary and reading comprehension tests, it appears that the vocabulary instruction might be responsible for both transfer effects. Thus, teaching children the meaning of words can improve comprehension because knowing the meaning of individual words makes the construction of passage meaning easier.

McKeown et al. (1985) obtained similar results in a more modest vocabulary intervention programme which aimed to teach 24 difficult words over a period of 12 30-minute lessons. They examined the effectiveness of three types of vocabulary instruction: rich instruction in which various aspects of word meanings were explored, rich/extended instruction which comprised the rich instruction together with a motivational programme designed to increase the students' use of words outside the vocabulary class, and traditional instruction in which word meanings were taught by the use of simple definitions or synonyms. The rich instruction was designed to produce a deeper understanding of the words than that provided by traditional instruction. It was found that all three instructional programmes were successful in teaching the meaning of the words. Following intervention, none of the groups differed in their performance on a multiple-choice vocabulary test comprising the taught words. However, children in the rich and extended/rich programmes showed better story comprehension.

A number of other investigators have reported similar effects (Kameenui, Carnine and Freschi 1982; Stahl, 1983). Stahl (1983) investigated the effects of vocabulary instruction on reading comprehension for fifth-grade average readers. The effectiveness of two forms of vocabulary instruction was examined: a definitional treatment method taught the students word definitions whereas a mixed treatment taught both definitions and contextual information about the target words. Compared with a control treatment that provided the students with no special training on the target words, both training

treatments produced significant effects. Post-test scores on two measures of sentence comprehension and a multiple-choice synonym test
were significantly higher for the trained groups. These results indicate that teaching children about the meaning of words has a significant effect on both comprehension and vocabulary. The results also
suggested that the mixed method of vocabulary instruction which
provided both definitional and contextual information about the target words produced superior comprehension compared with the
straight definitional method.

It can be seen that training studies have attempted to improve
reading comprehension skills by employing a variety of methods such
as teaching inferential comprehension skills, increasing metacognitive
awareness and improving background knowledge such as vocabulary.
In general, these studies have been successful insofar as performance
has improved on specially designed comprehension tests. However, it
has been notably difficult to produce corresponding gains on standardised reading tests (e.g. Paris, Cross and Lipson, 1984). The
absence of such transfer effects raises the possibility that comprehension skills have not actually improved; rather the children have been
taught specific study strategies to complete the trained task.
Furthermore, considering the immense effort devoted to teaching
comprehension, the improvements produced have typically been surprisingly small. As Pearson and Gallagher (1983) note:

> ... as one looks across these various attempts at removing the roadblocks of
> knowledge deficits, what is impressive, with very few exceptions, is how
> weak rather than how strong the effects are.
>
> (pp. 327–328)

Carver (1987) offers three major criticisms of training studies
aimed at improving comprehension skills. First, he notes that the
degree to which students can comprehend a passage can be
increased simply by using passages that are not too difficult; he terms
this the 'easiness principle'. He also points out that comprehension
can be improved simply by spending more time reading the passage:
the 'reading time principle'. Finally, it is acknowledged that students
ordinarily improve on any reading related task simply by practising
that task: the 'practice principle'. Carver argues that, if the improved
comprehension scores are explicable with reference to one of the
above three principles, then there is little evidence that the subjects
have actually increased their general reading ability. For example,
Carver refers to Hansen and Pearson's (1983) finding that strategy
training significantly improved poor readers' but not good readers'
comprehension. As the good readers were given materials to read

that were some two to four grade levels below their measured reading level, these results can be explained in terms of the easiness principle. He suggests that, if the poor readers had also received instruction on passages below their reading level, then they presumably would not have benefited from instruction either. Furthermore, Hansen and Pearson do not appear to have controlled how long the students spent reading the passages. Carver suggests that the instructions given to the experimental groups might have encouraged the poor readers to spend more time studying the passages. If so, the results can be explained in terms of the reading time principle. He argues that training children to spend more time reading and re-reading texts to improve comprehension should be described as a study skill and not a comprehension skill. This is open to question; the extent to which a strategy is considered to be a study skill or a comprehension skill is debatable.

Carver also criticises the conclusions drawn by Palincsar and Brown (1984). As noted above, Palincsar and Brown reported that reciprocal teaching produced an average gain of 15 months in comprehension as measured by a standardised reading test. Initially, these results seem very impressive. However, there is a major problem of interpretation. Only the reciprocal teaching group received this follow-up test. As Carver points out, because the poor readers were initially reading at least 2 years below grade level, it is quite possible that this substantial improvement actually reflects regression to the mean. Carver remains sceptical that such training studies actually improve comprehension.

Overall, the most effective means of improving comprehension appears to involve teaching new vocabulary, the results obtained by Beck and colleagues adding support to the view that impaired vocabulary might be an important factor underlying comprehension difficulties. It must, however, be stressed that conclusive evidence that vocabulary training enhances comprehension is still required. In particular, studies need to select children who have comprehension difficulties in the presence of normal decoding skills. If it can be shown that these children benefit from vocabulary training, then the case for teaching vocabulary as a means of improving comprehension can be argued more strongly.

Conclusions

The research reviewed in this chapter indicates that there is still a good deal of controversy surrounding the causes of reading comprehension difficulties in children. Many early theories focused on the idea that inefficient decoding skills might be an important source of comprehension problems. It is now clear, however, that most cases of specific reading comprehension deficits cannot be accounted for in this way; nor do they seem attributable to poor short-term or working memory skills.

Recent research indicates that children with reading comprehension difficulties typically have global language comprehension problems. It also seems reasonable to suggest that these children's generally poor verbal skills contribute to their difficulties with inferential skills, impaired metacognitive awareness and limited vocabulary knowledge. Consistent with this view is the observation that intervention programmes aimed at enhancing general language skills (e.g. teaching new vocabulary and inferential processing skills) have generally succeeded in improving these children's reading comprehension skills. Effective interventions for children with poor reading comprehension skills need to tackle the language deficits that underlie these children's difficulties with the comprehension of written and spoken language.

References

Aaron, P.G. (1989). *Dyslexia and Hyperlexia*. Boston: Kluwer Academic.

Anderson, R.C., Pichert, J.W., Goetz, E.T., Schallert, D.L., Stevens, K.V. and Trollip, S.R. (1976). Instantiation of general terms. *Journal of Verbal Learning and Verbal Behaviour*, **15**, 667–679.

Anderson, R.C., Stevens, K.V., Shifrin, Z. and Osborn, J.H. (1977). *Instantiation of Word Meanings in Children*. Technical Report No. 46. Centre for the Study of Reading: University of Illinois.

Arnold, D.S. and Brooks, P.H. (1976). Influence of contextual organising material on children's listening comprehension. *Journal of Educational Psychology*, **68**, 711–716.

Baker, L. and Anderson, R. (1982). Effects of inconsistent information on text processing. *Reading Research Quarterly*, **17**, 281–294.

Baker, L. and Brown, A.L. (1984). Metacognitive skills and reading. In P.D. Pearson, R. Barr, M.C. Kamil and P. Mosenthal (eds), *Handbook of Reading Research*. New York: Longman.

Barclay, J.R. (1973). The role of comprehension in remembering sentences. *Cognitive Psychology*, 4, 229–254.

Bartlett, F.C. (1932). *Remembering: A Study in Experimental and Social Psychology*. Cambridge: Cambridge University Press.

Beck, I.L. and McKeown, M.G. (1986). Instructional research in reading: A retrospective. In J. Orasanu (ed.), *Reading Comprehension: From Research to Practice*. Hillsdale, NJ: Lawrence Erlbaum Associates.

Beck, I.L., Perfetti, C.A. and McKeown, M.G. (1982). The effects of long-term vocabulary instruction on lexical access and reading comprehension. *Journal of Educational Psychology*, 74, 506–521.

Berger, N.S. (1978). Why can't John read? Perhaps he's not a good listener. *Journal of Learning Disabilities*, **11**, 31–36.

Bishop, D. (1983). *Test for the Reception of Grammar*. Available from the author, Applied Psychology Unit, 15 Chaucer Road, Cambridge.

Bransford, J.D., Barclay, J.R. and Franks, J.J. (1972). Sentence memory: A constructive versus interpretative approach. *Cognitive Psychology*, 3, 193–209.

Brown, A.L. (1975). The development of memory: Knowing, knowing about knowing and knowing how to know. In H.W. Reese (ed.), *Advances in Child Development and Behaviour*, vol. 10. New York: Academic Press.

Brown, A.L. (1980). Metacognitive development and reading. In R.J. Spiro, B.C. Bruce and W.F. Brewer (eds), *Theoretical Issues in Reading Comprehension*. Hillsdale, NJ: Lawrence Erlbaum Associates.

Brown, A.L. and Palincsar, A.S. (1982). Introducing strategic learning from texts by means of informed, self-control training. *Topics in Learning and Learning Disabilities*, 2, 1–17.

Brown, A.L., Palincsar, A.S. and Armbruster, B.B. (1984). Instructing comprehension-fostering activities in interactive learning situations. In H. Mandl, N.L. Stein and T. Trabasso (eds), *Learning and Comprehension of Text*. Hillsdale, NJ: Lawrence Erlbaum Associates.

Calfee, R.C., Arnold, R. and Drum, P.A. (1976). A review of the psychology of reading by E. Gibson and H. Levin. *Proceedings of the National Academy of Education*, 3, 1–80.

Carlisle, J.F. (1989). Diagnosing comprehension deficits through listening and reading. *Annals of Dyslexia*, 39, 159–176.

Carver, R.P. (1977). Toward a theory of reading comprehension and auding. *Reading Research Quarterly*, 13, 10–63.

Carver, R.P. (1987). Should reading comprehension skills be taught? In J.E. Readance and R.S. Baldwin (eds), *Research in Literacy: Merging Perspectives*. Rochester, NY: National Reading Conference.

Cohen, R. (1983). Self-generated questions as an aid to reading comprehension. *The Reading Teacher*, 36, 770–775.

Clay, M.M. and Imlach, R.H. (1971). Juncture, pitch and stress as reading behaviour variables. *Journal of Verbal Learning and Verbal Behaviour*, 10, 133–139.

Crain, S. and Shankweiler, D. (1990). Explaining failures in spoken language comprehension by children with reading disabilities. In D.A. Balota, G.B. Flores d'Arcais and K. Rayner (eds), *Comprehension Processes in Reading*. Hillsdale, NJ: Lawrence Erlbaum Associates.

Cromer, W. (1970). The difference model: A new explanation for some reading difficulties. *Journal of Educational Psychology*, 61, 471–483.

Cross, D.R. and Paris, S.G. (1988). Developmental and instructional analyses of children's metacognition and reading comprehension. *Journal of Educational Psychology*, 80, 131–142.

Curtis, M.E. (1980). Development of components of reading skill. *Journal of Educational Psychology*, 72, 656–669.

Daneman, M. (1987). Reading and working memory. In J.R. Beech and A.M. Colley (eds), *Cognitive Approaches to Reading*. Chichester: John Wiley & Sons.

Daneman, M. and Carpenter, P.A. (1980). Individual differences in working memory and reading. *Journal of Verbal Learning and Verbal Behaviour*, 19, 450–466.

Dooling, D.J. and Lachman, R. (1971). Effects of comprehension on the retention of prose. *Journal of Experimental Psychology*, 88, 216–222.

Fleisher, L.S., Jenkins, J.R. and Pany, D. (1979). Effects on poor readers' comprehension of training in rapid decoding. *Reading Research Quarterly*, 15, 30–48.

Garner, R. (1980). Monitoring of understanding: An investigation of good and poor readers' awareness of induced miscomprehension of text. *Journal of Reading Behaviour*, **12**, 55–63.

Garner, R. (1981). Monitoring of passage inconsistency among poor comprehenders: A preliminary test of the 'piecemeal processing' explanation. *Journal of Educational Research*, **74**, 159–162.

Garner, R. (1987). *Metacognition and Reading Comprehension*. Norwood, NJ: Ablex.

Garner, R. and Kraus, C. (1981–1982). Good and poor comprehender differences in knowing and regulating reading behaviours. *Educational Research Quarterly*, **6**, 5–12.

Garner, R. and Taylor, N. (1982). Monitoring of understanding: An investigation of attentional assistance needs at different grade and reading proficiency levels. *Reading Psychology*, **3**, 1–6.

Golinkoff, R. and Rosinski, R. (1976). Decoding, semantic processing and reading comprehension skill. *Child Development*, **47**, 252–258.

Goodman, K.S. (1976). Behind the eye: What happens in reading. In H. Singer and R.B. Ruddell (eds), *Theoretical Models and Processes of Reading*, 2nd edn. Newark, DL: International Reading Association.

Gough, P.B. and Tunmer, W.E. (1986). Decoding, reading and reading disability. *Remedial and Special Education*, **7**, 6–10.

Hansen, J. and Pearson, P.D. (1983). An instructional study: Improving the inferential comprehension of good and poor fourth-grade readers. *Journal of Educational Psychology*, **75**, 821–829.

Harris, P.L., Mandias, M., Meerum Terwogt, M and Tjintjelaar, J. (1980). The influence of context on story recall and feelings of comprehension. *International Journal of Behavioural Development*, **3**, 159–172.

Hess, T.H. and Radtke, R.C. (1981). Processing and memory factors in children's reading comprehension skill. *Child Development*, **52**, 479–488.

Hulme, C. (1988). Short-term memory development and learning to read. In M. Gruneberg, P. Morris and R. Sykes (eds), *Practical Aspects of Memory: Current Research and Issues*, Vol. 2: *Clinical and Educational Implications*. Chichester: John Wiley & Sons.

Hulme, C. and Snowling, M. (1992). Phonological deficits in dyslexia: A 'sound' reappraisal of the verbal deficit hypothesis. In N. Singh and I. Beale (eds), *Current Perspectives in Learning Disabilities*. New York: Springer-Verlag.

Jorm, A.F., Share, D.L., MacLean, R. and Matthews, R. (1984). Phonological confusability in short-term memory for sentences as a predictor of reading ability. *British Journal of Psychology*, **75**, 393–400.

Kameenui, E.J., Carnine, D.W. and Freschi, R. (1982). Effects of text construction and instructional procedures for teaching word meanings on comprehension and recall. *Reading Research Quarterly*, **17**, 367–388.

Kintsch, W. and Kozminsky, E. (1977). Summarising stories after reading and listening. *Journal of Educational Psychology*, **69**, 491–499.

LaBerge, D. and Samuels, S. (1974). Toward a theory of automatic information processing in reading. *Cognitive Psychology*, **6**, 293–323.

Levin, J.R. (1973). Inducing comprehension in poor readers: A test of a recent model. *Journal of Educational Psychology*, **65**, 19–24.

Marr, M.B. and Gormley, K. (1982). Children's recall of familiar and unfamiliar text. *Reading Research Quarterly*, **18**, 89–104.

McKeown, M.G., Beck, I.L., Omanson, R.C. and Pople, M.T. (1985). Some effects of the nature and frequency of vocabulary instruction on the knowledge and use of words. *Reading Research Quarterly*, **20**, 522–535.

Merrill, E.C., Sperber, R.D. and McCauley, C. (1981). Differences in semantic encoding as a function of reading comprehension skill. *Memory and Cognition*, **9**, 618–624.

Myers, M. and Paris, S.G. (1978). Children's metacognitive knowledge about reading. *Journal of Educational Psychology*, **70**, 680–690.

Oakan, R., Wiener, M. and Cromer, W. (1971). Identification, organisation and reading comprehension in good and poor readers. *Journal of Educational Psychology*, **62**, 71–78.

Oakhill, J. (1981). *Children's reading comprehension*. Unpublished DPhil thesis, University of Sussex.

Oakhill, J. (1982). Constructive processes in skilled and less-skilled comprehenders' memory for sentences. *British Journal of Psychology*, **73**, 13–20.

Oakhill, J. (1983). Instantiation in skilled and less-skilled comprehenders. *Quarterly Journal of Experimental Psychology*, **35a**, 441–450.

Oakhill, J. (1984). Inferential and memory skills in children's comprehension of stories. *British Journal of Educational Psychology*, **54**, 31–39.

Oakhill, J. and Garnham, A. (1988). *Becoming a Skilled Reader*. Oxford: Blackwell.

Oakhill, J. and Yuill, N. (1986). Pronoun resolution in skilled and less-skilled comprehenders: Effects of memory load and inferential complexity. *Language and Speech*, **29**, 25–37.

Oakhill, J., Yuill, N. and Parkin, A. (1986). On the nature of the difference between skilled and less-skilled comprehenders. *Journal of Research in Reading*, **9**, 80–91.

Palincsar, A.S. and Brown, A.L. (1984). Reciprocal teaching of comprehension-fostering and comprehension-monitoring activities. *Cognition and Instruction*, **1**, 117–175.

Palmer, J., MacLeod, C.M., Hunt, E. and Davidson, J. (1985). Information processing correlates of reading. *Journal of Memory and Language*, **24**, 59–88.

Pany, D. and Jenkins, J.R. (1978). Learning word meanings: A comparison of instructional procedures and effects on measures of reading comprehension with learning disabled students. *Learning Disabled Quarterly*, **1**, 21–32.

Paris, S.G. and Carter, A.Y. (1973). Semantic and constructive aspects of sentence memory in children. *Developmental Psychology*, **9**, 109–113.

Paris, S.G. and Jacobs, J.E. (1984). The benefits of informed instruction for children's reading awareness and comprehension skills. *Child Development*, **55**, 2083–2093.

Paris, S.G. and Lindauer, B.K. (1976). The role of inference in children's comprehension and memory for sentences. *Cognitive Psychology*, **8**, 217–227.

Paris, S.G. and Mahoney, G.J. (1974). Cognitive integration in children's memory for sentences and pictures. *Child Development*, **45**, 633–642.

Paris, S.G. and Myers, M. (1981). Comprehension monitoring, memory, and study strategies of good and poor readers. *Journal of Reading Behaviour*, **13**, 5–22.

Paris, S.G. and Oka, E.R. (1986). Children's reading strategies, metacognition and motivation. *Developmental Review*, **6**, 25–56.

Paris, S.G., Cross, D.R. and Lipson, M.Y. (1984). Informed strategies for learning: An instructional programme to improve children's reading awareness and comprehension. *Journal of Educational Psychology*, **76**, 1239–1252.

Paris, S.G., Lindauer, B.K. and Cox, G.L. (1977). The development of inferential comprehension. *Child Development*, **48**, 1728–1733.

Paris, S.G., Lipson, M.Y. and Wixson, K.K. (1983). Becoming a strategic reader. *Contemporary Educational Psychology*, 8, 293–316.

Paris, S.G. Wasik, B.A. and van der Westhuizen, G. (1988). Meta-metacognition: A review of research on metacognition and reading. In J. Readance and S. Baldwin (eds), *Dialogues in Literacy Research*. Chicago, IL: National Reading Conference Inc.

Pearson, P.D. and Gallagher, M. (1983). The instruction of reading comprehension. *Contemporary Educational Psychology*, 8, 317–344.

Perfetti, C.A. (1985). *Reading Ability*. Oxford: Oxford University Press.

Perfetti, C.A. and Hogaboam, T. (1975a). Relationship between single word decoding and reading comprehension skill. *Journal of Educational Psychology*, 67, 461–469.

Perfetti, C.A. and Hogaboam, T. (1975b). *The effects of word experience on decoding speeds of skilled and unskilled readers*. Paper presented at the Psychonomics Society, Denver, November 1975.

Perfetti, C.A. and Lesgold, A.M. (1979). Coding and comprehension in skilled reading and implications for reading instruction. In L.B. Resnick and P.A. Weaver (eds), *Theory and Practice of Early Reading*, vol. 1. Hillsdale, NJ: Lawrence Erlbaum Associates.

Perfetti, C.A., Finger, E. and Hogaboam, T. (1978). Sources of vocalisation latency differences between skilled and less skilled young readers. *Journal of Educational Psychology*, 70, 730–739.

Rosinski, R.R., Golinkoff, R.M. and Kukish, K.S. (1975). Automatic semantic processing in a picture-word interference task. *Child Development*, 46, 247–253.

Rumelhart, D.E. (1980). Schemata: The building blocks of cognition. In R.J. Spiro, B.C. Bruce and W.F. Brewer (eds), *Theoretical Issues in Reading Comprehension*. Hillsdale, NJ: Lawrence Erlbaum Associates.

Ryan, E.B. (1981). Identifying and remediating failures in reading comprehension: Toward an instructional approach for poor comprehenders. In G.E. MacKinnon and T.G. Waller (eds), *Reading Research: Advances in Theory and Practice*, vol. 3. New York: Academic Press.

Siegel, L.S and Ryan, E.B. (1989). Subtypes of developmental dyslexia: The influence of definitional variables. *Reading and Writing*, 2, 257–287.

Smiley, S.S., Oakley, D.D., Worthen, D., Campione, J.C. and Brown, A.L. (1977). Recall of thematically relevant material by adolescent good and poor readers as a function of written versus oral presentation. *Journal of Educational Psychology*, 69, 381–387.

Snowling, M. and Frith, U. (1986). Comprehension in 'hyperlexic' readers. *Journal of Experimental Child Psychology*, 42, 392–415.

Stahl, S. (1983). Differential word knowledge and reading comprehension. *Journal of Reading Behaviour*, 15, 33–50.

Stanovich, K.E., Cunningham, A.E. and Feeman, D.J. (1984). Intelligence, cognitive skills, and early reading progress. *Reading Research Quarterly*, 19, 278–303.

Stanovich, K.E., Nathan, R. and Zolman, J.E. (1988). The developmental lag hypothesis in reading: Longitudinal and matched reading-level comparisons. *Child Development*, 59, 71–86.

Stein, C.L., Cairns, H.S. and Zurif, E.B. (1984). Sentence comprehension limitations related to syntactic deficits in reading-disabled children. *Applied Psycholinguistics*, 5, 305–322.

Steiner, R., Wiener, M. and Cromer, W. (1971). Comprehension training and identification for poor and good readers. *Journal of Educational Psychology*, 62, 506–513.

Sternberg, R.J. and Powell, J.S. (1983). Comprehending verbal comprehension. *American Psychologist*, 38, 878–893.

Sticht, T. G. (1979). Applications of the audread model to reading evaluation and instruction. In L.B. Resnick and P. Weaver (eds), *Theory and Practice of Early Reading*, vol. 1. Hillsdale, NJ: Lawrence Erlbaum Associates.

Stothard, S.E. and Hulme, C. (1992). Reading comprehension difficulties in children: The role of language comprehension and working memory skills. *Reading and Writing*, 4, 245–256.

Sylvester, E. (1981). *Effects of prior knowledge and concept-building on good and poor readers' comprehension of explicit and implicit relations*. Unpublished doctoral dissertation, University of Minnesota.

Tierney, R.J. and Cunningham, J.W. (1984). Research on teaching reading comprehension. In P.D. Pearson, R. Barr, M.C. Kamil and P. Mosenthal (eds), *Handbook of Reading Research*. New York: Longman.

Torgesen, J.K. (1977). The role of nonspecific factors in the task performance of learning-disabled children: A theoretical assessment. *Journal of Learning Disabilities*, 10, 27–34.

Torgesen, J.K. (1982). The learning disabled child as an interactive learner. *Topics in Learning and Learning Disabilities*, 2, 45–52.

Tuinman, J.J. and Brady, M.E. (1974). How does vocabulary account for variance on reading comprehension tests? A Preliminary instructional analysis. In P.L. Nacke (ed.), *Interaction: Research and Practice in College Adult Reading. 23rd Yearbook of the National Reading Conference*. Clemson, SC: National Reading Conference.

Wagoner, S.A. (1983). Comprehension monitoring: What it is and what we know about it. *Reading Research Quarterly*, 28, 328–346.

Wechsler, D. (1974). *Wechsler Intelligence Scale for Children – Revised*. New York: Psychological Corporation.

Weinstein, R. and Rabinovitch, M.S. (1971). Sentence structure and retention in good and poor readers. *Journal of Educational Psychology*, 62, 25–30.

White, C.V., Pascarella, E.T. and Pflaum, S.W. (1981). *Problem Solving and Comprehension: A Short Course in Analytical Reasoning*. Philadelphia: The Franklin Institute Press.

Winograd, T. (1972). *Understanding Natural Language*. New York: Academic Press.

Winograd, P. (1984). Strategic difficulties in summarising text. *Reading Research Quarterly*, 19, 404–425.

Woods, W.A. (1980). Multiple theory formation in high-level perception. In R.J. Spiro, B.C. Bruce and W.F. Brewer (eds), *Theoretical Issues in Reading Comprehension*. Hillsdale, NJ: Lawrence Erlbaum Associates.

Yuill, N. and Joscelyne, T. (1988). Effect of organisational cues and strategies on good and poor comprehenders' story understanding. *Journal of Educational Psychology*, 2, 152–158.

Yuill, N. and Oakhill, J. (1988a). Effects of inference awareness training on poor reading comprehension. *Applied Cognitive Psychology*, 2, 33–45.

Yuill, N. and Oakhill, J. (1988b). Understanding of anaphoric relations in skilled and less skilled comprehenders. *British Journal of Psychology*, 79, 173–186.

Yuill, N. and Oakhill, J. (1991). *Children's Problems in Text Comprehension.* Cambridge: Cambridge University Press.

Yuill, N., Oakhill, J. and Parkin, A. (1989). Working memory, comprehension ability and the resolution of text anomaly. *British Journal of Psychology*, **80**, 351–361.

Zabrucky, H. and Ratner, H.H. (1986). Children's comprehension monitoring and recall of inconsistent stories. *Child Development*, **57**, 1401–1418.

Author Index

239

Subject Index